The Large-Scale Model Railroading Handbook

Robert Schleicher

THE LARGE-SCALE MODEL RAILROADING HANDBOOK

krause publications

700 E. State Street • Iola, WI 54990-0001
Telephone: 715/445-2214

Copyright © 1992 by Robert Schleicher
All Rights Reserved
Published in Iola, Wisconsin, 54990 by Krause Publications

Designed by Arlene Putterman
Cover photograph by Robert Schleicher
Manufactured in the United States of America

Library of Congress Cataloging in Publication Data

Schleicher, Robert H.
     The large-scale model railroading handbook / Robert Schleicher.
         p.   cm.
     Includes bibliographical references.
     ISBN 0-8019-8230-8 (hc)—ISBN 0-8019-8229-4 (pb)
     1. Railroads—Models.   I. Title
TF197.S338   1992   91-31607
625.1′9—dc20   CIP

   2 3 4 5 6 7 8 9 0   10 9 8

Contents

The Large-Scale Model Railroading Handbook

Chapter 1

Garden Model Railroading

THIS IS real railroading! Yes, the locomotives and rolling stock are models, but the world in which they operate is real—real sun; real plants; real dirt; and, yes, real rain, hail, wind, and snow. All of the models in this book are designed to be rugged enough for operation indoors or out.

If you ever have played in the sand or dirt, as a small child, digging tunnels and making roads and byways for cars or trains, this is a childhood dream brought to life. The digging and arranging the world at your fingertips is the same, but this time the trains move under their own power. It truly seems like magic.

Toy Trains

You may choose to view the models as toys, accurate scale miniatures, or magic in motion. Each of the brands and all the equipment shown and discussed

Fig. 1-1 *A 1/22.5 scale LGB Mogul creeps along a cliff in Bill and Dee Baldock's backyard.*

on these pages is designed to operate on a track with a gauge (the distance between the tops of the rails) of 1¾ inches. Modelers call it gauge 1, a scale that was popular in the 1930s.

These are the largest model trains in mass production today. Again, in the 1930s, the largest trains were about this size, stamped from tin-plated steel, and called "standard gauge." These pre–World War II toys usually ran on a three-rail track with a gauge of 2⅛ inches. Lionel is reproducing some of these models in metal, but they are strictly collector's pieces. The trains in this book are designed to be operated.

You can decide if there is a difference between "playing with toy trains" and "operating a model railroad." These gauge 1 trains are, perhaps, the size that offers the best of both models and toys. The most popular scale or size toy or model train in America is

Fig. 1-2 *Steve and Judy Arrigotti created a model railroad, rather than creating a garden.*

HO, with a track gauge of about ⅝ inch (between 0.650 and 0.667 inches); but the sales of gauge 1 models have increased in recent years to assume the number-two position in dollar sales drawing model trains in America.

You will find the majority of the mass-produced models discussed and/or shown in this book. The Supply Sources lists all the most-active manufacturers, but those firms range from strictly basement operations, making custom parts for true enthusiasts, to giant firms like Lionel in America, LGB (Lehmann Gross Bahn) in Germany, Bachmann in Hong Kong, and Aristo-Craft in China. Even the Playmobil toy trains, made in Germany, will operate on gauge 1 track. The degree of realism of these models is similar among these major makers; all except Playmobil are accurate reproductions of the shapes, at least, of real railroad equipment. These, then, are models built rugged enough to serve as outdoor toys.

Scale-Model Railroading

Whenever the subject of model railroading is described, one of the essences is that these are accurate scale miniatures of the real thing. The term "scale" is simply an expression of the proportion of the model as compared to the real thing. The HO scale toy and model trains, for example, are 1/87 the size of the real thing in every dimension. With the exception of some brass models imported from Korea, which sell for prices in excess of $4,000 (for a locomotive), not one model in this book is as accurate a scale reproduction as the HO scale plastic cars and locomotives in the toy train sets from firms such as Tyco, Bachmann, and Life-Like. Take a long look at the layouts in the color section of this book, in particular, and you'll see, nonetheless, that these gauge 1 models are as realistic as any model train.

With these larger-size models, precise scale is not as important as proportions—the size of one model relative to another. You won't find any odd proportions on these models, but if you measure them and compare the dimensions to the real thing, you will find that the scale will vary from as small as 1/32 to as large as 1/24.

Narrow and Standard Gauge Railroads

If you are bothered by the thought of operating a string of models where the locomotive is 1/22.5 scale with cars that may include 1/24, 1/32, 1/29, and 1/22.5 scale, you need to understand the difference between what the real railroads called standard gauge as compared with narrow gauge.

The first transcontinental railroad in America was

Fig. 1-3 *This 30-by-40-foot layout is in a basement, and the trees are dead weeds.*

Fig. 1-4 *Playmobil's toy trains are rugged enough for use outdoors.*

built with the rails spaced 4 feet, 8½ inches apart. By the 1880s, that became the "standard" gauge for railroads in America. Prior to that the track gauge ranged from as narrow as 2 feet to as wide as 7 feet and more. From about 1880, there also were thousands of miles of railroad built in America that had track with a gauge of 3 feet; these railroads became known as narrow gauge.

The 3-foot narrow gauge railroads were popular in the late 1800s because it was less expensive to build the right-of-way and the equipment itself was less costly. The locomotives and rolling stock were, as you could guess, about three-fourths the size of standard gauge equipment. The smaller size meant that the curves could be sharper, hence less dirt or rock needed to be moved and fewer bridges or tunnels needed to be constructed. Narrow gauge was the gauge of choice for building through the Colorado Rockies, in most logging areas, in parts of the Appalachians, and anywhere where a relatively cheap railroad was needed.

Naturally, modelers caught the idea of building models of narrow gauge equipment because it possessed its own unique charm; the narrow gauge was virtually a caricature in three-fourths of the standard gauge lines. Narrow gauge models were a natural choice for model railroads, where tight curves and lots of mountains were needed to help disguise the fact that the trains were hemmed in by the walls of the basement, spare room, or garage.

You can purchase narrow gauge models to HO scale as well as the other common indoor modeling scales, including 0 (1/48 scale), S (1/64 scale), and even some tiny equipment for N (1/160 scale). These narrow gauge models are built to the same specifications as the standard gauge version, but because they are to scale, they are three-fourths the size of the standard gauge version. An HO scale standard gauge model of the common 50-foot boxcar measures 7 inches in length while the HO scale version of the common 30-foot narrow gauge boxcar is just over 4 inches long. The height and width of the models is proportionally smaller for the narrow gauge models as well.

Gauge 1 Narrow Gauge

Now you understand that the real narrow gauge railroad locomotives, rolling stock, and track gauge were about three-fourths the size of the standard gauge

locomotives, rolling stock, and track. Remember this, because things can become a bit confusing from here on.

There are two distinct groups of models available to operate on gauge 1 track: replicas of narrow gauge equipment (primarily from LGB, Bachmann, Kalamazoo, D.A.N., and Delton) and a separate group of models based on standard gauge real railroad locomotives and cars (primarily from Aristo-Craft, Lionel, and MDC). Most of these brands, however, make both narrow and standard gauge models of at least some locomotives or cars. Remember, all of this equipment, whether narrow or standard gauge, is designed to operate on the same gauge 1 track; gauge 1 track is the only size shown in this book. For practical operating purposes and, as you can see in the photographs, from an appearance standpoint, narrow and standard gauge models in this size are completely compatible.

LGB helped to resurrect the interest in gauge 1 in the 1970s with the introduction of mass-produced models rugged enough for operation indoors or out. LGB selected real trains that were narrow gauge because these locomotives and cars would be more massive than standard gauge. Standard gauge equipment for gauge 1 track is 1/32 scale to match that 1¾-inch track gauge. If, however, you stipulate that 1¾ inches is the track gauge, and that 1¾ inches is supposed to equal 3 feet, then the models will be about 1/22 scale. Since they are 1/22 scale, they can be a bit larger (even though their prototypes are the three-fourths size narrow gauge) then a standard gauge model.

LGB elected to use 1¾ inches for its track gauge,

Fig. 1-5 *The full-sized Colorado & Southern number 8200 boxcar. There's a chart comparing the sizes of the models to this car in Chapter 14 (Fig. 14-3).* Richard Kindig photo, from the Hol Wagner collection, April 12, 1941, near Blackhawk, Colorado.

Fig. 1-6 *A Delton 1/24 scale boxcar painted to match a C & S car and available from Depot G Hobbies.*

Fig. 1-7 *A train of Aristo-Craft 1/29 scale equipment with a lone LGB 1/29 scale Rio Grande boxcar in front of the caboose on the Horovitz's layout.*

and because the real railroads it was modeling were German and Austrian, LGB trains operated on meter gauge track (about 39 inches rather than 36 inches between the rails). That resulted in the odd 1/22.5 scale that LGB uses for most of its models. In the late 1980s LGB began to produce models of American locomotives and cars, and they, too, were and are made to 1/22.5 scale. Bachmann entered the gauge 1 market in the late 1980s and also elected to duplicate

American narrow gauge locomotives and cars with the models built to about 1/22.5 scale.

Gauge 1 Standard Gauge

Lionel began to produce models to operate on gauge 1 track in the late 1980s. Lionel's first models were replicas of tiny 0-6-OT (engines with six drivers and no tender) and 0-4-OT narrow gauge locomotives with somewhat-foreshortened rolling stock to about

Fig. 1-8 *A Lionel 1/32 scale GP9 diesel, an LGB 1/29 scale boxcar, and two Lionel 1/32 scale reefers on Marc Horovitz's brass bridge.*

1/22.5 scale. After two or three years of production, Lionel introduced an ongoing series of slightly smaller models, still operable on the gauge 1 track. These were replicas of standard gauge equipment, including a Pennsylvania Railroad 4-4-2 (four leading wheels, four driving wheels, and two trailing wheels) a steam locomotive, models of EMD GP7 and GP9 diesels, and a variety of freight cars. These Lionel models were 1/32 scale replicas of the real thing. One of the major manufacturers of HO scale kits, Model Die Casting (MDC), also introduced some easy-to-build plastic freight cars to operate on gauge 1 track built with 1/32 scale proportions. American Standard Car (Great Trains) also offer 1/32 scale locomotives and cars.

The largest quantity of locomotives, rolling stock, and track based on standard gauge railroad equipment is the models produced by Aristo-Craft in China. Aristo-Craft decided that 1/29 scale was a much closer match to the 1¾-inch track gauge to produce a visibly larger model than a 1/32 scale model. Currently Aristo-Craft offers a variety of steam and diesel locomotives, freight cars, and passenger cars in 1/29 scale. USA Trains also offers boxcars, reefers, and work equipment in 1/29 scale. That reminder again: All of these models, whether 1/22.5, 1/29, or 1/32 scale, operate on the same gauge 1 track.

Accurate Scale Models

The only visible difference among the various scale models designed for operation on gauge 1 track oc-

curs when you begin to add buildings to your layout. The difficulty starts with the doors: A 1/32 scale model of a 6-foot-tall man is 2¼-inches tall while a 1/22.5 scale man is nearly an inch taller. The doors to accommodate these two sizes of men will, of course, be larger, which in turn means that a 1/22.5 scale building (made by Pola, among others) will be nearly one-third too large for 1/32 scale or even 1/29 scale trains. If you're worried about accuracy, pick either narrow gauge (1/22.5 to 1/24 scale) or standard gauge (1/32 to 1/29 scale) and use that scale for the people that will populate your model railroad and the buildings they will inhabit.

Frankly, gauge 1 is not the scale for those interested in superfine details, even though it is the largest popular scale. The concepts of "rugged" and "fine details" conflict. It is far easier to bend or break fine wire handrails or posts than the slightly oversized components on all of these models.

Delton, for one, decided that 1/22.5 was a ridiculous proportion for models of American locomotives or rolling stock, so their easy-to-build kits and locomotives are slightly smaller than LGB's. Delton models are built to the more common American scale of 1/24. There are thousands of plastic model car kits, tanks, trucks, and both mechanics and armed forces figures made in 1/24 scale. The difference between 1/22.5 and 1/24 is so slight that men and vehicles and structures from either scale can be used interchangeably. The Delton models are no more and no less realistic than LGB's; however, you might

Fig. 1-9 *A comparison of (l. to r.) an Aristo-Craft 1/29 scale boxcar, LGB 1/29 scale boxcar, and Lionel 1/32 scale boxcar. The dimensions for all three appear in Chapter 14 (Fig. 14-16).*

want to consider 1/24 scale if you really want to add greater details for an indoor railroad or diorama.

Similarly, several firms are importing brass models of both steam and diesel locomotives (selling for $4,000 and up) and rolling stock that are precise replicas of standard gauge locomotives and cars, with the models built to exact 1/32 scale. There is a wide array of plastic vehicle kits in 1/32 scale, and Preiser makes a selection of 1/32 scale people. The gauge 1 track, however, is still the same.

Indoors or Out?

The traditional model railroad is located in the basement, spare room, or garage—indoors. The best place to put these gauge 1 models is *outdoors*. The smallest-radius curved track sections are those included in the LGB, Lionel, and Bachmann train sets and are available as separate pieces from Aristo-Craft, Model Power, Kalamazoo, and Micro Engineering. These curves have approximately a 24-inch radius to the centerline of the track, which means you can fit an oval of track on a 5-by-9-foot Ping-Pong table with room for the cars and locomotives to overhang outside the curves. That's only a bit larger than the common 4-by-8-foot area considered minimum for HO scale trains.

Frankly, the gauge 1 trains look very toylike on the 24-inch radius curves. There's a charm to that, however. They can be used in a small garden or even an indoor setting. A layout indoors with gauge 1 equipment, however, should be at least 9 by 12 feet. That will allow the use of the larger-radius track—LGB's number 1600 or Micro Engineering's number 104— each with about a 4-foot radius. Matching switches

also are available from both LGB and Micro Engineering. Even with this radius, the curves are proportionally the same as those 18-inch-radius curves in HO scale toy train sets. Unless you are deliberately trying to make a caricature of a narrow gauge railroad with ultratight curves, I would suggest you consider these to be the minimum radius for a gauge 1 railroad, either narrow or standard gauge. The models simply look their best on the larger-radius curves.

When you consider that 6 by 9 feet is the minimum space for that basic train set oval, you can understand that some really massive spaces are needed for an indoor model railroad in gauge 1. Just reaching across the tabletop can be a problem because most of us cannot reach much more than 3 feet. You will see track plans in Chapter 3 that have a walk-in aisle to minimize the need to overreach for a derailed train.

In some homes the most practical space is on the floor. You'll see an incredible layout in the next chapter that fills a 30-by-40-foot area of a basement with LGB track and equipment. The outdoor layout of the Baldocks, also in Chapter 2, begins as an oval on the patio deck of their home. The Baldocks elected to continue the layout off the deck and around the back of the house, but there's plenty of operating pleasure available from just the patio portion of that layout.

Bill Bauer is building a traditional model railroad with benchwork made from 1-by-4-inch lumber and other techniques used by HO, N, and O scale modelers all around the world. His layout also is in Chapter 2. You'll find construction and scenery techniques in the *HO Model Railroading Handbook,* published by Chilton Book Company, that will be helpful in constructing an indoor model railroad in any scale.

The Great Outdoors

When I first became aware of the potential of gauge 1 modeling, I envisioned a railroad on shelves around the walls of a huge basement. This is the type of railroad that experienced modelers are making in HO scale to provide the maximum amount of mainline train running while still maintaining a scene. I've searched America for this mythical layout, however, and I have yet to find it. What I have located are the even more incredible outdoor layouts on these pages. Now, I'm completely convinced that gauge 1 is at its best outdoors.

These models offer model railroaders the potential to overcome the one pressing problem that plagues them: lack of space. There is more space in nearly anyone's backyard for a model railroad than in the largest basement. If you loop the layout around the perimeter of the yard, the curves can be 12- or even 20-foot radius, like those on Marc and Barbara Horovitz's layout in Chapter 2.

Fig. 1-10 *It's your garden railroad, so run what you like. This is Lionel's whimsical self-powered handcar.*

Fig. 1-11 *The LGB 1/22.5 scale replicas of the Alco DL-535E diesel are some of the largest gauge 1 locomotives. These are pulling a test train on Thomas Flynn's new layout.*

My personal dream has shifted from building a gauge 1 railroad around the walls of a basement to recreating a scale model environment like that of the layout built by Steve and Judy Arrigotti. That, however, is *my* preference. I've also realized that nearly any model railroad built outdoors is likely to be more realistic—given equal skill levels from the builder—than if built indoors.

Start with the lighting for an outdoor layout. It's perfect and doesn't need spotlights or hazy-day flourescents. The lighting makes even Playmobil's toy trains look more realistic than some HO models I've seen indoors. The dirt, of course, looks like dirt. If you select rocks with care, like the master Norm Grant, they are more realistic than anything cast from plaster.

Plants on an outdoor railroad should be a problem. I have seen virtually nothing that has accurate-scale leaves or needles for 1/32 to 1/24 scale. There are some tree and bush shapes and sizes that are nearly perfect, but the close-up sizes of the textures are simply too large. Yet it does not seem to matter. Even a grossly out-of-scale bush is more realistic than the typical tree on an indoor railroad because your mind somehow forgets the size differences and sees only a living plant. It seems like my mind, at least, forgets that scale is important in an outdoor railroad; what I see are real trains running through a real landscape under real sunlight with a real breeze in my face. There's only one place you can find that kind of realism: outdoors.

Chapter 2

Inspiration

THE DREAM of anyone who has watched a toy train circulating around a Christmas tree is to bring those scenes, that are so vivid in our imagination, to life. For most of us, there are moments where the presents and tree disappear and that train is snaking across a cliff, thundering over a trestle, diving into a tunnel, and emerging from a wooded glade. These gauge 1 trains allow us all to realize those dreams in nearly every sense of the word.

I have searched the country—from Los Angles to Burlington, Vermont, from Eugene, Oregon, to Miami—looking for gauge 1 model railroads, indoors or out. The layouts you will see spotlighted in this chapter are also the major layouts shown in the color section of this book. There are certainly some layouts around the equal of these, but, so far, there are none better. These scenes, then, are the dreams of their builders brought to life. Most often, the reality is brighter, clearer, and more exciting than the dream.

Do not, however, consider that you need to fill your basement or your backyard with trains to capture the scenes on these pages. A simple 6-by-12-foot oval of track around one corner of a yard or in a corner of a spare room can be enough for many of us to recreate our dreams of real railroading. In truth, nearly every one of these layouts started just the way; the Arrigotti's layout is simply an expansion of their 10-by-18-foot oval.

The Devonshire, Snail Park & Petunia Railroad

Bill and Dee Baldock freely admit they are just two grown kids. Their backyard slopes rather steeply into what would usually be useless land, but Bill has terraced the slope to create the cliffs and roadbed for the "garden" portion of their railroad. A loop around a small side yard encloses the half dozen buildings and two-story station at Devonshire. The towns of Snail Park and Petunia Junction—each with a station and at least one other structure—are located beneath the patio deck on the upper reaches of the backyard terrrace.

The Baldocks' railroad combines a simple large oval around the patio deck with a garden railroad. The patio deck also houses Dee's toys: a Playmobil castle and two-story Victorian house as well as the two-stall engine house for the locomotives.

The railroad is built on the native crushed sandstone with a unique roadbed that Bill developed, using three 1-inch-diameter PVC plastic lighting conduit tubes. The method is shown in Chapter 4, and it supplies a perfectly level roadbed that is virtually impervious to weather while automatically creating smooth-flowing curves.

Bill wanted a more realistic track than that supplied by LGB, Aristo-Craft, or Lionel with rail about half the size. Micro Scale now makes a series of track sections and turnouts with rail about three-fourths

Fig. 2-1 *The trains on the Baldock layout descend from the patio deck to a loop at the rear of this scene to travel beneath the deck, to a loop to the left of this scene, then back across the lowest level.*

the size of LGB or Aristo-Craft, but Bill's is even smaller, a code 197-size rail ($\frac{1}{5}$-inch tall) obtained from Old Pullman models. Old Pullman also makes turnouts and spikes. Bill cut 1/24 scale 6-by-8-inch ties from redwood and hand-spiked the rail to each tie.

The turnouts are controlled by LGB switch machines, but Bill modified Atlas switch controls by grinding the inside to eliminate a potential short with the 24 volt current. This is not a procedure recommended for inexperienced modelers, however. The railroad is powered by a Keller Onboard command-control system that allows many locomotives to be operated at once simply by installing a small electronic device in the cab or tender. The Onboard system also includes an optional steam or diesel sound synthesizer that can be installed so that whistles, bells, or horns can be controlled from the keypads that operate the locomotives. The Onboard keypads are about the size of a pocket calculator with a 20-foot tether cable that allows the operator to follow along beside the trains.

The three-tube roadbed method also simplified the task of obtaining smooth roadbed in a vertical plane; Bill simply sighted down the tubes and moved them up or down to eliminate dips or rises in the track. His railroad is unusual in that there are two very steep 8 percent grades (an 8-inch rise in 100 inches of track). He finds that either the LGB 2-6-0 or

Fig. 2-2 *An LGB number 2085 Mallet articulated 0-6-6-0 heads down grade below Petunia Station on the Bill and Dee Baldock layout.*

Fig. 2-3 *The large figure-8 layout in the Baldock patio deck can be operated in any weather. The cars and locomotives are stored here.*

the Delton 2-8-0 can pull a train of up to four cars. Many of the plants and groundcover that appear on John and Barbara Bierie's and on Bill and Joan Bradford's railroad setups (in this chapter and in Chapter 9) also appear on Bill and Dee Baldock's Devonshire, Snail Park & Petunia Railroad (DSP&PRR).

The Blackhawk & Devil Mountain Railroad

John and Barbara Bierie are completing a classic outdoor model railroad. The layout is part of a thoroughly planned backyard with a system of patio decks leading to a hot tub in a far corner and an observation deck in the opposite corner. Beneath and beside these decks wander a series of both dry and flowing streams. In all, it is a landscaping scene worthy of a professional. It is the railroad, though, that sets off the landscaping.

The railroad follows the natural flow of the streams and gulleys and adds an accent to the decking. Barbara has developed the landscaping using small-scale plants that are in proportion to the railroad if not in precise scale.

The trackwork is virtually all LGB, with most curves in the large-radius (about 46½-inch) number 1600 with matching turnouts. John used a few of the smaller-radius (about 23½-inch) number 1100 curves, but they have proved to be a constant source of aggravation. They cause trains to lurch in and out of

the curves and have caused a few derailments of the large White Pass and Yukon diesel pair he operates.

Bill utilizes two power systems for this railroad with a double-pole, double-throw (DPDT) switch to switch from pack to pack. The first system uses an Aristo-Craft power pack, the second a Power Systems Incorporated (PSI) Dynatrol command control that, similar to the Keller Onboard, allows dozens of locomotives to be operated at once on the same stretch of track with each locomotive under independent control. Each locomotive has a small electronic module wired in place, following Dynatrol's instructions, and a walk-around controller (about the size of a small pack of cigars) is used to control the trains. The controller is on a 20-foot tethered cable so the engineers can walk along beside their trains. Bill has the Dynatrol system in all but two of his locomotives; for the others, he switches the system over to the Aristo-Craft conventional power pack. Switches and electrical blocks in the track are controlled by LGB switches mounted inside a large wooden box (see Chapter 5).

The track plan for the Blackhawk & Devil Mountain Railroad (B&DMRR) includes a wye in one corner that allows trains to be reversed by running from the main line into the stub end of the wye from either direction. When the trains back out, they take the opposite route, and when they reach the main line again, they are pointing in the opposite direction from when they left the main line.

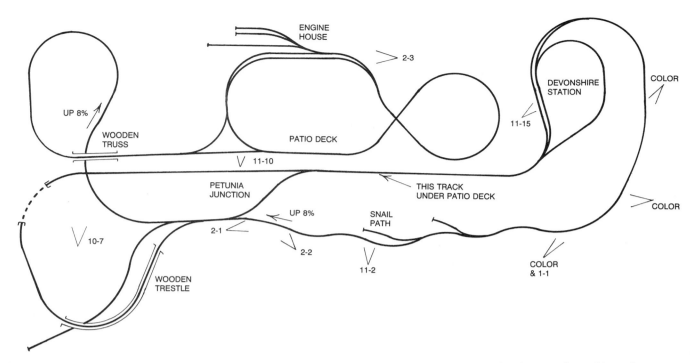

Fig. 2-4 A schematic diagram of the Baldock layout with the small angles indicating where the photographs in this and other chapters were located. The point of the angle is approximately where the camera was placed.

Fig. 2-5 The end of the wye stub and storage tracks run along the side of John and Barbara Bierie's home.

This layout, more than any other in this book, makes extensive use of scale people and animals. There are about fourteen small scenes that depict everyday life in a mountain community, from attending church to loading cattle. There are eleven buildings; most of them are in the town of Blackhawk.

The South Park & San Juan Railroad

Norm and Dale Grant have created one of the most spectacular gauge 1 model railroads in America. The railroad is part of the history of the hobby because, after thirty-nine months of construction, it was abandoned in November 1988. Fortunately, many of the bridges and some of the fifteen tons of rock were relocated to a new garden railroad that Norm and son Dale are building for Dick Schaffer.

This garden railroad was one of the first outdoor model railroads, with scenes and plantings matched to the scale of the trains. Here, the railroad came first and the "garden" was really scenery to support the realism of the railroad. Norm operates By Grant and Kenosha Railroad Supply which custom builds wooden bridges. There were fourteen of them on the South Park & San Juan Railroad, (SP&SJRR) including the 20-foot trestle shown here.

Norm was one of the pioneers of the concept that a backyard could serve as both a garden and the site for scale-size scenery. The yard at the Grant home was about 80 by 120 feet, and it was filled with railroad.

Inspiration

Fig. 2-6 *The station, water tower, and store are Pola buildings; most of the people and animals are Preiser on the Bierie layout.*

Fig. 2-7 *Preiser makes the pigs and Barbara Bierie found the fence and the water trough in a dollhouse miniatures store.*

The trackwork was all LGB ties with rail bent to fit the curves in a Lindsay Railbender. There were 424 feet of main line plus another 78 feet of sidings and branch lines. All turnouts were LGB's large-radius, operated on site with manual ground throws.

The leftover powder or dust from crushed granite (called "crusher fines") was used on the layout for ballast. Norm has tried a number of substances, but the rugged Colorado winter freezes and daily thaws shifted the track with nearly every other substance. The fine granite dust has a rough square shape while many other gravel powders are round—the rounded particles move more easily than the other materials, even in the severe spring rains.

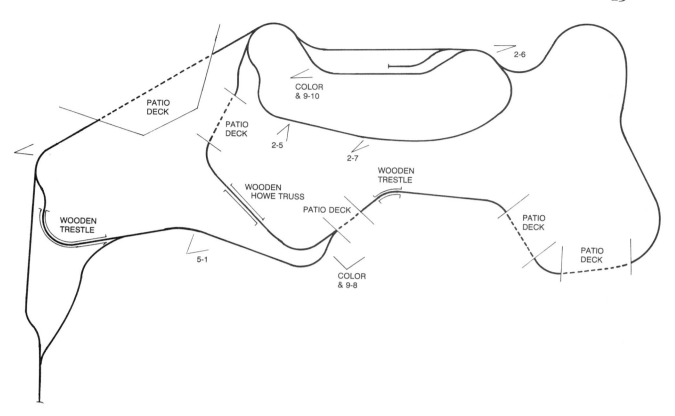

Fig. 2-8 *The Bierie layout follows the contours of the garden and the track runs from one corner of the backyard to the other.*

Fig. 2-9 *Norm Grant had just completed this redwood trestle, and this was the first work train across the span.*

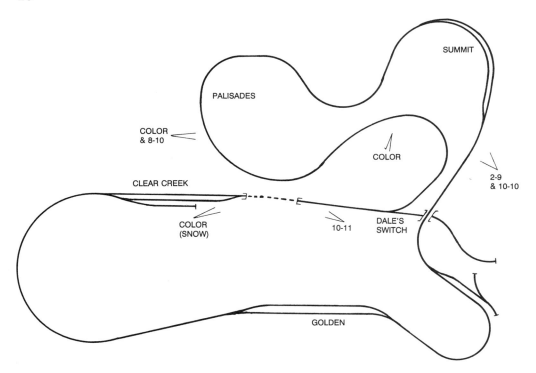

Fig. 2-10 *Norm Grant's South Park & San Juan layout gives an overview. There are photos of Norm Grant's spectacular layout in the color section and in Chapter 8.*

The rocks on the Grant layout were carefully selected so that moss-covered or "weathered" rock was used for the cliffs and peaks and the cleaner broken surfaces were used for cuts where the railroad company would have used dynamite to blast away the rock.

The uphill grades were limited to 2 percent so the LGB Mogul could pull seven cars anywhere on the layout. It was common, however, for the Moguls to double-head with twelve or more cars.

The Mother Lode Railway

Steve and Judy Arrigotti started with a simple 10-by-18-foot layout, which is shown on the far left of the track plan. The C-shaped layout was then expanded into the center a year later, and the following year, the mountain and sawmill area on the extreme right of the plan was added to create a layout that fills an 18-by-90-foot area. There are over 380 feet of track.

This layout is truly a model railroad built outdoors rather than a garden railroad. The layout is surrounded by 12-inch-square timbers to create an edge to the "tabletop." The land slopes down from the rear of the house so a single 12-by-12-inch timber is at the ground level nearest the house and a stack of four timbers is at the rear of the layout.

There is even "benchwork" of a sort: The Arrigotti's used garden-edge "bender board" to create a trough about 6 inches wide for the roadbed. They filled the trough with sheet plastic to stop weed growth, then filled to within ½ inch of the 6-inch-deep trough with a mixture of gravel and dry cement. Steve leveled the mix carefully and checked all grades with a level before gently watering the trough to set the cement. Loose gravel was then poured in and the track placed on that. The bender boards were spaced apart with 2-by-6-inch timber, and the track was nailed to the boards about every 2 feet to help anchor the track. The rock ballast, supported on both sides by the bender board, supplies most of the track-holding power, however.

The layout has its own drip-feed irrigation system with about 180 feet of ½-inch tube and 110 small water emitters located beside each major plant. The area within the timbers was filled with improved soil. Several tons of boulders were installed as cliffs and around the two waterfalls and lakes at the ends of the layout.

The track was laid using LGB's ties and rail with a homemade railbender similar to the Lindsay unit shown in Chapter 4. The turnouts are all large-radius LGB with hand-throw levers at the turnout. There are

Fig. 2-11 *A waterfall tumbles from the rocks at the left into the lake in the upper right on the original portion of the Arrigotti layout.*

Fig. 2-12 *Nestled in the shadows of the trees, a farmer plows with his horse on the Arrigotti layout. Judy's dad built the barn from redwood strips; the house is a Korber kit.*

photos of the specific plants Judy selected in Chapter 9.

The large sawmill and barn were built from strips of redwood by Judy's father. Steve made the redwood bridges and trestles. Most of the structures on this railroad, like the others in this book, are brought indoors when the railroad is not in operation.

The Ogden Botanical Railway

Marc and Barbara Horovitz have created a garden that also is occupied by a charming and mythical railway. The yard was surveyed with the help of a friend who is a professional surveyor. The area for the railroad was then built up with a variety of cribbing, most made as open boxes of 1-by-1-inch wood stringers to

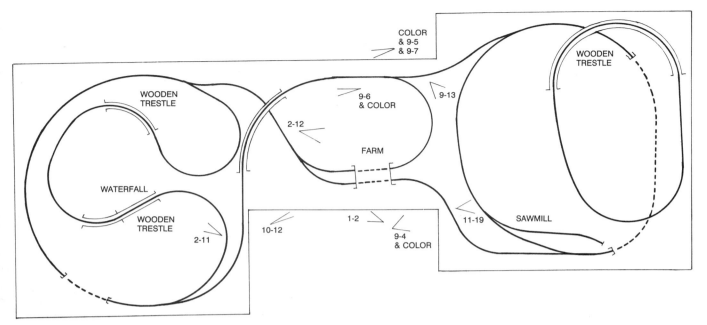

Fig. 2-13 *The Arrigotti's house is at the top of this plan, with their original 12-by-18-foot layout on the right, the addition in the center, and the latest enlargement (the sawmill and mountain) at the left.*

Fig. 2-14 *The Horovitz's garden railway is part of a carefully planned border of plants in boxes elevated about a foot from the lawn.*

make a level roadbed. These doubled as artistic planter boxes for Barbara's garden.

Barbara and Marc publish *Garden Railways* magazine, the leading bimonthly publication about this type of railroading. Their years of experience and Barbara's zeal for gardening were taxed to provide small-scale plants near the railroad as well as attrac-

tive larger plants to serve as a backdrop for both the railroad and the smaller plants. The layout and plants were illustrated in the November/December 1990 issue of *Garden Railways*.

Marc cut ties from redwood. Small holes were drilled for scale-sized spikes from Micro Engineering, and the spikes were pressed into place, to hold

Fig. 2-15 *This low wooden trestle, made from By Grant bents with Marc's scratch-built brass girder bridge, borders one corner of the Horovitz lawn.*

Fig. 2-16 *Marc Horovitz loves the obscure and eclectic, so the layout is built with dual-gauge trackage (gauge 1 and 0 gauge), and he builds curiosities like this brass free-lance gasoline-style locomotive and scratch-built wooden gondola.*

LGB rails, with pliers. Most of the track has three rails, with the center rail spaced 1¼ inches from one outer rail. This creates "dual gauge" track that allows Marc to operate some of his smaller powered and live steam locomotives over the same roadbed. Marc's hobby-within-the-hobby is creating whimsical loco-

motives, railcars, and rolling stock based very loosely on industrial American and British prototypes. Marc kindly allowed me to use the layout as a site to photograph some of the newer Aristo-Craft 1/29 scale standard gauge freight and passenger trains; they are certainly not the usual travelers over those rails.

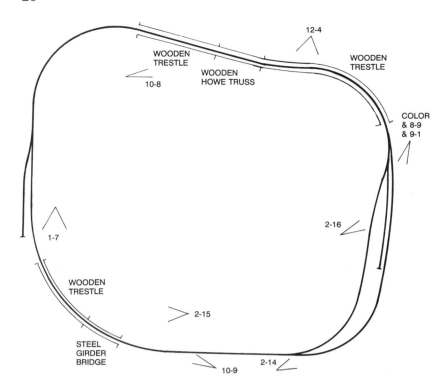

Fig. 2-17 *A professional surveyor friend helped the Horovitzs plan their garden railway in three dimensions before construction began.*

Fig. 2-18 *The Bradfords developed a small island of succulent plants in the center of their lawn and gracefully looped the railroad around it.*

The prespiked sections of track were inverted and ½-inch battens were nailed to the bottom to create what is essentially sectional track, but track made to fit the layout. The track itself was held in place with the same crusher fines granite dust and particles used by Norm Grant on his layout. The variety of curves allows the railroad to serve as a fine test bed for many of the newer locomotives and other items being introduced into the hobby through reviews in the *Garden Railways* magazine.

The Rare Bird Railway

Bill and Joan Bradford operate one of the stores that specialize in garden railways: Rara Avis in Concord, California. They also manufacture tunnel portals, bridges, and the water tower and station shown on their home layout. This one is a classic Sunbelt backyard garden railway. Here, the railway simply fits nicely into the casual backyard landscaping.

Bill has developed a unique method for laying his trackwork. He uses a ¼-by-6-inch strip of foam weath-

Fig. 2-19 *Bill used wooden ties and separate rails for the track. The station is a Rara Avis kit; the cars were built from wood with Rara Avis metal castings.*

Fig. 2-20 *A large grouping of boulders occupies the opposite end of the Bradford backyard, with a waterfall and small pond bridged by the railroad.*

erproofing material. He cuts redwood ties and cements them to the weatherstrip foam with carpenter's glue. The Micro Engineering code 250 rail is then spiked to each tie. Bill uses the rail to make his own turnouts from the same material. The long sections of track are then laid over a sheet of weed-blocking plastic, and the plastic, the foam, and the ties and track are all covered with fine gravel ballast.

The plants that Barbara uses are shown in Chapter 9. The right end of the layout is a forest of succulent plants, and the left end of the layout has a mountain of boulders with a small pond and pump-fed waterfall.

Inspiration

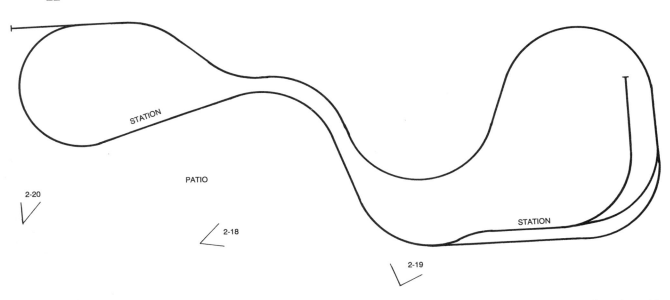

STATION

PATIO

2-20

2-18

STATION

2-19

Fig. 2-21 *The Bradford's track plan is simple enough, with a single passing siding to allow two trains to function with radio-controlled operation.*

The area aound the waterfall has Pola European-style buildings and a water tower to complement the European-style LGB cars and locomotives, whereas the "desert" area has a Rara Avis–brand station and water tower to complement a variety of handmade (again, from Rara Avis parts) small railroad cars pulled, here, by a Bachmann 0-4-0T locomotive.

The Shawmut Line

Bill Bauer's gauge 1 railroad is located in the most traditional of model railroad locations: his basement. Bill's favorite real railroad is the Pittsburgh, Shawmut & Northern (PS&N), a railroad that ran in northcentral Pennsylvania until abandoned in the 1950s. He has modified and repainted his locomotives and rolling stock to simulate the standard gauge PS&NRR, or the Shawmut Line, as it was known.

The layout benchwork fills about 15 by 17 feet of Bill's basement plus a 6-by-9-foot extension beneath the stairs. The major portion of the layout is a 15-by-17-foot rectangle. The benchwork is an open-grid style, similar to that shown in Chapter 6. However, he covered the wooden grid with sheets of ½-inch-thick plywood. The main line is laid over ⅛-inch sheets of cork directly onto the plywood tabletop. The extensive branch line begins at the tabletop but climbs a 2 percent grade on ½-inch plywood supported by ½-inch plywood risers attached with 1-by-1-inch cleats. The branch line, too, is laid over ⅛-inch cork to help reduce noise.

The branch line uses LGB number 1100 curved track sections and matching switches in most locations. The branch line is connected to the main line by an LGB number 1225 double-slip switch (turnout) that allows the trains to be routed either to the inside branch line, to the outside main line, or to cross from one to the other. The Shawmut main line runs around the outer edge of the 15-by-17-foot benchwork through the number 1225 switch, and the Kaul & Haul Lumber Company Railroad (K&HLRR) branch line leaves and enters the main line through the same switch.

Bill has modified and repainted every piece of rolling stock and locomotive to represent more closely the standard gauge Shawmut and branch lines that once fed the real railroad. The Shawmut cars are marked both Pittsburgh Shawmut & Northern (PS&N) and Saint Mary's & South Western Railroad (St. M&SWRR). The letter B on some of the cars was used on the real railroad to identify the brake wheel end of the car for emergency use. The locomotives and cars for the branch line are marked K&HLRR for the Kaul & Haul Lumber Company and EC&CC for the Elk Coal & Coke Company.

The locomotives are an unusual mixture of modified and rebuilt LGB and brass imports. The K&HLRR shay number 71 is a long-out-of-production KMT model, imported from Korea nearly ten years ago. The 2-6-2 number 2 has a chassis from the LGB number 2070 0-6-2T locomotive with a new boiler,

Fig. 2-22 *The area near Fitz Coal Mine No. 3 is finished with scenery and ballast on Bill Bauer's Shawmut Line.* Photo by Bill Bauer.

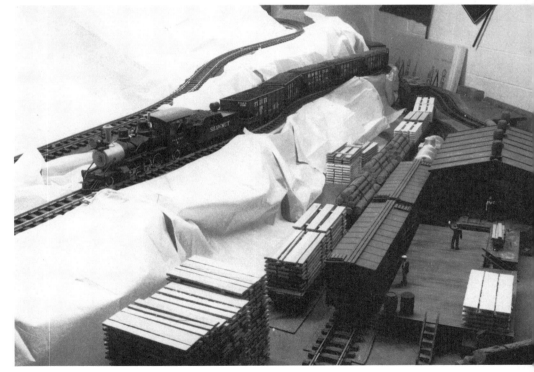

Fig. 2-23 *The sawmill started with a single Pola building, and Bill added a platform and stacks of wood cut from Northeastern basswood. The train is on the branch line loop, with a second branch climbing higher to reach timber.* Photo by Bill Bauer.

cab, and tender made from sheet brass by Bill Bauer. The Elk Coal & Coke 0-4-0T is a slightly modified LGB number 2076 0-4-0T locomotive.

The wooden Shawmut gondolas, passenger cars, caboose, boxcars, and reefers are from LGB. The log cars and railbus are Delton; the steel hopper cars are MDC. Decals and individual letters from William Mc-

Intyre and Robert Dustin are used on all the locomotives and cars. Bill uses scale-sized nonoperating knuckle-style couplers from George Randeall.

The railroad is designed for operation. Cars of coal, for example, from the J. A. Fritz Mine are picked up by Shawmut trains for imaginary trips to the outside world. A few cars of coal are picked up by

Fig. 2-24 *Bill used a rubber cooking dish to cast the forms for these coke ovens and carved the mortar lines while the plaster was still moist.* Photo by Bill Bauer.

Fig. 2-25 *Most of the rolling stock on the Shawmut Line has been repainted and new decals applied. The couplers are the correct size but nonoperative.* Photo by Bill Bauer.

K&HLRR locomotives to be taken up the branch line to the EC&CC trackage, where that road's locomotives move it to the coke ovens. Simulated loads of coke reverse the route to the mine to be, in turn, picked up by Shawmut trains. Similar paths are followed by log cars down the branch line to the saw-mill on the Shawmut main line, and loads of cut lumber move away from the mill.

Basement Floor-Level Railroading

This 30-by-40-foot gauge 1 layout fills most of a basement with LGB track and turnouts. Its builders wish

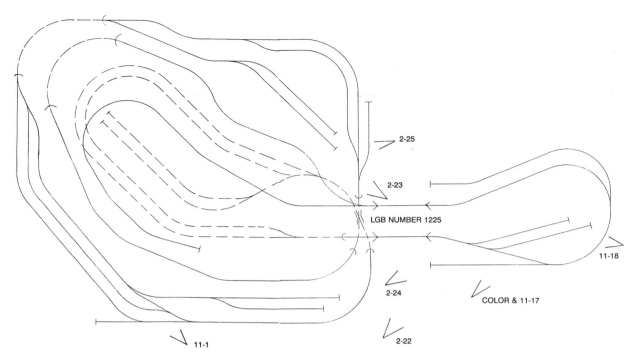

Fig. 2-26 *The Shawmut Line began on an old Lionel tabletop in a 15-by-17-foot area to the left. The gauge 1 track now crosses beneath the stairs to a 6-by-9-foot table.* Plan by Bill Bauer.

to remain anonymous but their efforts are worth sharing. About half of the track is laid directly onto the floor with the track sections connected by LGB's under-tie mount number 1150 clips. The curves are all LGB number 1500 with matching turnouts. The track is elevated from the floor on ¼-inch plywood with a series of 1-by-4-inch lumber risers. Each riser is ½ inch taller than the previous riser and the risers are spaced about the length of an LGB track section apart. The resulting grade is about 4 percent.

Virtually all of the LGB electric turnouts and wiring devices are used for remote control of the turnouts both manually through switches on the control panel and automatically by passing trains, using LGB's number 1701 magnets on the tender trucks and number 1700 track contacts between the rails. A Keller Onboard command-control system is used to control the trains so up to a dozen locomotives can be in operation, each under independent control of its engineer. Keypads the size of a pocket calculator are used to control each locomotive. A small electronic module is fitted to each locomotive so it responds only to its own controller. A sound system, also controlled by the keypad, is fitted with the system to simulate steam chuffing sounds, throbbing air pumps, whistles, and bells.

The track rises to nearly 30 inches from the floor and mountains soar almost to the ceiling. This base-

Fig. 2-27 *Thousands of weeds are used on this 30-by-40-foot basement layout to create a 1/22.5 scale forest. The mountains are plaster-soaked paper towels.*

Fig. 2-28 *The majority of the 30-by-40-foot space is just flat basement floor. The mountains provide a backdrop and some spectacular scenery.*

Fig. 2-29 *Eventually, a complete Western town will occupy this site, with a river valley painted on the floor.*

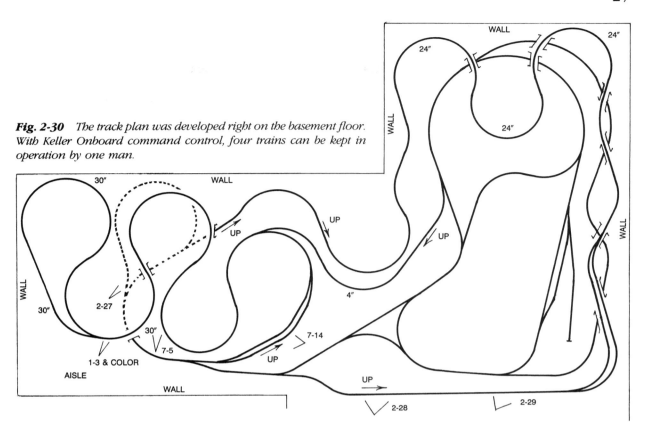

Fig. 2-30 *The track plan was developed right on the basement floor. With Keller Onboard command control, four trains can be kept in operation by one man.*

ment has a 7-foot ceiling, but even that would not be enough to allow mountains this tall if the railroad were built on a tabletop or benchwork that was 3 or 4 feet above the floor. If you want tall mountains, it makes sense to start from the floor rather than from a tabletop. The floor-level layout also makes it possible to walk across the tracks to reach remote areas. Later, the builders plan to paint and texture the concrete to simulate rivers and fields that the operators can walk on for access to derailed trains, for track cleaning, or for further construction.

Chapter 3

|||||||||||||||||||||||||||||||||||||||||||||||||||||||||||||||||||||||||||||||||||||||||||||||||||||||||||||||||||||||

Track Plans and Track Planning

THE JOY of model railroading is that it provides the basis and opportunity to dream, to envision the railroad empire you'll build. For some of us, the dream begins with a route for the trains, the configuration the track will take on our dream layout, or in hobbyists' terms, the "track plan."

You can use the track sections themselves to create a plan, and frankly, that is the most reliable method of ensuring that the track will actually fit in the space you have allotted. You can use a basic oval to plan a much larger layout by marking the position of the original track, then moving segments, marking them, and so on in hopscotch fashion until the entire layout is marked on the floor, the tabletop, or the earth itself.

Sectional Track Geometry

The gauge 1 train sets often include an oval of track that, save for its size, is identical to the oval of track supplied with the smaller HO, N, or O scale train sets. As you might expect, the track runs in the smallest possible circle that the train will negotiate without derailing. That allows you to fit the large-scale trains in about the same space as the smaller-scale trains. The basic train set track supplied in LGB, Bachmann, and Lionel gauge 1 train sets has a circle of track of about 4 feet in diameter. Modelers refer to it in terms of the radius, however; and the radius is measured to the center of the track circle. Hence, the nominal radius for a gauge 1 train set track is 24 inches.

The very shortest four-driver steam locomotives and short cars look okay on such a tight radius, but at best, they look like toys. For some of us, there is a certain charm to that tight-radius appearance and, if a caricature of a real railroad, rather than realism, is your goal, the train set curves are just fine. Matching turnouts (switches) to allow sidings, passing tracks, and alternate routes are available for the 24-inch radius curves from LGB, Aristo-Craft, and Lionel. The most common straight track sections are, again, a nominal 12 inches, and the turnouts match the length of the straights as well as the curves.

The 24-inch curved track sections in the train sets are designed so that it takes twelve sections to make a circle. Thus each section is 30 degrees (one-twelfth) of the circle. If you need a track that diverges from the circle at 45 degrees, half-curved sections are available from LGB and Micro Engineering.

I would recommend that you consider the nominal 48-inch radius curved track sections to be the minimum for a gauge 1 model railroad indoors or out. All of the models in this book are designed with special couplers so even the longest locomotive or car will negotiate the tight 24-inch radius curves. None of these models, however, looks much like a real train when it is lurching around a 24-inch radius curve.

Currently, only LGB and Micro Engineering offer 48-inch-radius curved track sections. Both brands use sixteen pieces of track to make a full circle so each

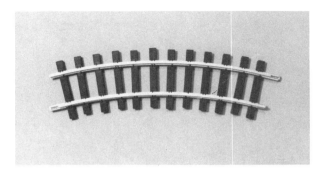

Fig. 3-1 *23.6-inch/600-millimeter-radius, 30-degree curved track sections: LGB number 1100, Aristo-Craft number 11100, Lionel number 82001, Bachmann number 94501, Model Power number 21100. 24-inch-radius/610-millimeter, 30-degree curved track section: Micro Engineering number 102.*

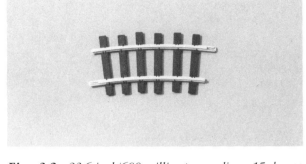

Fig. 3-2 *23.6-inch/600-millimeter radius, 15-degree curved track section: LGB number 1102. 24-inch radius/ 610-millimeter, 15-degree curved track section: Micro Engineering number 136.*

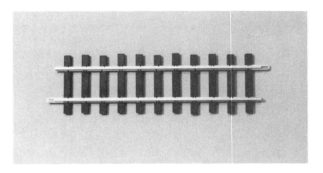

Fig. 3-3 *12½-inch/320-millimeter straight track sections: LGB number 1000, Kalamazoo number 1200, Bachmann number 94511, Model Power number 21000. 12-inch/ 309-millimeter straight track sections: Aristo-Craft number 11000, Micro Engineering number 001. 11¾-inch/300-millimeter straight track section: Lionel number 82002.*

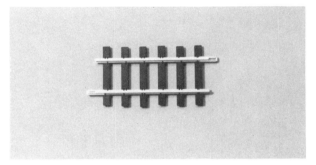

Fig. 3-4 *6¼-inch/160-millimeter straight track section: LGB number 1015. 6-inch/154-millimeter straight track section: Micro Engineering number 056.*

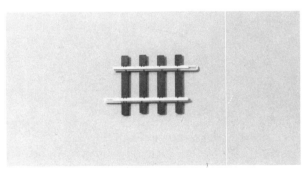

Fig. 3-5 *4-inch/102-millimeter straight track section: Micro Engineering number 054. (Note: two number 1005 LGB 52-millimeter track sections are close to 4 inches in length.)*

piece is 22½ degrees (one-sixteenth of the circle). Both LGB and Micro Engineering offer turnouts that will replace a section of 48-inch-radius curved track. The length of the straight track on both LGB and Micro Engineering 48-inch-radius turnouts is odd, a standard 12-inch straight plus a few filler pieces, as shown in Figs. 3-15 through 3-18, are needed so the turnouts match the length of two 12-inch straight track sections.

Expanding the Circle

The ends of the track sections must join firmly and with the rails in perfect alignment across the joint between the sections. That's easy enough to accomplish with a simple circle, provided you use the same brand of track for each section. If you wish to expand that circle into an oval, break the track at points diametrically apart and insert pairs of straight track sections. If you follow that rule, always inserting pairs of straight track sections at diametrically opposite

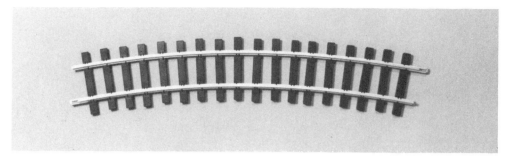

Fig. 3-6 46¼-inch/1175-millimeter-radius, 22.5-degree curved track section: LGB number 1500. 48-inch-radius/1220-millimeter, 22.5-degree curved track section: Micro Engineering number 104.

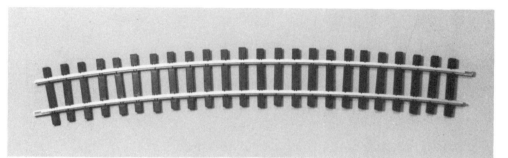

Fig. 3-7 46¼-inch/1175-millimeter-radius, 22.5-degree, 17¼-inch/440-millimeter-long turnouts (switches): LGB number 1605 (right hand) or 1615 (left hand). 48-inch/1220-millimeter-radius, 22.5-degree, 18.9-inch long turnouts (switches): Micro Engineering number 224 (right hand) or 204 (left hand).

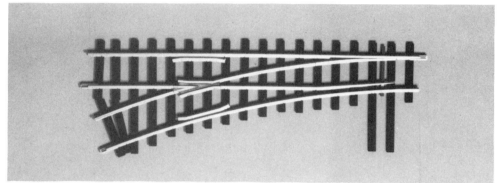

Fig. 3-8 80-inch/2032-millimeter-radius, 18-degree curved track section: Micro Engineering number 107.

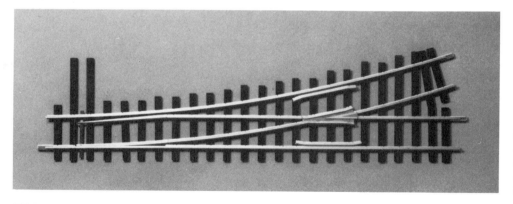

Fig. 3-9 80-inch/2032-millimeter-radius, 18-degree, 25.1-inch-long turnouts (switches): Micro Engineering number 227 (right hand) or 207 (left hand).

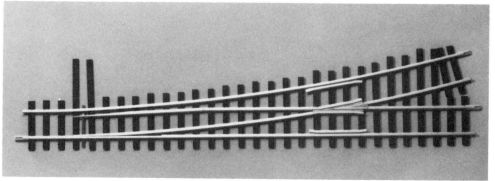

Fig. 3-10 120-inch/3048-millimeter-radius, 31.4-inch-long turnouts (switches): Micro Engineering number 230 (right hand) or 210 (left hand).

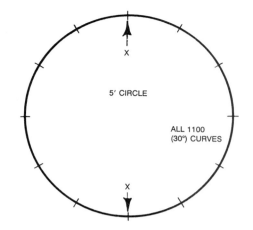

Fig. 3-11 *The basic 24-inch/610-millimeter-radius circle.*

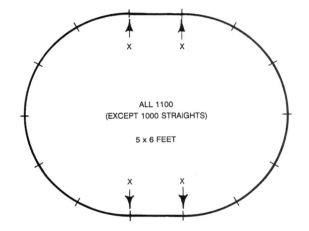

Fig. 3-12 *Add two 12-inch/305-millimeter straight sections to the circle.*

sides of the circle or oval or figure 8, you will know the tracks should align perfectly.

The turnouts are designed to replace either a standard curve or straight section. If you remove a straight section at E in Fig. 3-13, for example, you can insert a left-hand turnout. The part numbers on these diagrams refer to LGB track, but the photographs of the track sections list other brands with the same radius or length. Another left-hand turnout can be inserted at B in place of the curved section.

If you wish, the turnouts at A and B can be connected with the track sections you removed plus three more curves and, in this case, a short filler piece of LGB number 1005 straight track (Fig. 3-14). This is a passing or runaround siding, sometimes called a "through" siding as opposed to the two stub-end sidings created by the installation of just those two turnouts. The need for the short filler piece was created because we did not remove matching pieces of track that were diametrically opposite to each other.

Turnouts to replace the 48-inch radius curved track sections are also available from LGB and Micro Engineering. In Fig. 3-15, two curved sections have been replaced by a right- and left-hand pair of turnouts. The diagram also indicates that two filler pieces of LGB track (numbers 1008), will be needed so the straight portion of the new turnouts will match the length of two standard 12-inch straight track sections. If using Micro Engineering number 104 curved track sections, and the matching numbers 207 and 227 left- and right-hand turnouts, you will also need to add just one piece of Micro Engineering number 056 straight filler track to each turnout so the length of straight matches that of two standard straight tracks. In these simple circle and oval examples (Figs. 3-11,

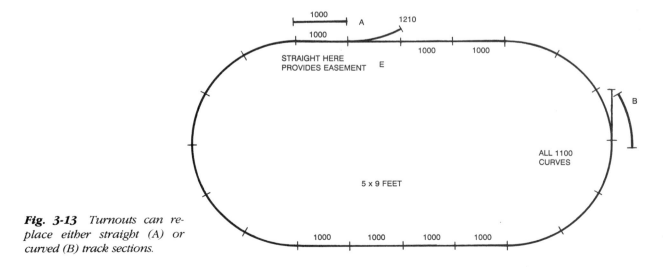

Fig. 3-13 *Turnouts can replace either straight (A) or curved (B) track sections.*

32

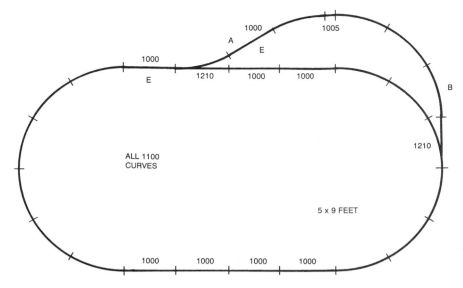

Fig. 3-14 *Filler piece number 1005 is needed for this outside passing siding.*

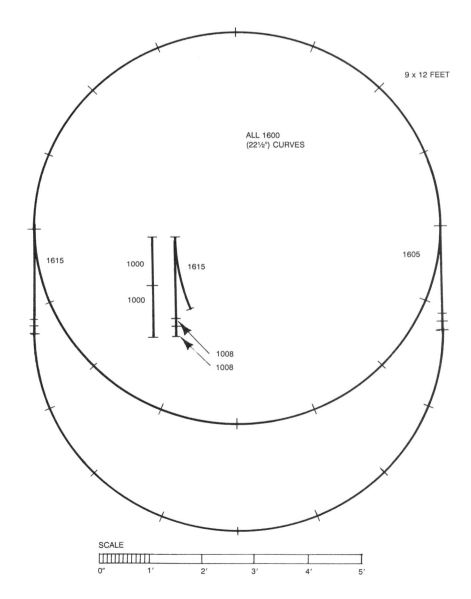

Fig. 3-15 *Two number 1008 filler pieces are needed to extend an LGB number 1615 turnout to equal the length of two number 1000 straight track sections.*

3-12, 3-13, 3-14, and 3-15), the filler straights are not needed, but it is wise to consider them essential to preserve the geometry of the system should you want to expand the plan or replace pairs of standard 12-inch straight tracks with the LGB or Micro Engineering 48-inch radius turnouts.

Smooth-Flowing Trains

One of the sights that identifies a toy train, as opposed to a realistic model, occurs when the toy train lurches into a curve as it leaves a straight segment of track. Real railroads avoid that problem by building the entry portion of the curve in an ever-tightening spiral that eases the train into an ever-tighter curve. For that reason, these gently tightening curves are called easements. Frankly, they are not necessary if you are using 48-inch or larger radius curves but, even with these larger radii, a segment of flexible LGB track (22½ degrees) will greatly improve the realism of the trains as they flow into the curve. If you are using Micro Engineering track, a piece of number 107 curved track with an 80-inch radius and 18 degrees of a cricle and a piece of number 156 curved track (4½ degrees of an 80-inch radius track) can be used to replace a piece of the number 104 48-inch radius curved track at the juncture between a curve and straight.

Fig. 3-16 *Seven short filler pieces are needed to fit the number 1310 LGB 90-degree crossing into a figure 8 with 24-inch/610-millimeter-radius curved track sections.*

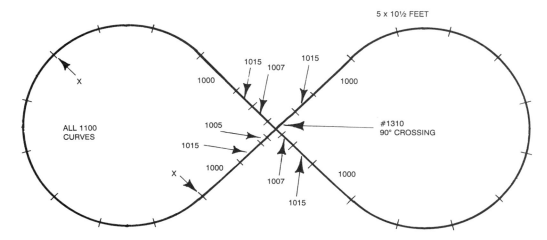

Fig. 3-17 *The same rules apply for extending the figure 8 with pairs of straights on opposite sides of the ends.*

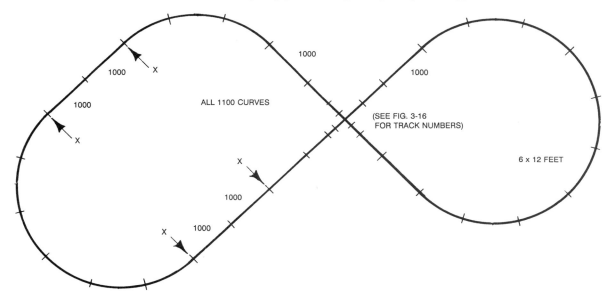

These easements are, essentially, scenic in that they make the trains look better as they swing gently in or out of the curves. Easements are needed even more (sometimes to prevent derailments with long locomotives or cars) in S-shaped stretches of track. If you think that a locomotive and train lurch when they dive from a straight into a curve, set up a pair of curves for which one curve goes left and the joining curve goes right to form the S. The locomotive's and car's sideways lurch when making the instant transition from right turn to left turn can be so severe that the train can actually be jerked right off the track.

Experienced model railroaders have developed a rule for using S-shaped track configurations: A straight track should be inserted between the right and left curves that is the length of the longest car or locomotive. Note that, even with the basic oval extended with a passing siding, I have placed the turnouts so at least one straight track section lies between the right and left curves (in Fig. 3-14).

The track diagram for the double-track oval (an oval inside an oval, Fig. 3-18) includes three crossover pairs of turnouts to allow trains to travel from the inner oval to the outer oval and back again. The turnout pairs on the left end of the diagram avoid any S-shaped curves. The turnout pair on the upper right, however, has a severe S bend. Remember, turnouts include curved track sections in their design. This pair of turnouts is also badly placed in that the inside turnout is placed right after the curve so trains traveling counterclockwise around the inner oval would lurch from left to right as they traveled through the crossover, then instantly lurch left again as they entered the outer oval.

Double-Track Layouts

LGB and Lionel offer curved track sections with a nominal 30-inch radius to allow double-track layouts in confined spaces. Fig. 3-18 shows the LGB number 1500 curved track sections on the right end of the layout. Lionel's similar-sized track section is number 82004. Neither Lionel nor LGB offers turnouts with curves of this radius. Another method of creating a double-tracked layout is shown on the left side of Fig. 3-18: Standard 24-inch radius curves are used with a single section of 12-inch straight track across the end. With LGB track, a number 1004 section of track is also needed to maintain the geometry and track align-

Fig. 3-18 *Two methods of making a double-track oval and the correct method of installing crossover pairs of turnouts from the inner to outer oval.*

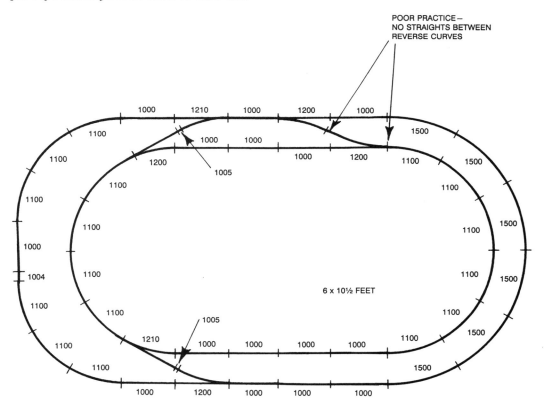

ment. A short piece of Lionel, Aristo-Craft, Bachmann, or Micro Engineering track can be cut as shown in Chapter 4 to fill this area.

Figure-8 Layouts

The figure-8 configuration is a popular choice for model railroad layouts in any scale. The shape allows the trains to stretch out with both longer curves and longer straights than you fit in the same space with a simple oval.

Many of the HO toy train sets include enough track for the figure 8 (Figs. 3-16 and 3-17) and some even include bridge supports for what they often call an "over-and-under" figure 8 (Fig. 3-19); one in which there is not a level crossing but for which one track rises above the other. Both configurations are possible using LGB's track sections. For most of these plans, you can freely substitute similar-sized pieces of track for LGB, but Figs. 3-16 and 3-17 require a 90-degree crossing and, so far, only LGB offers that with plastic ties.

The LGB number 1310 crossing is designed with varying lengths of straight track so two of the crossings can be used to cross a double-track main line or passing siding. The odd lengths, however, mean that a variety of sizes of filler pieces of track must be used, including one number 1005 (52 millimeters [2 inches] long), two number 1007 (75 millimeters [2$\frac{19}{20}$ inches] long), and four 1015 (150 millimeters [5$\frac{9}{10}$ inches] long). You can, of course, cut these from other

LGB track sections to avoid using so many short track sections. Track-cutting techniques are illustrated in Chapter 4.

The figure 8 provides a lesson in how to enlarge a track plan while still maintaining perfect rail alignment at each track joint. In Figs. 3-16 and 3-17 the basic figure 8 was broken apart at the joints marked with an *X*, and two pairs of number 1000 straight track sections were inserted diametrically opposite from each other. Obviously, any length of straight can be added as long as the same length is added on both sides of the half-circle.

Upgrade and Downgrade

Model trains can climb mountains at least as steep as the full-sized trains. In fact, the limits of adhesion (before the wheels or drivers of the locomotive spin), are remarkably similar between the twenty-times-larger real trains and these models.

Real railroad designers and model railroad designers both refer to the steepness of the uphill climb as a percentage based on inches (or feet) climbed per hundred inches (or feet) of track. Fig. 3-20 provides a sample of how far a model train will climb with various percentages of grades. Note that a 2 percent grade will carry the track twice as high as a 1 percent grade.

For gauge 1 model railroads, indoors or out, the steepest practical grade is about 8 percent; that's what Bill Baldock used on his DSP&PRR in Chapter 2, but

Fig. 3-19 *An over-and-under figure 8 needs eight extra straight sections to add enough track length to avoid too-steep uphill grades.*

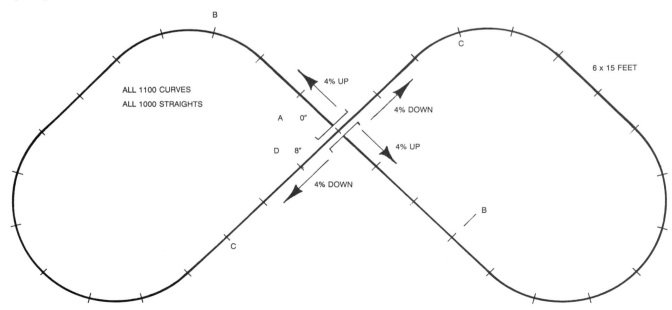

the locomotives will only pull three or four cars. For most modelers a 4 percent grade is about as steep as is practical; that will allow a powerful locomotive like the LGB Mogul (2-6-0) to pull up to about six cars.

It takes a bit more length of track for an upgrade or downgrade than is indicated by in Fig. 3-20, because you must allow room for the track to swoop, or make a vertical curve, upward. The grade cannot simply bend like a kinked sheet of paper or the locomotives and cars will derail when the couplers or pilots hit the ties. Similarly, the top of the grade must be curved (as shown in Fig. 3-21) so the locomotives or cars don't launch themselves into the air. Those upgrade and downgrade vertical curves need about 3 feet of track each, but you won't lose all that length in the grade because it does get ever steeper. As a rough rule, add about 3 feet to any grade, and you should have enough for both that uphill and downhill vertical curve.

If a 4 percent grade is considered maximum and if the vertical curves are included, it takes a bit of extra track to make an over-and-under layout in gauge 1 (Fig. 3-19). The overhead track's rails should clear the lower track's rails by at least 8 inches so you can operate large locomotives like the LGB Mogul or Bachmann's 4-6-0. In all, eight extra foot-long straight

Fig. 3-20 *Chart of grade percentages.*

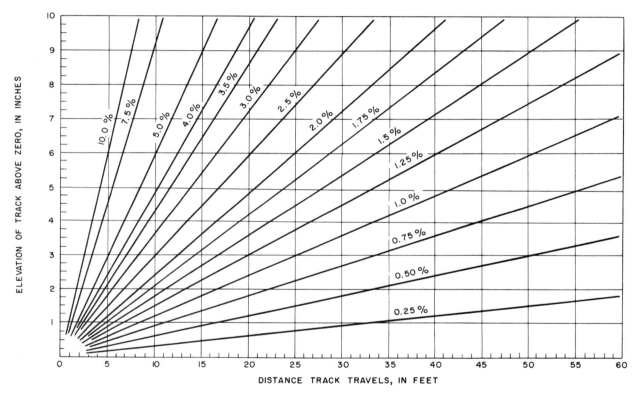

Fig. 3-21 *A side view of how the track must have gentle vertical curves at the bottom and top of all uphill sections.*

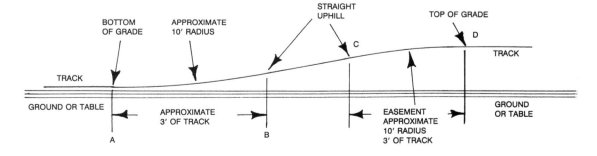

track sections must be added to the basic figure 8. The plan calls for LGB track, but in this case, the over-and-under figure 8 can be assembled with virtually any brand of track because the 90-degree crossing is not needed.

Mixing Brands of Track

The photographs of the track sections (Figs. 3-1 through 3-10) will give you an idea of how many different manufacturers make similar pieces of track. Because all the track has the same gauge, you might assume that all the brands are interchangeable. In fact, none of the different brands of track is completely interchangeable with another.

The LGB, Aristo-Craft, and Micro Engineering brands are nearly interchangeable because all three use similar rail joiners and all three have similar-sized track sections. LGB and Aristo-Craft use brass rail, but the LGB rail weathers to a brown and Aristo-Craft's to a dull gold. You can solve that problem by simply painting the rails a rust color. Micro Engineering offers aluminum rail but it, too, can be painted a rust color. The three brands use different types of rail joiners but all three can be used on each of the other brands.

Kalamazoo's track is similar to LGB, Aristo-Craft, and Micro Engineering, with brass rail and similar rail joiners. The Kalamazoo track, however, is only available in a 30-inch-radius curve—close to the LGB number 1500 30-degree curve with a 30⅛-inch (76-millimeter) radius. Kalamazoo also offers 12-inch lengths of straight track.

Lionel and Bachmann track are not interchangeable with any other brands: Lionel mates with Lionel;

Fig. 3-22 *LGB (left) and Aristo-Craft track both use solid brass rail.*

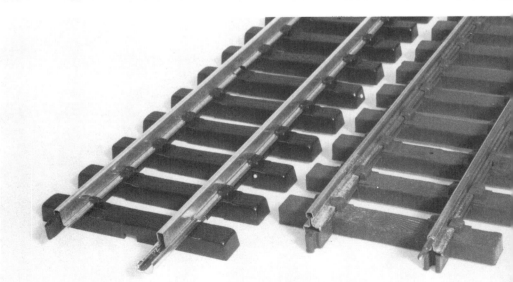

Fig. 3-23 *Bachmann track (left) and Lionel use sheet metal hollow rails.*

Bachmann with Bachmann. Both use a thin sheet (Bachmann's is steel; Lionel's is brass) shaped like a rail, which is hollow. If the rail is treated regularly with rust-proofing it can be used outdoors, but LGB, Micro Engineering, Aristo-Craft, and Kalamazoo track is far more rugged. The sizes of the Lionel and Bachmann track sections are similar to the other brands, however, and the other brands' rail joiners can be adapted to Lionel or Bachmann so you can mix brands.

Micro Engineering offers the option of a smaller and much more realistic rail size (code 250) on all their track sections. Most of the other brands use a code 332 (and Micro Engineering offers that, too). The code 250 rail is $\frac{1}{4}$ inch high and the code 332 rail is 0.332 inch high (about $\frac{3}{16}$ inch). The code 250 rail is also available in 6-foot lengths with a separate tie strip from Micro Engineering, Llagas Creek Railways, and Garich Light Transport.

Flexible Track

I will present more information about flexible track in Chapter 4, but it is an important element of layout planning because it frees you from the constraints of 30 or 22½ degree circles. In truth, the term "flexible" really only applies to the 3-foot lengths of track used for the smaller-scale model railroads like HO, N, and O scales. LGB, Micro Engineering, Garich Light Transport, and Llagas Creek Railways all offer 6-foot (1,500-millimeter from LGB) lengths of rail with a plastic tie strip that slides right on the rail. You can use two pieces of rail and the tie strip to make nice 6-foot-long pieces of straight track. Try to bend that code 332 or code 250 rail, however, and you will understand why gauge 1 track is really not "flexible." Lindsay, however, does sell the Railbender (see Chapter 6) so you can form accurate curves. You can lay out the curve you want on a piece of plywood, using a long board with a nail for a pivot and a pencil as a giant compass. You can also match the curves to Micro Engineering's larger-radius curves.

With separate ties and track, you literally can use the land as your guide in laying out an outdoor railroad. Most modelers, however, simply match the 48-inch or larger sectional track radius with the Railbender, then slip on the ties.

You can also use the rail and ties to make straight track section of any length up to 6 feet to minimize the number of rail joiners (and to save some money). That's the approach used by most of the layout builders in this book.

Planning an Indoor Layout

The major constraint when building an indoor layout is space. The planning, then, begins with an accurate scale sketch of the room itself. I find $\frac{3}{4}$ inch to the foot to be a workable scale for preliminary track plans because the $\frac{1}{16}$-inch marks on the ruler represent full inches. Use a drafting triangle and a compass to make reasonably accurate sketches. A 30/60-degree triangle is helpful when working with sectional track that has 30-degree curved track sections. You can make your own 22½-degree or 18-degree triangle from cardboard with a protractor to locate the angles. Those angles are needed if you are working with the larger-radius track sections or turnouts from LGB or Micro Engineering.

Once you have the room's walls outlined and the door and any windows that must remain uncovered located and drawn, you can begin to add the benchwork, or table, for the layout. You must, however, provide room for you and any visitors to stand while

Fig. 3-24 *Use a compass and triangles to draw plans like these for your layout.*

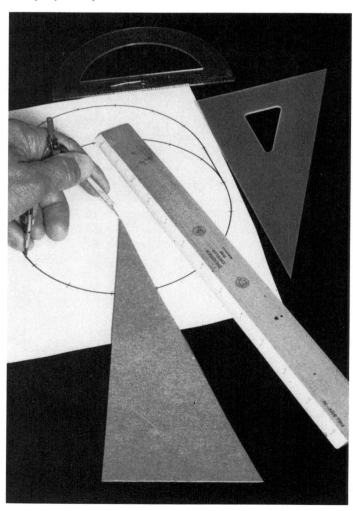

operating and viewing the trains. If you're working on the floor, with no benchwork like the 30-by-40-foot layout in Chapter 2, the operating and access aisles are not necessary.

If you put the track on a tabletop or open-grid benchwork, you will need to decide how high that benchwork will be. If you want the layout to be visible for children, the benchwork may be only 30 or 36 inches high. Modelers who like to look at their trains as though they were the real thing prefer benchworks that are about 54 inches high. The height of the benchwork will determine how far back you can reach. With a 54-inch-high benchwork, most adults can only reach about 30 inches back onto the table. With 36-inch-high benchwork, most can lean over and reach 36 inches or more back onto the benchwork.

The "reach" dimensions are important, because you will want to provide some kind of access aisle or opening in the center of the table so you can walk or crawl around to reach derailed equipment and to perform repair and maintenance work on the track and scenery.

A Loop-to-Loop Layout

Fig. 3-25 has a track configuration modelers refer to as "loop-to-loop." Each end of the layout has a reversing loop so that trains reverse their direction automatically as they travel over the layout. If you use the tight 24-inch-radius curved track sections, this layout can be fitted onto tables that fill an 8-by-8-foot space. Note, however, that it will take a larger room than 8 by 8 feet, because the lower and right ends of the layout cannot be placed against the wall; these ends must be left accessible to reach derailed trains. A 24-inch-wide aisle is enough for such emergency access. Another option would be to cut 24-by-24-inch access holes in the middle of the table, then the layout could fit in an 8-by-8-foot room.

Fig. 3-25 is designed with a center access or oper-

Fig. 3-25   *A simple walk-in layout for an 8-by-8-foot space.*

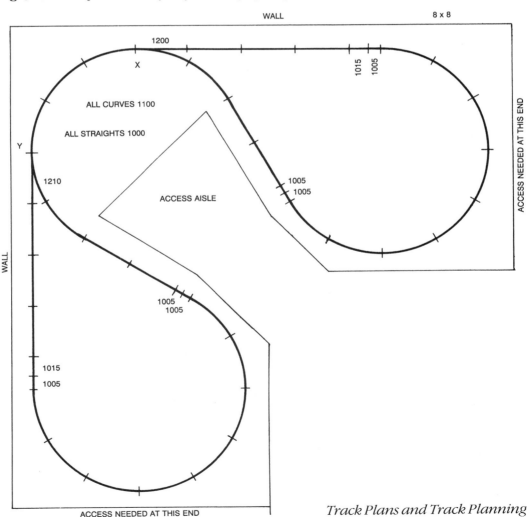

Track Plans and Track Planning

ating aisle, so you can literally walk into the layout. This feature makes operations more fun because you can get up close and personal with the trains (and their imaginary crew).

This plan can be expanded infinitely by simply inserting straight track sections at either point marked X or Y on the plan. If, for example, you want the layout to fill a 10-by-12-foot area, add two 12-inch straight track sections at Y and four 12-inch straight track sections at X.

This plan is deliberately simple to give you an idea of the basic shape. Remember, you can add a turnout (switch) in place of any straight or curved track section to make passing sidings or stub-end sidings like those on the point-to-point layout plan (Fig. 3-26), which follows.

Point-to-Point Layouts

"Point-to-point" is another model railroad term that describes the track configuration of most real railroads: They run from one major city or interchange yard, through many towns, to another major city—city-to-city, or point-to-point. Most model railroads, however, run around in circles, ovals, figure 8s, or loop-to-loops.

Modelers who want to simulate the operations of some particular real railroad, often create a track plan that will not run the trains in ovals or loops, but around the edges of the room or benchwork from one stub-end yard to another stub-end yard. The simplest form of point-to-point layout is just 12 feet of straight track with the train running back and forth from the left end, or point, to the right end, or point.

Modelers use point-to-point designs to avoid the boredom that can arise from watching a train run endlessly around an oval. That too-simple 12-foot straight layout, however, is even more boring. What makes a good point-to-point layout interesting is what happens to the trains at each of the points and in between.

An 11-by-12-Foot Indoor Layout

Most homes have a bedroom that measures at least 11 by 12 feet, or you might want to fit the layout shown in Fig. 3-26 into one corner of the garage, with parts of it cantilevered over the hood of the second car. Notice, however, that the plan will only fit in an 11-by-12-foot area if the doorway is in the lower right corner of the room, and even then, the tracks may need to be cut back to clear an inward-opening door. The plan can be built as a mirror image, however, if the room has the door in the lower left corner.

Notice, too, that access is needed at the end of peninsula A and that would require another 2 feet or a 13-by-12-foot room. You can get around that—and fit the layout in 11 by 12 feet—by providing a 24-by-24-inch access hole in the center of peninsula A. The access aisles are shaped so you always can keep the back edges of the layout within 30 inches of the aisle for easy reach.

This is a true point-to-point layout, because the trains travel from point A to point E. There is, certainly, much, much more to this layout than that simple path. If, for example, a train departs from A, it passes towns and industries at B, C, and D before reaching E. Each of those places provides a chance for the train to pick up a car or drop one off; "switching" is the term modelers use for such operations.

When the train gets to E, it can use the triangular-shaped trackage at D (called a "wye" by modelers and real railroaders) to reverse direction so it can actually back into any of the three sidings at D, ready for its return trip to A.

When the train heads out of E, it will pass D, C, and B once again and, perhaps, the cars left before are ready to be picked up or more cars from E are destined to be left ("spotted" is the railroad term) at D, C, or B. When the train returns to A it can travel around the reverse loop at R and back into the siding at A, ready for its return trip to E.

Those movements, as the terms suggest, are exact duplicates of what happens on a real railroad. You can increase the realism by using real or imaginary commodities like coal or lumber or cows at the industries and, like many modelers, even imagine that most of the carloads arrive on this railroad from some outside railroad (in this case, by being carried from the storage shelf by your hand rather than by train).

If you want excitement, operate two trains at once and have them pass at the passing siding at C. Add more excitement with a third train. Make it more interesting by using one of the command-control power systems shown in Chapter 5 and run three trains at once, each under independent control.

If you want the thrill of hands-off coupling and uncoupling, install Kadee couplers (as shown in Chapter 15) on the cars and locomotives. The Kadee magnetic uncoupling ramps would then be located at the K track sections to serve all the sidings.

Like the previous loop-to-loop plan (Fig. 3-25), this one can be expanded by adding more sidings in place of nearly any curved or straight track section. I'd suggest at least two more stub-end sidings at A. When you understand the runaround switching movement shown in Chapter 15, you'll see the need for the double-end sidings at C and D. In fact, the switching sequence shown in Chapter 15 takes place on trackage like that between B and C (but constructed from the larger 48-inch-radius curves and matching turnouts).

This plan can also be expanded by adding foot-long straight track sections at X or Y to fill nearly any space. Add eight foot-long straights at Y, and the plan would fill an 11-by-22-foot area. You would not likely settle for just another eight straights, of course; you might include another passing siding like that at C or simply use several large curves for a smooth-flowing series of S-bends like those on Bill Baldock's outdoor layout shown in Chapter 2.

There's no room for a passing siding at A; however, the reversing loop itself can serve as a run-around siding. If your train is traveling clockwise around the reverse loop at R, it can stop and uncouple from the cars at the letter R. The locomotive can then proceed around the loop through the turnout at Y, reverse direction and back clockwise around the reverse loop, and be at the opposite end of the cars it just left at R. The movement accomplishes the run around described in Chapter 15 and also serves as a train-reversing loop.

Fig. 3-26 *A walk-in layout with point-to-point operations for an 11-by-14-foot area.*

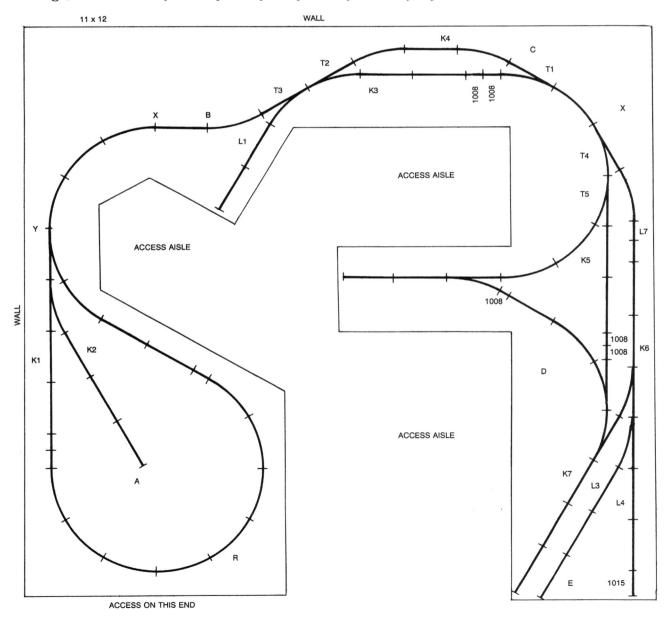

Chapter 4

||||||||||||||||||||||||||||||||||||||||||||||||||||||||||||||||||||||||||||||||||||||||||||||||||||||||||||||||

Basic Track-Laying

THESE GAUGE 1 trains are some of the most reliable and rugged models (or toys) ever produced. Much of their reliability stems from the sheer size, some from the magic of modern plastics. Any of the equipment is perfectly suitable for operation indoors on the carpet or floor. With HO and smaller-scale models, it is essential that the track be mounted on a tabletop, even if that tabletop rests on the floor. That operating reliability of gauge 1 makes the track truly portable—just pull it apart and stash it away along with the cars and locomotives.

All of the brands of track that fall within the scope of this book—including Aristo-Craft, Bachmann, Kalamazoo, LGB, Model Power, Lionel, and Micro Engineering—are available in sections that simply push together. Lionel has a system that is really only compatible with Lionel, and Bachmann has a system that is really only compatible with Bachmann. Aristo-Craft, Kalamazoo, LGB, and Micro Engineering track sections will connect with one another even if, as described in Chapter 3, there are some minor differences in the length of the track sections and the rail material.

Reliable Trackwork

Lionel and Bachmann track is perfectly suitable for use indoors on the floor or on a tabletop. These two brands have sheet-metal rails that are hollow inside and thus not as rugged as the solid rails used by the other brands. Bachmann once offered all-plastic track

with their first radio-controlled gauge 1 train set, and that track is, of course, only suitable for use with battery-powered models. New Bright produces somewhat smaller-scale toy trains that also use plastic track, but those are a bit too much like toys to be included in this book. Conversely, the Playmobil metal track is virtually the same as LGB, and the Playmobil trains are rugged enough for use outdoors even though their proportions are certainly whimsical rather than accurate attempts at scale models. The locomotives sold by Kalamazoo are also somewhat whimsical but they, and the Kalamazoo track, are rugged enough for use outdoors or in.

Aristo-Craft, Kalamazoo, LGB, and Railway Engineering use similar styles of rail joiners. The joiners must be tight around the bottom or web of the rail to maintain both track alignment and electrical current flow. Aristo-Craft includes locking screws, but although they will help hold the rails together, the rail joiners must still grip tightly.

Use common pliers to grip the sides of the rail joiner and to clamp it down tightly over the web of the rail. Squeeze on the outside web, as shown in Fig. 4-2, then reach inside the track and squeeze the inside of the rail joiner and rail web in the same manner.

Rails as Electrical Cables

A few modelers in gauge 1 are converting their locomotives to battery power, using rechargeable

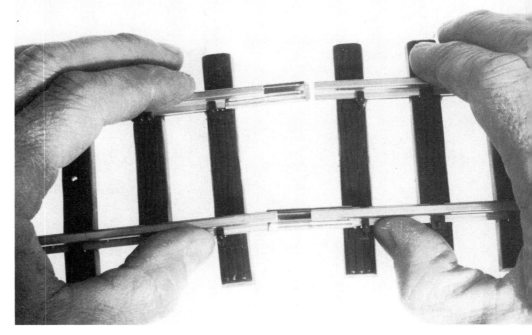

Fig. 4-1 *The standard LGB, Aristo-Craft, Delton, Micro Engineering and Kalamazoo track sections have these simple slide-in rail joiners.*

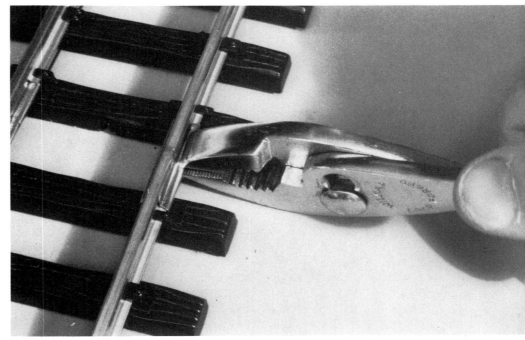

Fig. 4-2 *For a tight fit, squeeze the rail joiners against the outside web of the rail, as shown, as well as the inside web of both rails being joined.*

batteries from radio-controlled model race cars. A few modelers are even operating locomotives that are actually powered by live steam and burn butane or alcohol fuel. The vast majority of modelers, however, are operating their models as the manufacturers intended, using the track rails to deliver power to the locomotives' wheels, or drivers, and then to the 12- to 18-volt DC motor inside the locomotive.

If you consider the rails of your model railroad to be electrical cables as well as the guidance system for the trains, you might worry about the dozens, maybe hundreds, of plugs that can work loose. Every rail

Fig. 4-3 *Apply a small dab of electrically conductive grease, like LGB number 5101, into each rail joiner for more reliable contact.*

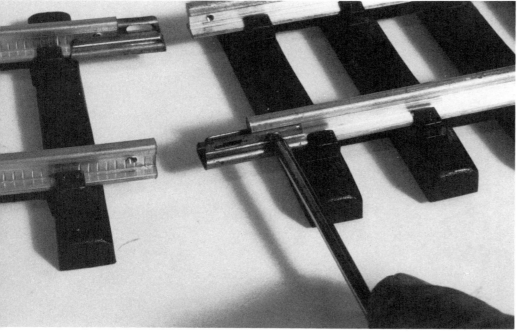

Fig. 4-4 *One of the screw holes in the Aristo-Craft rail joiner is a slot to leave room for any slight misalignment.*

joint is, in essence, an electrical plug and socket. Yes, you will experience breaks in that flow of electricity, particularly if you operate outdoors, even if the rails appear to be tightly joined. The single most frustrating factor (after falling leaves) with outdoor railroading is the unpredictable flow of electrical current across the rail joiners.

You can minimize the chances of a break in the flow of electricity by packing each rail joiner with a dab of electrically conductive grease. LGB offers a small container of LGB Leitpaste and larger hardware stores may carry Molykote BR2 Plus. Use only a small dab and carefully wipe any excess from all surfaces of the rail after the track is joined. The grease serves

Fig. 4-5   *Derailment and Track Troubleshooting*

Trouble	Probable Cause of Trouble	Solution
Train derails frequently at one particular place.	1. Offset rails at joiners.	1. Align rails and rail joiners with steel ruler and needlenose pliers.
	2. Excess plastic "flash" or wisps from ties on inside edges of the rails.	2. Trim "flash" with a hobby knife.
	3. Plaster, glue, or some foreign object stuck to track.	3. Remove it.
	4. Ends of rails burred or rough.	4. Smooth the tops and inside edges of the rails with number 400 sandpaper.
Train derails at switch.	1. Switch points not throwing far enough to make firm contact with "through" rails.	1. Remove any foreign matter from area around points and check the action of switch lever inside the switch machine.
	2. Switch twisted or bent, so all rails do not align in both "main" and "siding" switch positions.	2. Bend the switch into perfect alignment.
	3. Coupler pins hitting switch rails or frog.	3. Cut pins to proper length.
	4. Any of four problem areas for "regular" track.	4. Correct, as outlined above.
Train derails everywhere.	1. Running the train too fast.	1. Run it slower.

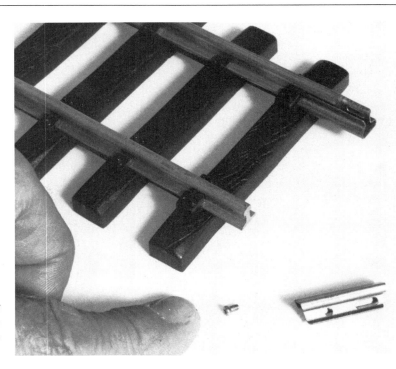

Fig. 4-6 *Aristo-Craft sectional track has a screw through each rail joiner into both rails to ensure a tight fit at each joint.*

three purposes: it keeps dirt and water from working into the joiner, it prevents the oxidation of the rail and joiner, and it will actually conduct electricity.

The electrically conductive grease is a relatively new development in outdoor railroad operations, but in two or three seasons, it does seem to do the job, particularly if the rails or track are mechanically bonded so they can physically move apart. The mechanical bond can range from a screw (like Aristo-Craft's track sections) to clamp-on rail joiners (like Micro Engineering's) to actually soldering the rail and rail joiner together. Or you can simply screw the track sections to a joiner plate of plywood.

The most reliable method of ensuring electrical

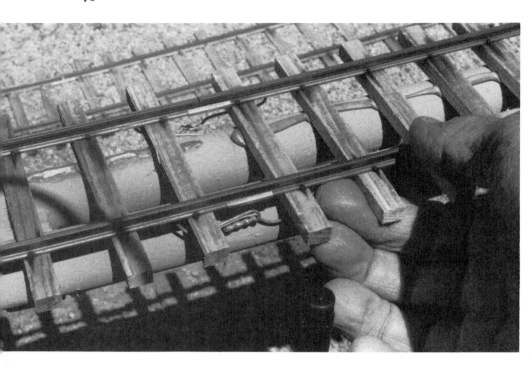

Fig. 4-7 *Bill Baldock solders a wire to the bottom of each rail and twists the ends into this pigtail, then solders the pigtail.*

flow across the rail joiners is to solder the rails together. That, though, is a relatively difficult task. It is far easier to simply run small number 18 gauge solid copper wires across the rail joint as Bill Baldock does on his outdoor railroad. Bill solders a 3-inch piece of wire to the bottom of the rail, about ½ inch from the end so it will not interfere with the rail joiner. He solders those wires to both ends of every rail before assembling the track. Those dangling little strands of wire are twisted together after the track is assembled. Usually, the wires are invisible beneath the rails and they are above the ballast so they can be inspected to see if they have worked loose. The twisted connection in Fig. 4-7 is located at the site of a future bridge; it will be hidden by the bridge supports.

Continuous and Fault-Free Rail

The real experts in outdoor model railroad construction seem to prefer as few rail joiners as possible. Norm Grant, for one, solders every connection on both his own railroad and on the railroads he custom builds for customers of his layout-building service. Norm uses a small propane torch (available at hardware stores) for most joints. Recently, Norm purchased a resistance soldering outfit like those sold by PBL. These devices use high electrical current to heat a relatively small area of the metal being soldered. The resistance soldering method minimizes the chances of melting the plastic ties and spikes.

Norm Grant uses wet ballast or sand from the layout itself as a heat sink on each side of the solder joint. He also pushes the ties back about 3 inches from the joint. The rail itself and the inside of the rail joiner must be scraped clean so no oxidized metal remains, because the solder will not bond to oxided metal surfaces. He uses a rosin core solder (also available at most hardware stores) to solder the rail joiner to the rails.

Some electrical gaps are needed in the rails, as described in Chapter 5, but Norm Grant also prefers to leave turnouts free so they can be replaced or removed for repairs. He uses the clamping metal rail joiners at the six places where a turnout connects to the rails of the layout. Those same clamps, incidentally, can be used to attach the electrical connections to the layout. Clamping rail joiners like these are available from San-Val. Other styles of clamping rail joiners with set screws are available from John Row, Micro Engineering, and Richard Hillman.

One of the easiest ways to improve the mechanical joint at a rail joiner is to simply drill the sides of the rail with a number 53 drill, then gently thread the hole with a number 1-72 tap held in a pin vise. Use Aristo-Craft or Micro Engineering stamped-metal rail joiners. Drill out the holes in the Aristo-Craft rail joiners or drill new holes in the Micro Engineering rail joiners with a number 48 drill. It is easier to install the undrilled rail joiners and both rails first,

Fig. 4-8 Norm and Dale Grant solder the rails to the rail joiners using a propane torch and piles of wet sand to soak up the heat.

Fig. 4-9 A resistance soldering tool, from PBL, makes a quick solder joint with little chance of the heat spreading down the rails.

then drill through both the rail joiner and rail with the number 53 drill. Remove the rail joiner and enlarge its hole with a number 48 drill and thread the number 53 holes in the rail with the 1-72 tap. The rail joiners can then be held in place with a roundhead 1-72-by-$\frac{3}{16}$-inch brass machine screw with the screw heads on the inner faces of the rails so the protruding length of screw will not hit the wheel flanges. If you can find hex-head 1-72-by-$\frac{1}{8}$-inch machine screws, they can be installed from the outside to look a bit like real railroad bolt-on rail joiners. Hobby stores sell the drill bits, taps, pin vises, and screws.

Fig. 4-10 *Clamp-on rail joiners, like these from San-Val, also can be used to attach the electrical wires from the power pack.*

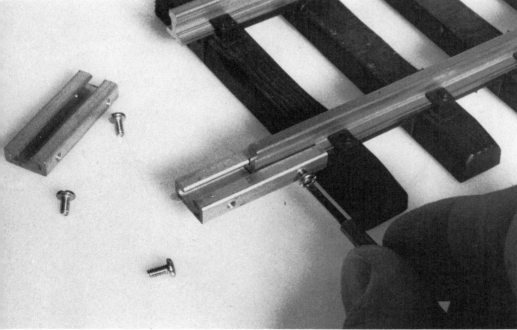

Fig. 4-11 *Micro Engineering offers this aluminum rail joiner with set screws that clamp the web of the rail.*

The easiest method of ensuring a tight joint between the rails is to join the track sections themselves with a 4-by-4-inch block of $\frac{1}{4}$- or $\frac{1}{2}$-inch plywood. If you are working outdoors, use pressure-treated plywood and apply two coats of waterproof sealer to each plywood block. Drill a $\frac{1}{8}$-inch hole in the end tie of each track section. Join the sections with some electrically conductive grease and clamp the rail joiners tight. Attach the track to the 4-by-4-inch block of plywood with two number 3-by-$\frac{5}{8}$-inch screws. This system works fine for layouts on the floor indoors or for any outdoor layout where the plywood blocks will simply be buried in ballast. If you are building a layout indoors on a tabletop or open-grid

Fig. 4-12 *Norm Grant attaches the turnouts to the rails with set screw-style clamps so the turnout can be removed for maintenance.*

benchwork, the plywood blocks will not be needed; the track can be screwed directly to the tabletop or subroadbed.

Custom-Fit Track

LGB, Aristo-Craft, and Micro Engineering offer short sections of straight track and partial sections of some curves. It is relatively simple to cut your own track to fit the needed gaps. Use a razor saw (available from hobby shops) to cut the rail. Support the track on a sturdy block and align the saw blade with the ties to make a vertical cut. You can saw through the ties from below the rails.

Use a jeweler's rectangular file (again, available from a hobby shop) to smooth away any burrs left by the saw blade. A jeweler's saw makes a very fine cut with a minimum of burrs, but it is still necessary to file the edges lightly.

Separate rail, with plastic ties to fit, is available from LGB, Micro Engineering, Garich Light Transport, and Llagas Creek Railways. The rail is designed simply to slide into the molded-on plastic spikes as shown in Fig. 4-19. The rail is sold in 6-foot lengths so it makes a relatively inexpensive method of producing long lengths of straight track.

The rail used for gauge 1 railroads is usually either code 332 (about $\frac{5}{16}$-inch high) from LGB and Micro Engineering or code 250 rail ($\frac{1}{4}$ inch high) from Micro Engineering, Garish Light Transport, and

Fig. 4-13 *If you use slide-on rail joiners, they can be attached with screws by drilling a number 53 hole through both rail joiner and rail.*

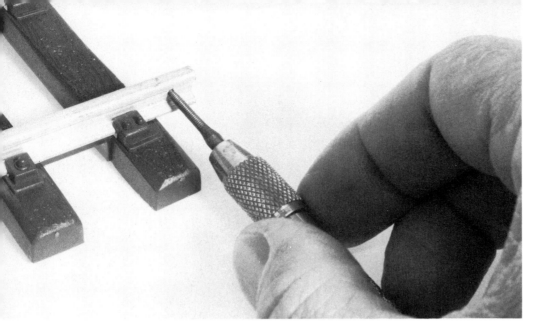

Fig. 4-14 *Enlarge the rail joiner hole with a number 48 drill, then tread the hole in the rail with a number 1-72 tap in a pin vise.*

Fig. 4-15 *The simplest mechanical rail joint is a piece of 4-inch-square plywood screwed to the track. Drill holes in the ties at the ends of the section.*

Fig. 4-16 *Use a roundheaded wood screw to attach both sections of track to the 4-by-4-inch plywood support.*

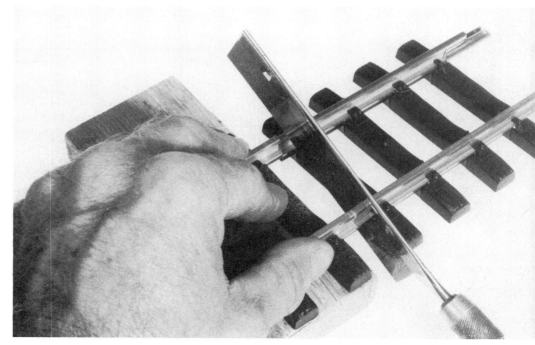

Fig. 4-17 *Use a razor saw to cut track sections to special lengths.*

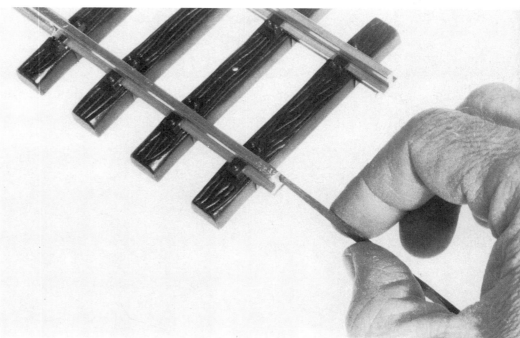

Fig. 4-18 *Smooth the cut ends of the rail with a rectangular jeweler's file.*

Llagas Creek Railways to match those manufacturers' molded plastic ties. That size rail is too stiff to bend by hand to form curves. The Lindsay Railbender in Figs. 4-20 and 4-21 includes three rollers that force the rail into a curve as the rail is drawn through the tool.

The Lindsay Railbender is sold with a 4-inch-long-

handle so you can manually turn the taller wheel to draw the rail through the tool. The knurled knob on the back of the tool moves the center wheel closer or farther from the two idler wheels; the closer the third wheel, the tighter the curve will be in the track. If you want curves tighter than a 48-inch radius, it's far easier to curve the 48-inch radius first, then run the rails through the tool a second (or even a third) time with the large wheel set close enough to bend the rail into the curve you need. The curve can be matched to a spare piece of sectional track or you can draw the curve on a sheet of plywood with a compass made from a length of 1-by-4-inch lumber with a nail for the pivot and a pencil to mark the desired curve. The rail can be moved an inch or so by hand, but it's best to get the curve to within a $\frac{1}{2}$ inch or less of the precise radius you need.

Norm Grant has modified the Lindsay Railbender in Figs. 4-20 and 4-21. He replaced the handle with a clevis pin from a hardware store. He inserted a piece of $\frac{3}{8}$-inch aluminum rod with a hole drilled to fit the clevis pin. A variable speed drill with a $\frac{3}{8}$-inch chuck is attached to the aluminum rod to turn the drive wheel electrically. However, the Railbender must be clamped firmly to a workbench or attached with screws through the holes provided in the tool.

A few modelers, including Bill Baldock and Bill Bradford, whose layouts appear in Chapter 2 and in the color section, wanted more realistic track with smaller rail. There's a photo of Bill Baldock's track earlier in this chapter. These builders used code 197 rail with ties cut from redwood. Old Pullman, Precision Scale, and Rara Avis offer code 197 rail in addition to the code 250 rail mentioned earlier in this chapter. Micro Engineering, Old Pullman, and Rara

Fig. 4-19 *The LGB number 1000/5 rail slides easily into the 1000/3 tie sections to make longer sections of track.*

Fig. 4-20 *Bend the exact curves into the rails before inserting them into the ties by using a Lindsay Railbender tool.*

Fig. 4-21 *Norm Grant uses an electric drill to drive the Railbender for easier and quicker movement of the rail through the device.*

Avis provide scale-sized spikes to hold the rail. The California & Oregon Coast Company, Bill Gagne, Old Pullman, and Rara Avis also offer precut wooden ties. Old Pullman, the Parker Company, and Rara Avis also offer switch kits in code 197 rail, with the switch rails and frog (where the rails cross) soldered together and ready to spike to the ties.

Detailing Turnouts

The turnouts (switches) from LGB, Lionel, and Aristo-Craft include self-locking mechanisms so the points (the moving parts of the turnout that actually change the route the trains will take) will snap firmly into position. Some type of throw lever will be needed for the Micro Engineering turnouts or for any of the turnout kits. This will allow you to operate each turnout by moving either the lever or the points. Caboose Industries makes a low-level lever that can be used to move the points. Ozark Miniatures also makes a lever that can be used to move the points from one route to the other.

So far, only LGB makes a remote-controlled turnout (switch) that can be moved by throwing a lever on a control panel. LGB also provides the electrical levers. If you want a remote-controlled turnout, this is the easiest method; just by LGB's turnout and switch levers. Peco offers number 6 size (about a 14-foot radius) turnouts and 1-meter-long (about 39-inch) track that can be curved with a Railbender. The Peco

Fig. 4-22 *An Ozark switch stand can be used to add detail to LGB turnouts. The stand sits on wooden ties to extend the LGB ties with a second pair of longer wooden ties buried beneath and attached with wood screws beside the rails.*

Fig. 4-23. *Peco makes gauge 1 track, with code 250 nickel silver rail that can be shaped into curves and large-radius turnouts with the Railbender.*

track has code 250 (¼-inch high) nickel silver (an alloy of tin and brass) rail.

1/32 Scale Track

The track in all of the photographs in this book has ties matched to 1/22.5 scale narrow gauge. Standard gauge (gauge 1) ties reduced to 1/29 or 1/32 scale are much slimmer and more closely spaced. Aristo-Craft produces some sectional track and turnouts with these types of ties.

Steve and Judy Arrigotti have covered every inch of their outdoor railroad with ground cover, miniature or dwarf bushes and trees, or fine bark. The windmill is from Rara Avis. A list of these plants appears in Chapter 9 (Fig. 9-7).

The third "annual" addition to Steve and Judy Arrigotti's railroad included this sawmill with a log pond fed by a waterfall. A list of the plants in this photograph appears in Chapter 9 (Fig. 9-4).

Bill Bauer's Shawmut Line is a traditional indoor model railroad with rebuilt locomotives, repainted cars and some scratch-built buildings. There is a plan and more photographs in Chapters 2 and 6. Bill Bauer photograph.

This is the mountainous area of a 30-by-40-foot layout that begins on the basement floor and climbs to 30 inches. The trees are dried weeds covered with ground foam.

Bill and Dee Baldock's Devonshire, Snail Park & Petunia Railroad runs downhill from a patio deck across dramatic rock cliffs.

John Bierie at work on his Blackhawk & Devil Mountain Railway, a layout that complements the landscaping. The plants in this scene are listed in Chapter 9 (Fig. 9-8).

Bill and Joan Bradford used native California rocks and succulents to landscape their backyard layout. The locomotive is a Bachmann 0-4-0T with a caboose built from wood and Rara Avis metal parts.

A pair of LGB White Pass diesels pull a string of MDC ore cars lettered to match the diesels on John and Barbara Bierie's layout.

A train of standard gauge models including Aristo-Craft's 1/29 scale Alco FA-1 and GB-1 diesels, covered gondola, flatcar with trailers, flatcar and boxcar and reefer, an LGB 1/29 scale boxcar, an LGB 1/22.5 scale tank car, and an Aristo-Craft 1/29 scale caboose on Marc and Barbara Horovitz's layout.

Real water, a real sunset, and the real world make these large-scale models something more than models. James Pearson photo from the Norm Grant collection.

Tom Flynn is just completing his garden layout with help from Norm Grant. He left the plant labels as a personal reminder. These plants are listed in Chapter 9 (Fig. 9-3).

Chapter 5

▌▌▐▌
▌▌▐▌
▌▌▐▌

Wiring and Train Control

ALL OF the trains in this book, whether replicas of steam locomotives or diesels, are powered by 12- to 18-volt DC electric motors. Models are available that are powered by real steam, but the smaller ones are imported on a limited basis from England or Europe and the larger ones are imported from Korea or Japan with prices of $3,000 and up; they are beyond the scope of this book.

If you have experience with a model electric train, you already understand most of what there is to know about how to control gauge 1 locomotives and trains. The 115-volt AC household current is simply converted to 12- to 18-volts DC current by a transformer and a rectifier inside what modelers call a "power pack." Most power packs also have a speed control (called a "throttle"), an on-off switch, a reversing switch (to change the direction the locomotive will travel), and a circuit breaker.

The power pack is connected to the track with two wires, one to each rail. The rails, in turn, carry the electrical current to the locomotives. The locomotive wheels or drivers pick up the electrical current from one rail, route it through a small electric motor, and return the current through the opposite rail. The rails are an integral part of the electrical circuit and, as such, certain rules must be followed with some track configurations to avoid short circuits. For most layouts, all you need do is connect the two wires, plug in the power pack to a wall outlet, and turn on the throttle.

Electric Train Control

The diagram (Fig. 5-2) includes the major components of the power packs supplied with Bachmann, Aristo-Craft, LGB, Playmobil, and Lionel train sets. These firms also offer separate power packs, and accessory power packs of a similar design are available from these same firms as well as Model Rectifier Corporation (MRC), San-Val, and PH Hobbies. ITTC and Starr-Tec offer power packs with the heavy transformer and rectifier mounted in a separate box from the throttle and reverse controls. These controls are mounted in a lightweight box small enough to hold in one hand. The hand-held throttle control is on a long-tether electrical cable (usually about 20 to 50 feet). The tether allows you to walk closer to the trains or to walk along with them and, for this reason, these control systems are called "walk-around" throttles. There are also some radio-controlled throttles that qualify as walk-around, but we'll discuss them later in this chapter.

A third style of electronic control for model trains is also a walk-around throttle on a tether cable, but these units use electronic signals, sent through the rails, to a small receiver in each locomotive. The rails carry full power and the signal activates the receiver to allow more or less power to pass into the motor. These units are usually called "command-control," because the throttle commands the locomotive's receiver to slow down, speed up, or reverse. Some even offer the option of sound with the whistle, bell,

Fig. 5-1 *John Bierie has the ideal power pack arrangement: He locks it inside the weatherproof box when the layout is not in use.*

or horn controlled from the hand-held controller. PSI's Dynatrol and Keller Engineering Onboard are two currently available command-control systems. Both brands offer the advantage of completely independent control of two or more (up to 80) locomotives on the same track at the same time. A separate controller and receiver is needed for each locomotive.

The multiple-locomotive feature of the command-control systems utilizes different frequencies, transmitted through the rails; so that only one locomotive's receiver will respond to the commands from the controller. Several of the layouts in this book have command control but most modelers only operate three or four locomotives at a time. That means that three or four controllers are needed and three or four receivers must be mounted in the three or four locomotives. You can mount receivers in all your locomotives (assuming you have more than four) and change the frequency by merely removing and replacing a plug-in chip. The controllers also have a frequency-change device so you can match the controller's frequency to the receiver's frequency. If you want to operate a fifth locomotive, simply change the controller's frequency to match the frequency of the fifth locomotive.

Fig. 5-2 *Power pack and throttle electrical wiring. (Note: wires are numbered to correspond with their locations on other wiring diagrams.)*

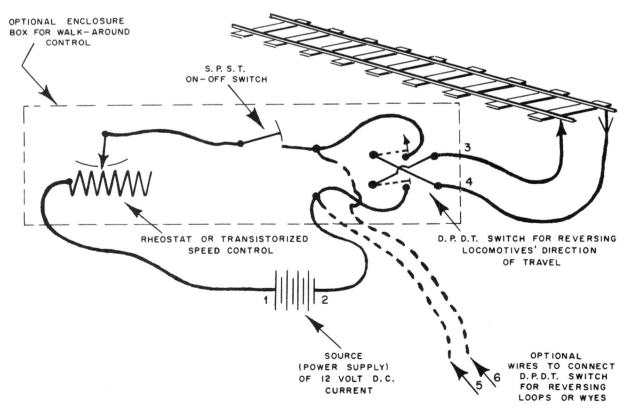

Fig. 5-3 Model Rectifier's power pack includes a "Mode" switch for slow-speed running. Do not use "Mode" with sound-equipped locomotives.

Fig. 5-4 San-Val makes this heavy-duty power supply with a simple knob, on-off switch circuit breaker, and built-in cooling fan.

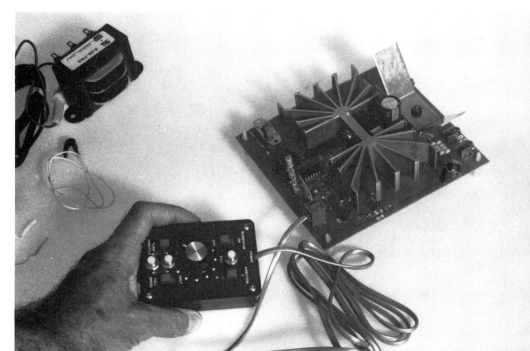

Fig. 5-5 The ITTC 1000 power pack has a walk-around throttle on a tether cable, an electronic circuit that mounts on the layout, and a separate transformer (upper left).

Fig. 5-6 *Starr-Tec Model 80M Hogger power pack has the electronics and transformer in a single case with a tethered walk-around throttle.*

Fig. 5-7 *The PSI Dynatrol walk-around throttle and command-control electronics are also in just two boxes, with a receiver in each locomotive.*

The disadvantage of the command-control system is that each locomotive must be equipped with a receiver or it cannot be operated on the layout. There are two ways around that problem: Simply disconnect the command-control from the rails and connect a conventional power supply (with or without walk-around) or divide the track into electrically isolated blocks as shown later in this chapter. Connect the conventional power supply to the "Train A" terminals on the DPDT ("block selector") switch and the command-control to "Train B" terminals. When you want to operate with command-control, flip the switches to Train B. If you are very, very careful, you can operate two trains, one on conventional power and one on

Fig. 5-8 *The Keller Onboard command-control system has a walk-around throttle with a receiver in each locomotive and an optional sound system.*

command-control, on the same layout. You must, however, keep a "dead" or no-power-on block between the trains, because conventional power can burn out the command-control receivers and the command-control power can throw instant full-power to the conventional (nonreceiver-equipped) locomotives, throwing them off the track, burning the motor wires, or ruining the motor.

Radio-Controlled Trains

Radio control sounds like something you would only need for model racing cars, airplanes, or boats. "R/C," as modelers call it, is another exciting option for operating a gauge 1 model railroad. There are four companies currently making radio control for gauge 1 trains: Remote Control Systems, EDA, Economy R/C (T.I. Miller), and On Track (sold by Rara Avis). All offer a system that utilizes batteries—carried by the locomotive or a following car—to provide the power; no electrical current flows through the rails. You can, of course, operate a second train with conventional power at the same time you are operating the battery-powered radio control train or, if you have command-control, operate two or three or four trains with command-control and a fifth with radio control. There is no limit, either, to how many trains you can operate with the radio-controlled systems, but you must purchase a complete transmitter, receiver, and battery setup for each train.

The advantages of the radio-controlled systems include the following: The track need only be clean enough so the locomotives and cars do not derail, and loose rail joiners and electrical connections have no effect on the locomotive's power. Almost equally important is the use of the hand-held transmitter with no tether wires; you can follow the train anywhere on the layout or simply lay back in a lounge chair.

Remote Control Systems also provides the option of using track power, rather than rechargeable batteries, for the locomotive's power.

EDA, Remote Control Systems, Economy R/C, and On Track offer the choice of a gel-cell battery that will fit inside a gauge 1 boxcar and power the train for several hours before needing to be recharged. An option for the systems is a pair of rechargeable nicad battery packs, similar to those used in R/C race cars. These smaller batteries will fit in the tender of an LGB Mogul (if there is no sound system). If you are willing to settle for half-throttle performance and your layout has no steep grades, you may want to fit just one of the nicad battery packs; it can be mounted beneath a high coal load in an LGB tender with sound. The nicad battery packs usually last for forty-five minutes to an hour before needing to be recharged.

There is also a rechargeable nicad battery in the receiver and in the transmitter of these radio-controlled systems, but they usually last more than a dozen hours before recharging is necessary. In all, you may need three recharging systems. If you opt for the nicad batteries, you also may want to invest in a

Fig. **5-10** *Bill Baldock and John Bierie use the On Track radio-control system sold by Rara Avis with batteries for power in a following freight car.*

spare set of batteries so one can set can be recharging while you operate with the other set. Hobby shops that sell radio-controlled race cars provide battery charges that can recharge the nicad batteries in less than an hour.

The process of unplugging and replacing a battery with a freshly charged battery is simple—far simpler than the maintenance needed to keep the track clean enough for perfect performance with either conventional or command-control systems. The primary disadvantage of the radio-controlled systems is the need to have a car carrying the batteries or to modify the

Fig. 5-11 *The EDA radio-control system also mounts the batteries for power in a trailing freight car, but smaller batteries to fit the tender are optional.*

tender (if, indeed, there is one) to fit the batteries. The nicads can probably be worked into the body of an Aristo-Craft FA-1 diesel but you may have to use special one-pack battery packs to jam them into an Aristo-Craft U-28B or Lionel's GP7, GP9, or GP20 diesels. There are several configurations of six C-cell batteries available for radio-controlled racing cars in addition to the traditional row of six cells side by side. These packs produce about 7.2 volts, which is enough for half-speed operations; two of these packs are used for full performance of gauge 1 locomotives.

EDA, Remote Control Systems, Economy R/C, and On Track offer radio-controlled transmitters and receivers, but you can supply your own. The toy radio-controlled cars, boats, or planes do not have accurate enough signals for this purpose. The most common brands used for radio-controlled trains are Futaba (On Track recommends the Attack 4) and Aristo-Craft. Usually one lever operates the forward and reverse speeds. Push the lever right for forward, and the farther you push, the faster the locomotive will travel. Push the lever left and the locomotive will slow, then stop, and then reverse. Continue pushing the lever left and the locomotive will travel faster and faster in reverse. Some of the systems are developing ways of triggering LGB and other sound systems so the bell, whistle, or horn also can be actuated by radio control.

Basic Wiring Rules

The track and turnouts produced by LGB and Aristo-Craft are designed to minimize the need for extra electrical wires and insulating gaps in the rails. With the exception of track configurations for reverse loops or reversing wyes (both are shown in Chapter 3 and later in this chapter), you can install an LGB or Aristo-Craft turnout anywhere on the layout. You can also connect the electrical power wires to the track anywhere and the power will carry through the turnouts.

The LGB and Aristo-Craft turnouts are designed so that both routes out of the turnout have power regardless of which direction the turnout is thrown. That means that you cannot park a locomotive on a siding and operate a second locomotive on the main line; the "parked" locomotive will move. We'll show you how to turn-off the power to the siding later.

The turnouts sold by Micro Engineering and the various turnout kits described in Chapter 4 are designed so that there is power available only to the route selected by the turnout's points. With these turnouts, you can move a locomotive onto a siding and then move the switch points to direct the trains onto the main line; the train on the siding will not move. It's an easy way to "park" a second train. If you use these turnouts, however, there are some wiring and rail insulation rules that you must follow if you

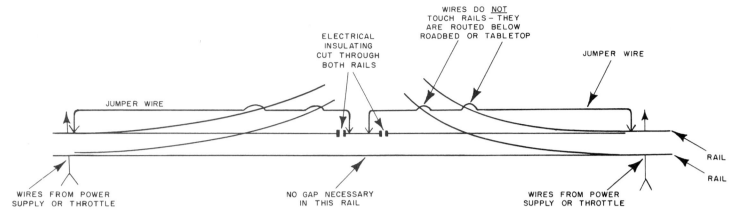

Fig. 5-12 *Rail gaps and extra wires allow train operation between two facing switches.*

want to avoid a short circuit every time you move the switch points. These are called "power-routing" turnouts.

When the wires are connected to the rails, they must "feed" the power-routing turnouts from the entry end of the turnout. Fig. 5-12 indicates the proper positions for the wires to be connected. You can feed a whole string, or "ladder," or turnouts, either right or left handed, as long as all the points face the wire-attaching points. Whenever the frogs or diverging ends of the turnouts face each other, the inside rail between the facing turnouts must have an insulating gap. LGB sells plastic rail joiners (number 5026) for this purpose, or you can cut the rail and insert a strip of plastic as shown later in this chapter. The electrical power must, then, be carried around the turnout, as shown in the diagram, with a separate "jumper" wire. Remember, these gaps and jumper wires are only necessary with Micro Engineering ready-made turnouts and with the turnout kits to be spiked to wood ties, these steps are not necessary with LGB or Aristo-Craft turnouts.

Wyes and Reversing Loops

When a model railroad is powered by electricity carried through the rails, one of those rails will always have a positive flow of electrons and the other rail a negative flow. If the rails cross, just as when two wires cross from a household outlet, there is going to be a short circuit. With model railroads, you are only dealing with low voltage, 12 to 18 volts DC, so there is little chance of personal injury. There is enough heat generated with a short circuit on a model railroad to start a fire, however, so there is a very real danger. A short circuit also can destroy expensive locomotive

motors and the electrical devices that move turnouts, and there's enough heat to loosen solder joints. You can avoid short circuits by installing insulated rail joiners or insulated spacers in the rails and wiring the wyes or reversing loops as shown in Figs. 5-13 and 5-14. Even with these precautions, be sure that the power supply has a built-in fuse or circuit breaker.

The wye or reversing loops allows a train (or at least the locomotive) to reverse direction. Usually, wyes on model railroads do not have long enough stub ends to allow a complete train to reverse, but they could be long enough to accommodate at least a locomotive. Some interesting switching maneuvers can be developed if you leave the stub end of a wye so short that only a locomotive and tender will fit and specify in your rules that cabooses and some passenger cars must also be turned or reversed. Reverse loops are generally long enough so that entire trains can be turned. Both of these track configurations are, incidentally, based on real railroad practice: the Durango, Colorado, narrow gauge yards had a reverse loop to allow complete passenger trains to be turned as early as the 1920s, and there are others. Wyes are common in nearly every medium-sized town in America.

On a model railroad, the very process of reversing means that what began as the positive-charged rail must become the negative-charged rail by the time the locomotive completes its path through the reverse loop or wye; that's the only possible way for the locomotive to change its direction. When that positive rail touches the negative rail, as shown in Figs. 5-13 and 5-14, a short circuit will result unless insulated rail joiners or inserts are installed in the rails.

Another problem arises when that model locomotive reaches the point of reversing: The power that

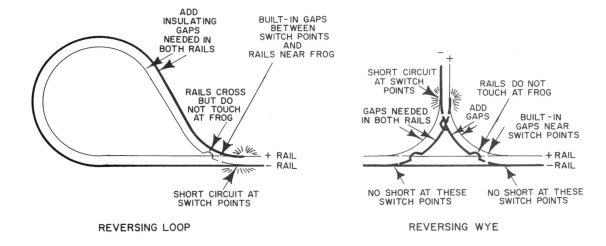

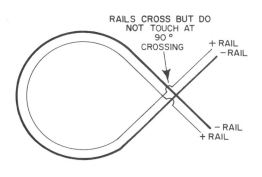

Fig. 5-13 *Short circuits will occur at wyes and loops unless gaps are cut through both rails.*

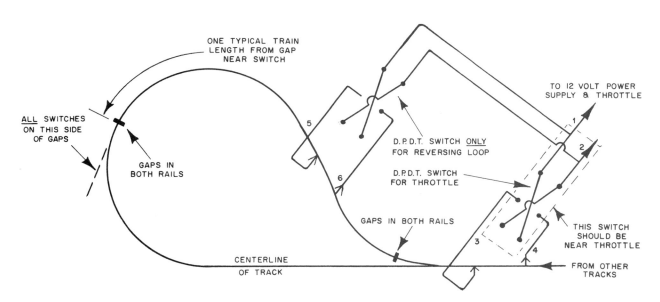

Fig. 5-14 *Special wiring is required for all reversing loop tracks.*

was used to make it go forward must be reversed to allow it to continue to move forward after it has completed its reversing move. On a model railroad, a portion of the reverse loop or wye is wired into a separate, electrically isolated segment of track that modelers call a "block." That block has its own DPDT toggle or slide switch wired to reverse the polarity in that block. You find one of these blocks in the reversing loop and in both types of wyes on these pages. The block is needed so the locomotive can continue going forward for a short distance during the reversing process while the rest of the reverse loop or wye (or even the rest of the layout) is reversed. When the locomotive enters that block, the rest of the layout's polarity to the track is reversed so, when the locomotive exits that block it finds "friendly" rails with a polarity that allows it to continue in the direction it is heading. The block is located in specific positions in Fig. 5-14 to make the movement of the train as smooth as if no extra block existed.

LGB has devised a pair of track sections with built-in polarity, or block reversing, in its number 1015K

Reverse Loop Set. The set includes two 150-mm ($5\frac{9}{10}$-inch) lengths of straight track with automatic train detection and power-reversing circuits that need no wiring. Just install the two track sections precisely as described in LGB's instructions. With all of these systems, the wiring diagram, and LGB's number 1015K, you must decide which direction the train will travel through a reverse loop, clockwise or counterclockwise, and install the electrically isolated block and reversing DPDT toggle switch as indicated by the arrow showing direction of train travel. Similarly, one of the two track sections in the LGB number 1015K set must be placed at the entrance to the loop and the second at the exit from the loop.

Special Wiring for Reversing Wyes

There are two types of wye tracks possible on a model railroad or, for that matter, on a real railroad: a wye that simply allows a train or locomotive to change directions and a wye located between the junction of two railroad main lines. With the first type of wye (seen in Fig. 5-15), one of the three legs of the

Fig. 5-15 *Wiring for stub-end reversing wye tracks.*

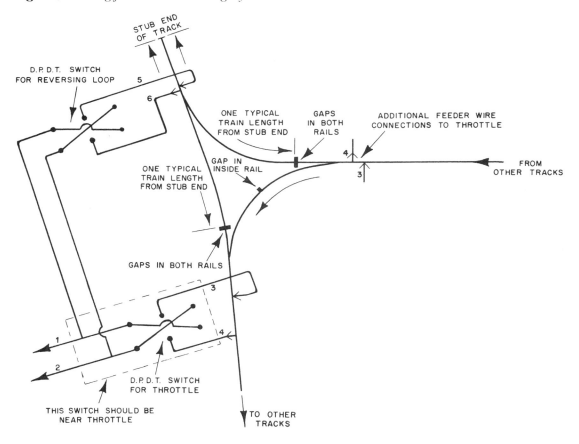

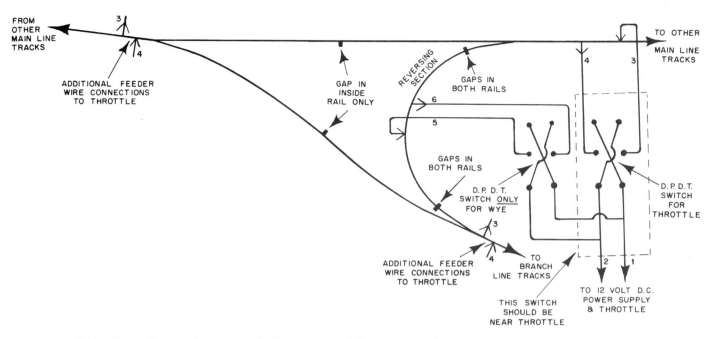

Fig. 5-16 *Wiring for wyes between main line tracks and diverging branch tracks.*

wye, at least, will be a stub end. That is the leg of the wye that will be used primarily to reverse the locomotive; the other two legs may lead to other towns or more turnouts and switches. The stub end will be used only for locomotive turning, although there is no reason why an industry or freight house could not be located on the stub end of the wye. The other two legs, however, are both active portions of the railroad.

The wiring diagram (Fig. 5-15) shows where to install two insulated rail joiners (to put an electrical gap in a rail) or insulated rail inserts, when the stub end of the wye is the least-traveled portion of the area. The extra reversing DPDT toggle, or slide switch, would need to be operated more frequently for normal train movements if the wiring were altered. There, the DPDT only needs to be turned (as does the main reversing switch) when you are actually turning a locomotive. This would be the wiring diagram for the wye on the track plan at the end of Chapter 3 (Fig. 3-26).

When the wye is located between two main line tracks (or between a main line and a branch line, as in Fig. 5-16), it is the inside leg of the wye that is the least-used portion of the track. There, the "reversing section" is on the connecting track between the main line and branch line. This, again, will minimize the number of times that the reversing DPDT slide or toggle switch needs to be thrown.

Turntables for Reversing Locomotives

There is a third device for reversing locomotives: the turntable. This is simply a rotating bridge, pivoted in the center, that swings the locomotive end for end. The locomotive moves onto the turntable and stops; the turntable is then rotated 180 degrees and the locomotive moves off in the opposite direction. With a turntable, it is only necessary to turn off the power while the locomotive is on the turntable. When the power is turned back on to allow the locomotive to leave the turntable, the reversing DPDT slide or toggle switch for the entire layout can be set in the opposite direction. It is wise to make any tracks that run off of the turntable to store locomotives as separate blocks so you can park locomotives. There is no special wiring needed for a turntable, however. LGB offers a small turntable with twelve tracks diverging from the pivoting bridge (number 1400).

Storage Track Sections for Locomotives

There are a variety of options available to a modeler with the gauge 1 equipment to operate two trains without any special track wiring; all were described earlier in this chapter, including command control for the operation of sixteen or more locomotives at once, radio control with the battery power for the locomotives carried on the train, or a combination of battery power and radio control for one (or twenty) trains and conventional control (or command-con-

Wiring and Train Control

trol) for another train. If, however, you want to use a conventional power pack or one with a walk-around throttle for each train, then the layout must be divided into electrically isolated blocks, each with its own on-off switch that also will select which power pack will control that block.

The simplest way to operate two locomotives on a layout with a single conventional or walk-around power pack and throttle is to designate some of the extreme stub ends of the sidings for "locomotive storage." Install an insulated rail joiner in just one of the rails to electrically isolate the stub end of the siding. Connect a wire to that electrically isolated rail, then to a simple on-off, single-pull, single throw (SPST) toggle or slide switch. Connect the other side of that on-off switch to the rail on the "live" side of the railroad. By turning the on-off switch to the "off" position, you can park or store a locomotive on the stub end of that siding while you operate the rest of the layout. You will need two such sidings (or ends of sidings), however, so you'll have a place to park the first locomotive while you activate the second locomotive. If you have four locomotives, make five of these locomotive storage sidings. The same system would be used to connect the locomotive storage tracks that lead off a turntable to the main line of the layout, with a single on-off switch for each siding.

Making Rail Insulators

LGB sells a plastic rail joiner (number 5026) that can be used on most brands of track with the code 332 rails used by LGB. The joiner simply replaces the metal rail joiner on one rail. The joiner is not quite as strong as a metal joiner so the track should be fixed to a piece of plywood or linked firmly beneath the ties with LGB's number 1150 clip. That rail joiner, however, is a large block of bright yellow plastic. That can be helpful if you want to see where the end of the block is located, but it also destroys the realism of that area. If you wish, the joiner can be painted brown to match the ties or rail.

You can install your own electrical-isolating blocks in the rails with this simple system. Use a razor saw to cut the rail right between the spike heads on the tie. Work carefully so you cut clean through the rail but as little into the tie as possible. Use a screwdriver to pry the cut gently apart by moving one or both rails about $\frac{1}{64}$ inch; just enough to know you've cut clean through.

Buy a .010 × .250-inch strip of Evergreen styrene plastic (or cut your own, with scissors or a paper cutter, from a plastic "for sale" sign). Dip the tip of the plastic in thickened hobby-type cyanoacrylate cement or Super Glue and shove the glued end down into the gap you just cut in the rails. Let the cement dry overnight or spray-on a quick dash of the "kicker" or accelerator for cyanoacrylate cements (hobby dealers sell these products). Use a hobby knife to carve the excess plastic flush with the sides and top of the rail. If you need insulated rail joiners in both rails (for a reversing loop or wye) cut the second rail at least four ties down the track from the first rail (an eight-tie spacing is better) so you don't weaken the track at one place.

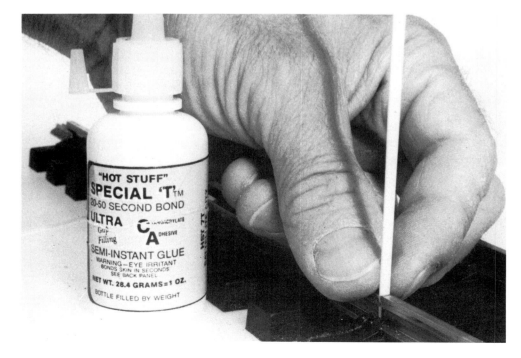

Fig. 5-17 *Make an insulating gap by cutting one rail and then inserting a strip of 0.020-inch-thick plastic dipped in cyanoacrylate cement.*

Fig. 5-18 *Finish the insulating gap by trimming the plastic flush with the rail head.*

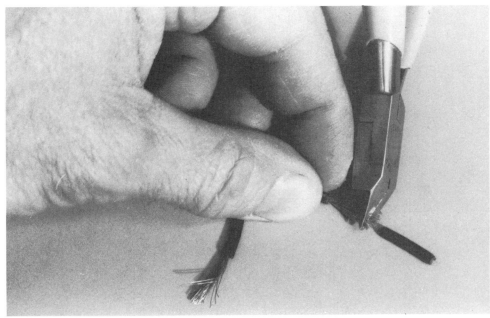

Fig. 5-19 *Strip the insulation from the ends of the wires for any wire connection.*

Basic Wiring Technique

The least expensive wire for gauge 1 railroads is common 14 gauge household copper or aluminum stranded wire. Use the type with indoor insulation for an indoor track and the thicker outdoor type for an outdoor layout (or use buried PVC plastic conduit, as shown later in this chapter, for the outdoor layout with indoor-style insulation on the wires). Sometimes you can buy complete extension cords on sale for less than the price of bulk wire. You can use much smaller solid wire (of about 20 gauge) for simple 2- or 3-inch connections, but the 14 gauge should be adequate for most outdoor layouts.

Buy a wire-stripping tool if you have an extensive layout to wire. For most of us, a pair of diagonal cutters can be used to cut through just the insulation and pull it from the wire. The trick is to avoid even nicking any of the copper strands, and it can be done with practice. I make two bites with the cutters, the second at exactly the same point but 90 degrees from

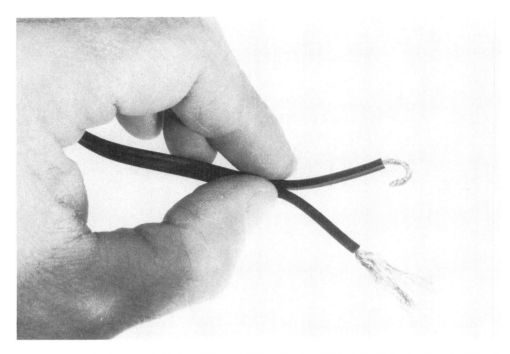

Fig. 5-20 *Twist the stranded wire into a solid cable and bend a C-shaped loop.*

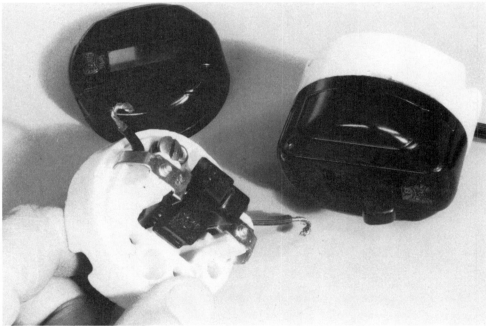

Fig. 5-21 *This heavy-duty on-off switch can be sealed for use outdoors, but only with 12 to 18 volts of DC current. The wires enter from the ceramic back.*

the first to cut through the insulation from four sides. I find I can easily pull 1 to 2 inches of insulation from the wire without any damage to the copper strands.

If you are going to loop the wires around a screw on the back of a power pack or an electrical switch, the wires must first be twisted tightly to form a single strand. The strand must then be looped to fit around

the thread of the screw. *Never* just stick an untwisted, straight wire under the side of a screw. Make the loop open like the letter C so the loop is pulled tighter when the screw is tightened.

It's best to solder any wires to the track, but you can buy crimp-on terminals at hardware and electronics stores. Buy a matching crimping tool. The

Fig. 5-22 *A row of these on-off switches can be attached to a board and placed near the control panel.*

smallest single-hole connectors can be bolted to the track with the various types of screw-on rail joiners shown in Chapter 4. Use the crimp-on terminals to make connections to rail joiners if you are using aluminum rail, but apply some of the special grease sold by these stores to avoid electrolysis.

You can obtain heavy-duty electrical switches that are designed for use outdoors. Hardware stores sell the type shown in Fig. 5-21. Smaller electrical switches with a rubber insulation cover over the handle are available at electronics supply stores like Radio Shack or Allied Radio. Exposure to rain and sun can damage the plastic in electrical components, but the actual track wiring is only 12 to 18 volts, so there is no major danger from electrocution in wet weather. Still, it's wise to house any control panels in weather-tight boxes when they are not in use. The 115-volt power packs should be disconnected and moved indoors when they're not in use or, again, mounted in completely weatherproof boxes with any outdoor 115-volt wiring installed by a licensed electrician according to the building codes in your area.

Conventional Two-Train Control

If you wish to use one of the conventional power packs or one of the packs that have the tethered walk-around throttle controls, it is wise to wire the layout for the operation of two or more trains. The system shown in Fig. 5-23 has been developed by model railroaders with indoor layouts over decades of ex-periments. There are at least a dozen other systems that will work as well. With this system, a SPDT slide or toggle switch with a center "off" position is used to control the power to each electrically isolated block. This is a common rail system where only one rail need be cut or insulated and only one wire connected.

Briefly, the DPDT switch is used either to select power pack A, to select power pack B, or simply to turn the unit off. The system makes it impossible for both power packs to be turned on in the same block at the same time. Each block should be about the length of a train because you will want to have at least one "off" block between each train. The system also requires two complete power packs, each with its own on-off, reversing, and throttle switches. Each of those packs can, of course, have a walk-around tethered throttle.

Some modelers use a command-control system for one of the power packs and a conventional (with or without the walk-around feature) for the second power pack. The danger with this system is that the locomotives (and the power pack) from one system virtually can be destroyed if command-control power reaches a locomotive without a receiver. If you are disciplined enough to keep at least one block between the trains and that block is off, there is little chance of any problem. A single metal wheel from a tender or rolling stock, can, however, span any of the insulating gaps to carry command-control power into

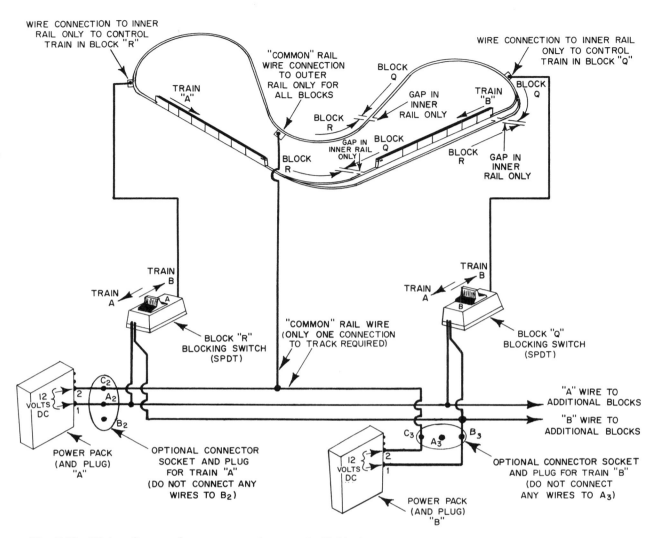

Fig. 5-23 *Wiring diagram for true two-train control with blocks.*

Fig. 5-24 *Wiring diagram for telephone sockets and plugs for walk-around control. (Note: socket only is shown; for plug wiring, connect the power pack's 12- to 18-volt DC terminal number 1 to both A and B and connect 12- to 18-volt DC terminal number 2 to C on plug.)*

CONNECTING PLUG AND SOCKET WIRING

CONNECT WIRES: C_2, C_3, ETC., TO C TERMINAL
A_2, A_3, ETC., TO A TERMINAL <u>ONLY</u>
FOR POWER PACK "A" SOCKETS
B_2, B_3, ETC., TO B TERMINAL <u>ONLY</u>
FOR POWER PACK "B" SOCKETS

that dead block. If, by sheer fate, a metal wheel spans the gap from the conventional power pack into the dead block, then the two incompatible power systems can connect and either or both systems and locomotive motors can be destroyed. If two "off" blocks are kept between the trains, then even this problem can be avoided and any potential danger becomes a matter of human error.

The system, as shown in Fig. 5-24, also has the provision for one of the older-style round telephone jacks to be used to connect a walk-around throttle into the system. If you place plugs every 20 feet or so around the edges of the layout, you can limit the length of tether cords on the walk-around throttles to 20 feet. If several people are operating at once, the tether cables can be a problem if there are only two outlets.

Wiring Remote-Controlled Turnouts

For now, LGB and Lionel are the only firms offering remote-controlled turnouts for gauge 1 railroads, although Aristo-Craft and Micro Engineering are working on their own systems. Lionel supplies a two-button actuator with each of its turnouts. The LGB number 5175 or older number 5075 turnout controllers must be purchased as separate items. Both the Lionel and LGB controls are bulky and do not lend themselves to being positioned directly on a schematic diagram of the track plan on a control panel like those in this chapter. It is possible to use any

DPDT toggle or slide switch as long as it has a momentary contact and can withstand 24 volts. If you want to leave the panel outdoors, the switch should also be waterproof. If you are using crimp-on connectors rather than soldering the connections, the terminals must be compatible with connectors to match your crimping tool. Electronics hobby stores like Radio Shack and Allied Radio should have a variety of sizes and styles available that match all these specifications.

Two wires must be connected to the back of the DPDT switch as shown in Fig. 5-26. Two more wires

Fig. 5-25 *Wiring diagram to use DPDT center-off switch to control electric switch machines at turnouts.*

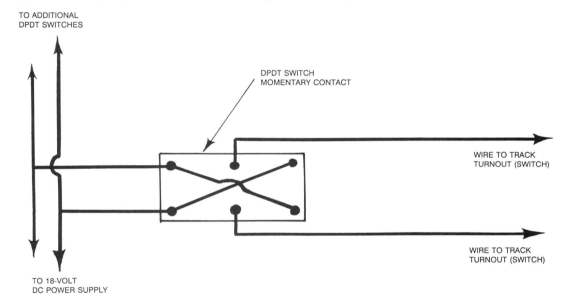

Fig. 5-26 *This is the control panel for the 30-by-40-foot layout in Chapter 2. It is made from sheets of $\frac{1}{8}$-inch hardboard with the track diagram scraped in the face. Small DPDT switches control the turnouts.*

lead from one pair of terminals on the edge of the switch to the 18- to 24-volt DC power supply and also to more DPDT switches. Notice that the two wires that lead to the turnout connect to the center pair of terminals.

The control panel itself can be constructed from $\frac{1}{8}$-inch thick Masonite or similar hardboard like the two shown in Figs. 5-26 and 5-27. An alternate material would be Plexiglas, but avoid metal because there is too much danger of a short circuit if a wire works loose and hits the back of the panel. One of these panels uses small DPDT switches similar to the Radio Shack number 275-673. Fig. 5-26 shows the panel for the basement-floor layout shown in Chapter 2 and in the color section. In Fig. 5-27, Bill Baldock used Atlas switch control boxes (number 56) but he used a hobby-type motor tool to grind out the backs of each so they would make a momentary contact and not burn through the thin copper with 24 volts. Bill connected the wires into a tethered cable so he can move the control panel indoors when he is not operating. During operating sessions he mounts the board on an old camera tripod.

Fig. 5-27 *Bill Baldock has lightly penciled a diagram of his layout on a piece of plywood. The Atlas controls for the switch machines are modified and the wires grouped into a cable so the panel can be moved indoors.*

Outdoor Electrical Cables

There can be a considerable number of electrical wires in an outdoor model railroad to power electrical blocks, remote-controlled turnouts, streetlights, interior lights in buildings, water pumps for real water streams and waterfalls, and low-voltage garden spotlights. You may also want some plug-in terminals for walk-around throttles at some of the remote locations on larger layouts.

If you use conventional indoor wiring outdoors, the insulation will crack and disintegrate in a season or two; maybe faster if the wires are buried in damp ground. Heavy-duty insulated wire is expensive, but some types are rugged enough to be buried. The least expensive method of burying wires is to use conventional indoor insulated 14-gauge stranded copper wire and route it to the layout inside PVC plastic conduit as shown in Fig. 5-28. Larger hardware and building-supply outlets sell entire systems of conduit with junction boxes and end caps. Make a rough wiring diagram of the wiring for your layout, buildings, and lighting to determine how you can best group the wires into the least amount of conduit. In some cases, it might be worthwhile to purchase a foot or two of the outdoor-insulated wire if only one or two wires have a short run outside the conduit.

The electrical conduit systems include optional end caps to seal the ends of the PVC conduit pipe. When all the wires are in place, the area around the wires can be sealed with silicone caulking so water cannot find its way inside the pipe to freeze and corrode the wires. Do not be tempted, however, to run any 115 volt wires with this system. Because there are systems of low-voltage patio lights available, even yard lighting need not be 115 volts. The yard light wires can, of course, share the same conduit with the model railroad electrical wires.

LGB's Wiring and Control System

LGB has a complete array of power packs, throttles, and switches as well as magnetically acutated switches to flip turnouts automatically for predetermined train routes and to actuate the whistle or bell in LGB's locomotive sound system. For more information on the LGB system, I would suggest the *LGB Track Planning and Technical Guide,* sold by LGB dealers, or my book, *Model Railroading with LGB* (the Greenberg division of Kalmbach Publishing Company) as sources for information on the LGB electronic components. LGB also offers some special turnouts (switches), including a three-way (right, left, and straight) turnout and a double-slip switch that is a combination crossing and four switches compressed

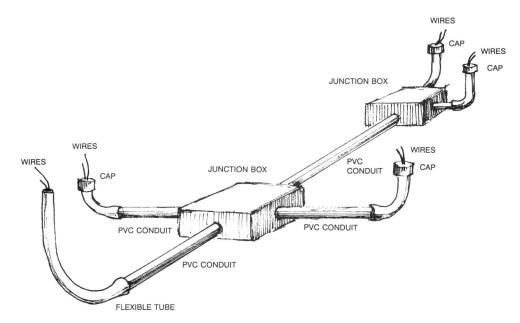

Fig. 5-28 *A typical underground wiring arrangement using plastic PVC conduit with matching junction boxes and end caps.* Artwork by Dave Etchells.

Fig. 5-29 *The dark black strips across the ties are the LGB number 1700 reed switches used, in this case, to throw turnouts automatically in reversing loops.*

into the space of a single crossing. Bill Bauer utilized one on the indoor layout in Chapter 2.

The LGB number 1700 reed switch can be used in conjunction with a number 1701 magnet located beneath a car or locomotive to allow the train to throw its own switches to negotiate, for example, a reverse

loop with no need for the enginner to turn any on-off switches or move any turnouts.

Sound Systems for Locomotives

Many of the LGB, Lionel, Bachmann, and Aristo-Craft gauge 1 locomotives include sounds. The diesels

Wiring and Train Control

Fig. 5-30 *The magnets under the LGB locomotives (or number 1701 add-on magnets) actuate the number 1700 reed switches as the train passes.*

emit hearty growls similar to the diesel engine sounds of the real locomotives, and a remote-controlled horn is available in the LGB diesels. The LGB Mogul is available with a sound system that includes the chuffing sound of steam as well as separate bell and whistle sounds. Lionel uses digital recordings for more authentic steam and diesel sounds in its locomotives.

There are also some accessory sound systems available from Starr-Tec, Keller, MRC, Roanoake Electronics, and others. The Roanoake system uses speakers hidden beside the track, but a system for locomotives is under development. The Roanoake system uses digital recordings for accurate steam and diesel sounds. Starr-Tec has a system using sythesized sound that mounts in a tender or following car. Keller offers sound for diesel or steam as part of its Onboard command-control receivers shown earlier in this chapter. PSI's Dynatrol command-control system also offers sound as an optional feature. MRC has a power pack that includes synthesized steam and diesel sounds with a beside-the-track speaker so no modifications to the locomotive are needed.

Many of the sound systems that utilize track power can be destroyed if you operate the locomotive with the special slow-speed circuit built into some power packs. This circuit is labeled "pulse power mode," or "slow speed," and it usually appears on a switch on the power pack. When you turn the "pulse power" or "slow speed" switch on, the power pack delivers short bursts of higher voltage that allow the motors to run much slower than with conventional power. If you use one of these power packs with a locomotive that has track-powered sound, tape the switch into the off position so it cannot accidentally be turned on. The sound systems that are powered by batteries in the locomotive or a following car are not, of course, affected by pulse power. The command-control systems have their own sound or a bypass circuit that will allow you to use the locomotive's built-in sound so they should not affect any sound systems.

Chapter 6

Indoor Right-of-Way and Benchwork

MOST GAUGE 1 railroads have their birth around a Christmas tree with the track laid right on the bare floor or carpet. The solid-rail track is rugged enough to step on, so the floor is a reasonable site for these large trains. There are examples of basement-floor empires and outdoor railroads that began on patio deck floors in Chapter 2. Gauge 1 trains, like their smaller-scale counterparts, can also be built onto tables or "benchwork" (as modelers call it) like Bill Bauer's Shawmut Line in Chapter 2.

Floor-Level Modeling

The large-scale, gauge 1 trains were designed to operate in an environment far worse than the floor; they were designed to operate on *less* than a floor—the bare earth. There is little in the way of dust or lint or pests that will attack these trains on an indoor floor that will not reach them outdoors. Frankly, HO scale trains really never were designed to be operated on the floor; the track was created to be nailed or screwed to a tabletop. Tables are not really necessary with gauge 1, however.

If you choose to model directly on the floor, you'll have the advantage of being able to reach any part of the layout instantly, without ducking under benchwork or running around fragile flowers and plants; just step over (or even on) the tracks and walk to where the train has derailed. The wiring can be tucked under the tracks and, if the floor is painted

brown to match the wiring, the wires will be nearly invisible.

You will not likely want to nail the track to the floor or apply real ballast to hold the track in place. Some brands, like LGB, Aristo-Craft, Bachmann, and Lionel, have clips that help hold the track together more securely than slip-on rail joiners. Some modelers use 4-by-4-inch-squares of $\frac{1}{4}$-inch plywood at each track joint, as shown in Chapter 4, with screws to hold the track to the wood. If you are going to have uphill grades, you may want to run $\frac{1}{2}$-inch plywood under the entire length of the track, raising it with vertical boards as shown on the 30-by-40-foot basement layout in Chapter 2. Bare concrete floors seem to create their own dust. A coat or two of concrete-sealing paint will greatly reduce the dust level. The dust level on any basement layout can be reduced to upstairs levels by placing some kind of ceiling paneling above the layout so dirt and dust pounded through the floor from above won't filter down to the layout.

Building Tables for Your Trains

If you are going to build a model railroad indoors, there are some definite advantages to elevating the trains at least 3 feet from the floor on their own tables. The major advantage is that you can see your trains from an angle close to the one that you have to view the real trains. The minimum is about 3 feet, a

Fig. 6-1 *Bill Fleisher built this compact LGB layout on simple tables made of 1-by-4-inch boards with a ½-inch plywood tabletop.*

worthwhile height if you want the railroad to be seen by small children. For most modelers, a height near chest level is a more comfortable layout level, something between 48 and 54 inches from the floor. The higher the layout, however, the less distance you can reach, so the tables must be kept fairly narrow or access must be provided as shown in Chapter 3. You also might want to consider how high you want the uphill tracks to reach and how tall you want the mountains; you may find that you need to move the track back down to the floor to fit 6-foot-high mountains beneath your ceiling like in the 30-by-40-foot layout in Chapter 2.

Tables for the layout should begin with a track plan for the layout. You can draw the layout to scale

on paper, like those in Chapter 3, or you can simply lay the actual track on the floor, mark off the future edges of the table right on the floor, and build the tables to match. The sectional gauge 1 track will disassemble and reassemble easily. At least make a sketch of the plan before you tear the layout apart to begin working on the tables.

Some modelers are not willing to settle on just one plan or track arrangement. There is no reason why the track needs to be permanent, even on a tabletop. You might want to attach every third or fourth section to the table with a wood screw just to keep the track together, but those screws can be easily removed to shift the track into new positions. If you feel you may want to experiment with track plans on the tabletop, then build a table slightly larger than what you perceive as the minimum size you would want. Again, refer to Chapter 3 for some ideas of how much space these layouts require. I would suggest that a table 5 by 12 feet is about the minimum and the 12-foot sides must both be accessible because you cannot reach across 5 feet. An ideal experimental layout space might be a 5-by-17-foot table down the center of a single garage stall or, better, if you can squeeze 3 feet of aisle on each side, a 9-by-16-foot table would allow you to use the large-radius curves and turnouts. If you like the plans in Chapter 3, build tables to match those outlines. The *LGB Track Planning and Technical Guide* (available from LGB dealers) has dozens of other track plan ideas, including some large freight and passenger terminals.

You could start with a Ping-Pong table kit from a lumber-supply dealer. Ping-Pong tables are generally 5 by 9 feet in two 4½-by-5-foot sheets of plywood. The conventional 4-by-8-foot sheet of plywood is too narrow even for the smallest-radius gauge 1 curves. It's easy enough to build your own tables, however, using common 1-by-4-inch and 2-by-4-inch lumber for the supports and ¾-inch plywood for the tabletop.

Open-Grid Benchwork

Model railroaders never refer to their layouts as being built on tables; to them, the layouts are built on "benchwork" or, in some cases, on shelves. You're a model railroader by the fact that you've read this far—thousands of modelers never get beyond what they call the "armchair" stage of modeling—they read and collect models and *maybe* build or paint. We are all part of the hobby, but I can assure you, having tried both armchair modeling and just about everything else beyond, that it's far more fun to do it than to read about it. If you really don't want to do some aspect of the hobby yourself, you can find it

Fig. 6-2 *Use an electric drill with a special pilot bit to form the holes for number 8 screws to assemble all benchwork joints.*

ready built. Ask any large hobby shop in any major city for the names of custom layout builders in your area; there are nearly always three or four people that will build any part of the layout for you—from benchwork to wiring to track laying to scenery or any one of those that you'd really rather not do yourself. If you need to get someone to run the trains for you, however, then you may want to consider staying back at the armchair stage.

You may want to build your first layout on a flat tabletop. That allows the option of shifting the tracks just about anywhere without modifying the tables—whoops, the benchwork. I would recommend, however, that you build the supporting members of the benchwork so you can cut away part of the tabletop if you want uphill grades or depressions for rivers or lakes. Support the plywood tabletop with an underframe around the edges made from 1-by-4-inch lumber on edge. Run cross braces every 18 inches if you want to use $\frac{1}{2}$-inch plywood for the tabletop; every 24 inches if you want to use $\frac{3}{4}$-inch plywood. The plywood tabletop can be common BC grade plywood, which means one side is smooth but the holes are filled and the opposite side is rough with unfilled holes.

If you do not support the $\frac{1}{2}$-inch plywood every 18 inches or so, it will eventually sag and warp; similarly, the thicker $\frac{3}{4}$-inch plywood can span slightly larger areas without sagging. If the table is more than 30 inches wide, the 18- or 24-inch gaps should be filled with cross braces to be sure that no area larger than about 18 by 24 inches is unsupported with $\frac{1}{2}$-inch plywood and no area larger than 24 by 30 inches is unsupported with $\frac{3}{4}$-inch plywood. Make these supports from the same 1-by-4-inch lumber, placed on edge, as the outer framework.

Figs. 6-3 and 6-4 show the benchwork for a 5-by-9-foot layout with a rectangular extension for a small yard. This benchwork was made in relatively small segments so it could be disassembled and moved out a standard doorway. The two ends are 30 by 60 inches with two 18-by-24-inch panels that space the ends apart to leave a 24-by-48-inch access area in the middle. Modelers call this type of benchwork "open grid." The plywood sheets would be cut to match the sizes of the open grid boxes so the layout could be disassembled into five components. If you are building a layout in a spare room or basement, it's wise to consider what you will do if you ever want to move it; this type of door-sized box construction will ensure that you can break the layout into movable segments. When you get track and scenery on a pair of Ping-Pong table $4\frac{1}{2}$-by-5-foot panels, it can weigh as much as a thousand pounds. The smaller panels are far easier to manage.

Assemble the individual open-grid panels with number 8 by $1\frac{1}{4}$-inch flathead wood screws, but predrill all the holes with a number 8 by $1\frac{1}{2}$-inch pilot bit. It's about as good to simply use drywall screws but you will not be able to remove any of the cross braces if you need to move them to put in a river or large lake. When the component panels are assembled, join them with either the number 8 by $1\frac{1}{2}$-inch flathead wood screws or with $\frac{1}{2}$ by 2-inch stove bolts, flat washers, and nuts so you can disassemble the panels if the layout is moved. A pair of large clamps can be used to hold the panels together while you install the screws or stove bolts. Use a variable-speed electric drill to install the wood screws.

Cut legs from the cheapest 2-by-4-inch lumber available and attach them with $\frac{1}{4}$-by-$2\frac{1}{2}$-inch stove bolts, flat washers, and nuts. You will, of course, need to drill $\frac{1}{4}$-inch holes for the stove bolts. The legs can then be removed to move the layout or to replace them with longer or shorter legs if you want to raise or lower the height of the layout.

Do not use anything but those wood screws to attach the plywood tabletop. You may want to remove

Fig. 6-3 Design the bench-work open grids so they can be bolted together into the final size but are small enough to be moved out a standard door-way.

Fig. 6-4 This large layout can be broken down into five units. The legs are 2-by-4-inch boards attached with carriage bolts, washers, and nuts.

Fig. 6-5 Clamps make it much easier to build open-grid benchwork. The clamp aligns the parts perfectly while you drill the pilot holes for wood screws.

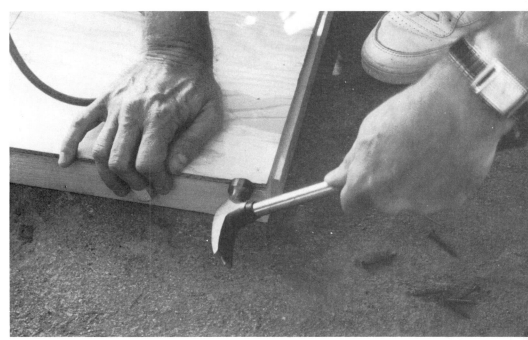

Fig. 6-6 *If the tabletop is likely to stay in place, it can be attached with drywall nails driven with a hammer.*

Fig. 6-7 *Mark the location of the track right on the tabletop with pencil marks along both edges of the ties.*

all or part of the plywood—and that's difficult indeed if it is nailed down. The wood screws can simply be removed.

Cookie-Cutter Construction

If you are certain that you have the final track plan, you can mark the position of the track on the plywood and use a saber saw to remove any plywood from places where there is no track. Mark the locations of any buildings, however, because you'll want to leave plywood supports for the buildings. Modelers call this "cookie-cutter construction" because you are cutting the plywood almost as if it were cookie dough. When the plywood is only below the track, it's a simple matter to raise both plywood and track for uphill grades. Hold the plywood aloft with scraps of 1-by-4-inch lumber screwed to those 1-by-4-inch open-grid cross members. There's no limit to how far you can raise the track as long as you limit the grades to 4 percent or so as described in Chapter 3.

It is also possible to leave the plywood tabletop intact and add another layer of ½-inch plywood placed below only the tracks that will climb upgrade. This is the type of construction Bill Bauer used on his Shawmut Line in Chapter 2. Bill wanted a lot of sidings and industries on the lower level and it was easier for him actually to lay the track and at least temporarily mark the positions of all the buildings on the plywood.

When the zero-level track and buildings were in

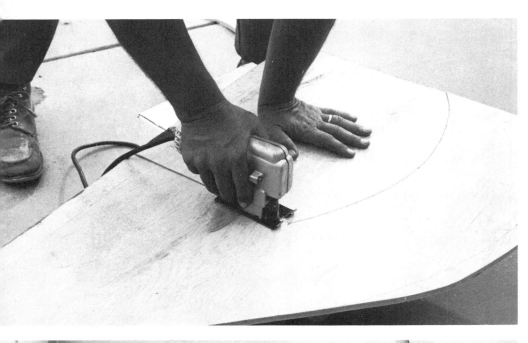

Fig. 6-8 *Use a saber saw to cut along the pencil lines in those areas of the layout where the track will be pushed upward into uphill grades.*

Fig. 6-9 *There is no limit to how far the track can climb above the basic open-grid benchwork with the 1-by-4-inch boards as vertical risers. This is Bill DeFoe's HO scale layout.*

Fig. 6-10 *Bill Bauer added upper-level tracks to an existing tabletop using vertical 1-by-4-inch supports with 1-by-1-inch cleats at the top and bottom. Photo by Bill Bauer.*

place, Bill routed the tracks that would climb upward by placing them right on the tabletop. He was able to see, in three dimensions, if he had looped the tracks far enough so the trains could climb 8 inches to run over the table-level tracks and still maintain less than an 8 percent grade. When he was satisfied with the climbing track configuration, he disassembled sections of it and traced them onto $\frac{1}{2}$-inch plywood. The plywood was then attached to the table with number 8-by-1$\frac{1}{2}$-inch flathead wood screws at the lower level and gently raised with 1-by-4-inch blocks to create a smooth vertical beginning of the uphill run (see Chapter 3 for the use of vertical curves). Then, 1-by-1-inch cleats were attached to the bottom and top of the longer 1-by-4-inch risers to mount the risers on the tabletop and below the upper-level tracks' plywood roadbed. When the railroad reached the scenery stage of construction, a few small areas of the plywood tabletop were cut with a saber saw for streams and lakes that were to be placed below track level.

Roadbed and Ballast

The majority of experienced modelers who build with HO and smaller-scale models add a layer of roadbed between the track and the plywood tabletop. Some modelers use cork roadbed, others use a $\frac{1}{2}$-inch-thick cardboardlike wallboard called Homosote or $\frac{1}{4}$-inch-thick gypsum board. These roadbeds serve two purposes: They elevate the track enough so the track will look like the real thing with its sloping ballast (the crushed rock that holds the ties) shoulders and the cork or cardboard serves to reduce the noise and rumbling that can be caused by trains, which sets up a drumming effect on bare plywood. I would strongly recommend a noise-reducing roadbed because the gauge 1 trains are far heavier and produce more running noise than the HO scale trains. The $\frac{1}{8}$-inch cork is available in sheets from larger lumberyards, but for gauge 1, Homosote would be the best material if you can find a lumberyard willing to order it for you. The plywood tabletop can be covered with Homosote, but you will still need the recommended $\frac{1}{2}$- or $\frac{3}{4}$-inch plywood and 1-by-4-inch braces because Homosote is not self-supporting. Homosote can be cut with a knife blade in a saber saw (Sears sells the blades, as do most larger hardware stores). Cut the Homosote to the shape of the track using the techniques Bill Bauer used to cut the plywood for his upper-level trackage.

Chapter 7

||||||||||||||||||||||||||||||||||||||||||||||||||||||||||||||||||||||||||||||||||||||||||||||||||||||||||||||||||

Scenery for Indoor Layouts

THE QUICK and easy way to create realistic scenery for a gauge 1 model railroad is simply to move the model railroad out into the real world—build a garden railroad. Since these trains are rugged enough to operate outdoors, you won't have to compromise with make-believe dirt or leaves or sun or rain or snow. For some modelers, however, the appeal of these models is more important than the desire to move them outdoors. There are even some of us who would rather not work in a garden, and especially not with our favorite hobby.

Trackwork as Scenery

Indoors or out, scenery for a model railroad begins with the track. The most common size of rail for gauge 1 is the code 332 (about $\frac{5}{16}$ inch high) used by LGB, Aristo-Craft, Kalamazoo, Model Power, Lionel, and Bachmann and available from Micro Engineering. If you are modeling accurate-scale narrow gauge, the most common rail size is about 55-pound rail (the railroads' method of sizing rail by the inch), which was about 4 inches high. That reduces to about $\frac{3}{16}$ inch in 1/24 scale. Old Pullman offers code 197 rail, which is about $\frac{3}{16}$ inch tall, with matching ties and turnout kits.

If you are modeling 1/32 or 1/29 scale standard gauge, using Aristo-Craft, MDC, Great Trains, Lionel, or USA Trains equipment, you might want rail sized to common standard gauge sizes. Main line rail is often about 155-pound, which is about 8 inches high (which reduces to about $\frac{1}{4}$ inch in 1/32 scale). Micro

Engineering and Peco offer track sections and turnouts with code 250 rail and Llagas Creek Railways and Garich Light Transport offer plastic ties and rail, but all of these have ties spaced wide apart to match narrow gauge practice. These brands will work nicely if you want easy-to-lay track for 1/22.5 or 1/24.5 scale, because there is little visual difference between the correct scale code 197 rail and this slightly oversized code 250 rail. Garich Light Rail also has plastic ties spaced closer together to match standard gauge and matching code 250 rail. Aristo-Craft is producing sectional track with ties spaced like standard gauge railroads, but it has code 332 rail. An alternative, if you want code 250 rail for 1/32 scale, would be to use Micro Engineering's code 250 rail and spikes with either Micro Engineering code 250 aluminum rail or Llagas Creek Railways code 250 nickel silver rail and turnout frog and points sets.

Oversized rail has been a tradition with toy trains; the common rail used in HO trains sets is at least 20 percent oversized. The larger rail is more rugged, and some modelers feel that the slightly exaggerated rail emphasizes the concept of narrow gauge trackwork. Reduce the effect of oversized rail by painting it or, in the case of LGB's rail, just leaving it outside for a season or two to achieve a natural brown color. Micro Engineering offers rail precolored with chemicals or you can simply paint the rail with one of the brown paints sold by model railroad shops, like Floquil's Roof Brown or Santa Fe Mineral Red.

You can improve the appearance of any of the ties

by painting them a lighter gray-brown color to match weathered cresote on real railroads. The creosote color only lasts a few years, and the narrow gauge, in particular, often left ties in place for decades. All but the very newest stretches of track have a variety of tie colors that can range from dark reddish brown newly installed ties to pale gray weathered ties. Bill Baldock has done an especially fine job of staining his wooden ties to match the various colors of the prototype. Photos of his DSP&PRR appear in the color section.

Real railroad track uses ballast—golf ball–sized stones—to hold the ties in place. If you are building an outdoor layout, you will want to use ballast for that same purpose, although some modelers nail their track to boards buried beneath ballast. Ballast is not needed on an indoor railroad for track retention, but ballast is needed if you want to duplicate real railroad track. None of the indoor layouts in this book are completed to the stage at which their builders have elected to install ballast, with the exception of the mine scene on Bill Bauer's Shawmut Line that appears in Chapter 2 and in the color section.

Model railroad shops sell bags of ballast, but most of it is far too small for gauge 1 layouts. The most popular choice of ballast for outdoor layouts is crushed granite. It can be obtained as "crusher fines"

from building construction firms. Crushed rock is also sold as a diet supplement for chickens. Large feed-supply stores should be able to provide "starter grit," a finely crushed granite. You may be able to find similar-sized crushed rock at a local garden supply center. Common pea gravel, however, is far too large for even 1/22.5 scale ballast, although some modelers, again, like the way it makes a caricature of the already oversized track. Some modelers also use a gravel product intended for driveways and walkways called "squeegee" that is similar to the granite crusher fines but utilizes a different rock color.

The ballast can be glued permanently in place on an indoor layout but it should be left loose outdoors. To apply the ballast, simply pour it slowly over the track to minimize the dust. You can also pour the ballast through a tea strainer and save just the parts that are left in the strainer; the dust and smaller particles that flow through the strainer can be used for ballast on an early era narrow gauge model railroad or just as "dirt."

Use a toothbrush to spread the ballast and to shape it into an angled shoulder. If you are modeling narrow gauge, the shoulder can lead right off any embankments. If you are modeling standard gauge, however, notice that there is a flat shelf at the foot of the ballast before any embankment goes on down a

Fig. 7-1 *This roadbed has relatively fine-grain ballast and a second shoulder (see lower right). A dirt road crosses the double-track main line just in front of the semaphore signals.* Union Pacific Railroad photo.

Fig. 7-2 *Narrow gauge track was often this crude—with the full ends of the ties hanging out in the air. This is the Rio Grande Southern railbus called the "Galloping Goose" at the Colorado Railroad Museum.*

Fig. 7-3 *Use a tea strainer to sift the powder and dust from dirt and spread what falls through the stainer to simulate dirt.*

slope and a similar shelf before any cut goes up from the track. Those ballast shoulder shapes and the amount of tie ends that protrude (note that the full end of the tie is usually visible on narrow gauge track) can increase the realism of your model railroad. Sweep any excess ballast from the tops of the ties and from the turnouts with a 1-inch-wide paintbrush.

For an indoor layout, the ballast can be set firmly in place by flooding the entire ballast area with a mixture of equal parts artist's matte medium and water and a drop or two of liquid detergent to break the water's surface tension so it will soak into the ballast. The matte medium dries with a flat finish and is relatively flexible, whereas common white glue dries to a shiny finish and can crack and transmit noise. It is essential that the ballast be completely awash in the fluid so the matte medium will penetrate down into the lower layers and not just make a thin shell over loose ballast. The technique will not work outdoors because the weather turns the matte medium white and cracks the surface. Outdoors, simply spray the crusher fines or squeegee lightly with water and the dust in the ballast hardens enough to hold the track.

Ballasting Turnouts

There is an element of danger in applying ballast with any kind of cement or matte medium; it is far too easy to glue the moving points and mechanism of the turnouts solid, thus ruining some very expensive trackwork. There are some ways to avoid gluing the turnouts, including not covering them with as thick a layer of ballast. Keep the moving parts well clear of the ballast as you spread it with the toothbrush and paintbrush. When the ballast is settled, apply a few drops of LaBelle number 102 plastic-compatible oil (hobby stores can order it) to all the working parts. The oil should keep the cement from the working parts. If you're still worried, don't use the matte me-

dium near the working parts of the turnout, just flood those areas with plain water and a drop or two of detergent and let the dust solidify as it does outdoors. You may need to wet the area occasionally to keep the ballast tight.

Making Mountains Indoors

There are dozens of methods of shaping mountains for an indoor model railroad, but the most popular ones at present are paper towels soaked in Hydrocal plaster or carved beaded foam sheets covered with plaster. There are examples of the results of both techniques in Chapter 2 and in the color section. The 30-by-40-foot layout on the basement floor has mountains formed from plaster-soaked paper towels, and Bill Bauer's Shawmut Line has mountains around the Ajax Mine shaped from extruded beaded foam insulation board.

The plaster-soaked-paper-towel method begins with the rough shapes of the mountains and valleys. The peaks of the mountains can be formed with 1-by-2-inch lumber braced from the benchwork or, if on the floor, with 1-by-2-inch tripodlike triangular braces. The skyline of the mountains or valleys at the rear of the layout can be formed with used household wire or duct tape that is strong enough to support the wet plaster temporarily. The final shape of the mountains can be formed with wadded-up newspapers.

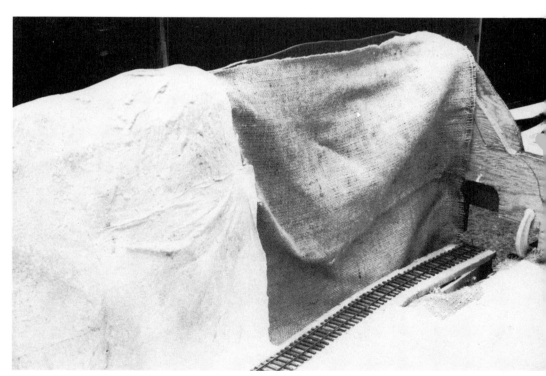

Fig. 7-4 *Shape the mountains with either wet paper towels or old burlap bags.*

Large empty corrugated boxes can fill the major areas so you don't have to pile wadded-up newspapers into 6-foot-high mounds. Cover the wadded-up newspaper with a single layer of industrial-grade brown-colored paper towels. The paper towels will conform to the shapes more easily if they are sprayed with water. Old burlap bags are an alternative cover for the wadded-up paper towels.

The plaster-soaked newspaper system allows you to preview the final shapes of all the mountains and valleys with the bare water-soaked paper towels or burlap. If you want a taller mountain or a deep valley, you can change the shape quickly and easily. Be wary of two-steep mountain slopes; it is rare to find any mountain near the tracks of a railroad with a slope greater than about 45 degrees. If you really do want rock cliffs, make the mountain about 3 or 4 inches back from where you want the rock faces; we'll add the rock faces later from foam or plaster castings. This is a good time, too, to push your longest and tallest locomotives or cars around the track to be sure the scenery doesn't protrude far enough so it will be hit by moving trains. It's wise to keep this initial shaping stage at least 1 inch away from the trains.

The shaping stage is the time, too, to position all the bridges and tunnel portals. Remember, each bridge must be supported by some kind of abutment. There are a variety of simulated stone, brick, and wooden bridge abutments, or you can simply make a stack of three ever-shorter pieces of $\frac{3}{8}$-inch-square (for 1/32 or 1/29 scale) or $\frac{1}{2}$-inch-square (for 1/22.5 or 1/24 scale) pine, redwood, or balsa. Make the bottom piece 7 inches long, the middle piece 6 inches long, and the top piece 5 inches long and stack them in a pyramid shape. Stain or paint them a dark reddish brown color like cresote. Later, the edges of the abutments will be buried in plaster, but for now, the abutments must be in place so the paper towels or burlap can be shaped into smooth 45-degree slopes. Study photographs of real railroads and look at the outdoor railroads to see how real dirt is formed by rain and wind erosion (or by its natural shape) around bridge abutments and tunnel portals.

Find a large building supply company that is willing to order Hydrocal brand plaster from U.S. Gypsum. You'll need at least 100 pounds for the smallest gauge 1 layout and the plaster is sold in 100-pound bags. Hydrocal sets to a rock-hard surface that is virtually the same as alabaster, and that property is what makes the paper-towel soaked mountains self-supporting. When the plaster dries, all those wadded-up newspapers and boxes can be removed.

Buy a dozen packages (about 288) industrial-grade paper towels. The towels are a bit easier to work with if you cut or tear them in half; into about 6-by-12-inch strips. Mix the Hydrocal with water by slowly adding

Fig. 7-5 *These mountains, on the 30-by-40-foot basement layout in Chapter 2, are industrial-grade paper towels soaked in Hydrocal plaster.*

John and Barbara Bierie's Blackhawk & Devil Mountain Railway flows through a Southwest-styled garden landscape. A list of the plants in this photograph appears in Chapter 9 (Fig. 9-9).

Norm Grant operated his SP&SJRR year-round with snowplows on the pilots of two LGB Moguls to buck the drifts. James Pearson photo from the Norm Grant collection.

The bridges, trees, and rocks on Dick Schaffer's layout were salvaged from Norm Grant's layout when it was abandoned. This bridge is just visible behind a bush in the color photograph of the canyon in Norm's layout.

Norm Grant's South Park & San Juan Railroad was one of the most spectacular outdoor layouts ever built. The redwood Howe truss in the background will weather to the color of the foreground trestle in about a year.

The footpath behind Bill and Dee Baldock's home allows visitors to view the trains at shoulder height with a rock and dirt wall supporting the railroad on a real cliff.

Steve Arrigotti built this bridge from half-inch redwood strips. There are more photographs and a plan of the layout in Chapter 2 and a list of these plants in Chapter 9 (Fig. 9-6).

Bill Baldock's choice of trees includes the dwarf boxwood in front of the Delton 2-8-0 and a dwarf boxwood. The large bushy tree will be removed.

Paul Bussey, of Garden Railways in Cincinnati, builds and installs layouts like this one, often with waterfalls and old railroad ties for scenery.

Marc and Barbara Horovitz's Ogden Botanical Railway has the charm of an English country garden. The locomotive and rolling stock are Bachmann. A list of the plants in this photograph appears in Chapter 9 (Fig. 9-2).

Bill and Dee Baldock's DSP&PRR descend's from the deck of the patio above the top of the photo through a series of loops beneath the patio and down these wandering tracks.

The first portion of Steve and Judy Arrigotti's layout ran around a 12-by-18-foot area beneath this tree. A list of the plants in this photograph appears in Chapter 9 (Fig. 9-5).

the plaster to a quart-sized bowl of water. Keep stirring until the plaster becomes the consistency of thick milk. A quart-sized glass cooking bowl may be easier to clean than a plastic bowl and a quart is about all you can work with before the plaster cures. Dip the strips of paper towel into the plaster and submerge them so they are completely soaked with the plaster. Do one strip at a time: Dip it, pull it out, and then drape it over the mountainside. Overlap the first strip by about half with the second strip, the second strip by about half with the third strip, so you effectively have at least two layers of plaster-soaked paper towels. Continue working around the mountains until they are completely covered. Protect the track and tunnel portals and bridges and abutments with plastic bags. Quickly scrape the mixing bowl clean after you consume each batch of plaster. You'll find this work goes very quickly; if you have the mountains shaped and the track, bridge portals, and abutments protected, you can apply the plaster-soaked paper towels to a 5-by-9-foot area in an evening. Let the plaster dry overnight.

You have two choices for coloring plaster: mix color into the plaster or apply latex paint after the plaster is in place. I would recommend that you mix color with the plaster so that any chips or unpainted areas will show as colored plaster rather than stark white. Building supply firms usually stock powdered colors intended for use in concrete. A mixture of about two parts brown to one part black provides a reasonable shade of dirt. The ratio of dry color to plaster will be listed on the dry color container. When the scenery is complete, I'd also suggest that you use brown latex paint as both a coloring and a

cement to hold surface textures—the precolored plaster is really just an undercoat for later work.

Foam Insulation Board Mountains

The second popular method of of shaping mountains and valleys uses 2-inch-thick sheets of extruded, beaded plastic insulation board. Styrofoam is one common brand but there are others. Some stores refer to the material as beadboard. When you buy the 2-by-8-foot sheets, purchase a contractor's cement (and a caulking gun to apply it) that is designed to glue the beadboard. Some cements will actually melt the surface and common white glue is not quite thick enough to bond the beadboard.

Use a large carving knife or a hacksaw blade in a handle that holds one end of the blade to cut the beadboard. Stagger the material into pyramids to match the shape of the mountains and valleys you envision for the railroad. Small scraps can be used to fill-in around tunnel portals and bridge abutments. Cement the beadboard in place on the layout and cement the upper layers to the lower with the caulking gun and construction cement. When the cement dries, shape the slopes with the carving knife or hacksaw blade. The material cuts easily, and if you remove too much, you can cement the "mistake" back in place. Bill Bauer used some 1-inch-thick beadboard on his Shawmut Line in these photographs (Figs. 7-6 through 7-9); the thinner material requires more layers, but it is a bit easier to shape because there are fewer "steps."

When you are satisfied with the shapes of the beadboard mountains and valleys, coat the entire sur-

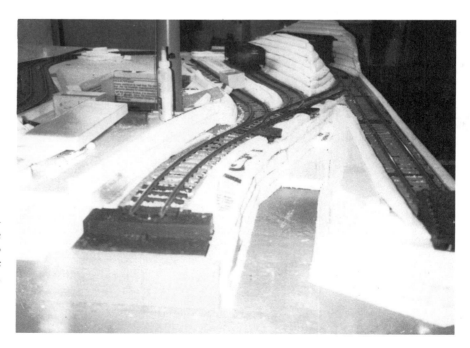

Fig. 7-6 *Bill Bauer used plastic beadboard insulation board, stacked in piles three to ten layers deep, to shape his mountains.* Photo by Bill Bauer.

Fig. 7-7 *After the beadboard insulation is cut to the ever-smaller sizes to make pyramid-shaped hills, the corners are rounded off with a rasp.* Photo by Bill Bauer.

Fig. 7-8 *The beadboard is coated with patching plaster and roughed by hand as it begins to cure. Bill Bauer embedded bits of broken cork to simulate rock.* Photo by Bill Bauer.

Fig. 7-9 *In areas where the ground will be visible, brush on a thick coat of artist's matte medium and install fiber weeds and sifted-on real dirt.*

face with a thick layer of plaster. There's no need to search for Hydrocal for this work, common patching plaster will do fine. Again, it is wise to precolor the plaster so any unpainted or chipped areas won't show through as pure white. Bill Bauer embedded small chunks of broken fishing float cork into the surface to simulate rocks.

Casting Stones (and Rocks)

Mountains-in-Minutes sells a variety of cast foam plastic rock cliffs with textures and colors to match the geology of most parts of North America. These foam rocks are easy to cut with a carving knife or hacksaw blade. The rocks are also lightweight, an important factor when mountains scaled to gauge 1 are being created. Position the rocks to simulate dynamite-blasted rock near the tracks but far enough away so they will not hit passing cars or locomotives. Some of the castings can also be used to simulate rock cliffs or rock outcrops on more gentle slopes. Bury the edges of the foam plastic rocks with earth-colored patching plaster; later it can be textured to match dirt or weeds.

If you are not concerned about the weight of the layout, use rocks cast in plaster. The rocks available to modelers are at least as realistic as real rocks because they are literally copies of real rocks. Mountains-in-Minutes makes their copies in foam plastic. Mountains-in-Minutes also sells a two-part foam plastic that you can mix to pour your own rocks in molds available from them as well as several other manufacturers. Hobby dealers usually have a copy of Walthers's 800-page *The World of HO Scale* that lists tools, paints, raw materials, books, and scenic items useful in all scales. Walthers also publishes the 200-page *The World of Large Scale Trains,* which is devoted exclusively to gauge 1 items in 1/24, 1/22.5, 1/29, and 1/32 scales. You'll find several brands of latex rubber molds to make your own rocks from foam or plaster as well as ready-to-use rocks cast in plaster or Hydrocal.

If you wish to make your own rocks from plaster, Hydrocal, or Mountains-in-Minutes foam, buy two or three of the rock molds. These molds are made with cloth-reinforced latex rubber directly from real rocks. You can, in fact, make your own molds from your choice of real rocks. Mountains-in-Minutes and others sell the latex rubber. To make a rock mold, simply spray the chosen rock with Pam or a similar nonstick cooking spray. Do not, however, use any kind of oil or grease, it can disintegrate the latex. Brush a thick coat of the latex over the rock and let it dry. Brush on a second layer and, while it is still wet,

Fig. 7-10 *Purchase (or make your own) latex rubber molds of real rock surfaces, fill the mold with plaster, let it harden, and then peel back the mold.*

cover it with some common surgical gauze and apply a third layer. When that dries, apply a fourth coat of latex, more gauze, and a final coat of latex. The gauze will reinforce the rock mold so it won't tear as easily when you remove it from later plaster rock castings. When the latex has cured overnight, peel it gently from the rock and your rock mold is ready to use.

Again, it's wise to use precolored plaster in case it chips or you fail to paint some hidden corner. Use the same powdered pigment intended for concrete driveways suggested earlier. Experiment with some small batches of plaster and colors until you arrive at a color that is a few shades lighter than the rocks you are trying to recreate. I prefer patching plaster because it takes stains easier, but others prefer Hydrocal for its strength in the delicate fissures of the real rock.

There are two methods of using your own cast plaster rocks: Simply make replicas of the real rock and attach them to the simulated dynamite-blasted cuts and cliffs or slap the still-wet plaster rock against the plaster mountain faces. The second method is really the easiest because you can contour the still-wet plaster to the shape of the mountain. Later applications can actually overlap earlier "rocks" so you can produce a 2-foot-high by 12-foot-long cliff with essentially the same texture but with varying patterns.

Fig. 7-11 *Find rocks that match the texture and shape found in the real world. The smooth rock at the right would be used to simulate weather-worn granite outcrops, the rough rock for cliffs and cuts dynamited through rock.*

Feel free to rotate the molds or, if you are modeling a stratified rock, to align the fissures as you work along the layout. The plaster for the rock molds is mixed to the same thick milk consistency suggested for Hydrocal and paper towel mountains. If you simply want rocks, wait until the plaster has just set—you can tell because it suddenly turns from cold to warm. Remove the latex mold before the plaster is completely hardened to minimize the tearing inside the mold. For wet plaster applications, hold the plaster-filled mold in two hands and gently rock it back and forth. The moment the plaster will no longer rock, slap the mold and plaster against the mountain. The plaster will adhere a bit better if the face of the mountain is dampened with water. Hold the mold against the mountain until you feel that warmth that indicates the plaster has set and gently peel back the mold. Expect some mistakes as you practice the technique; just scrape off the mess and try again.

The cast plaster or foam rocks should be painted with a stain or wash made of equal parts water and latex paint. Look at the darker areas of the real rocks and mix a dark gray, a greenish gray, a brown, or a bluish gray to match the real thing. Mix that paint with about nine parts water and a drop or two of liquid detergent. Brush the mix (called a "wash") over the rock faces and you'll find that it just naturally builds up in the crevices and falls off the highlights to give perfect shadow and multihue effects. For some rocks you may need a wash of a second color. Look carefully at the real rocks you want to recreate; most of

Fig. 7-12 *This 4-foot-high wall of Hydrocal is being faced with rock textures, with the still-wet plaster and the mold slapped against the Hydrocal cliff so the casting can harden in place. Then the mold is peeled away.*

the rocks in the Sierras and Rockies are about 80 percent pale olive green. That green is a hard moss, and it can be duplicated by simply mixing a matching color of acrylic paint, then cutting that color with about an equal amount of water, and then a drop or two of liquid detergent so you can spray the stuff through a laundry-type hand spray bottle or an old household cleaner hand pump bottle. Apply the green moss as the final coat, hitting mostly the exposed surfaces of the rocks.

Getting Down to Earth

One of the "real-world" items you can bring indoors with as much realism as working outdoors is the dirt itself. The trick to making realistic scenery indoors lies in getting the slopes right. Make relatively gentle hills, not sheer dirt cliffs. In the world of real dirt, when you build a model railroad outdoors, you can make the hills as steep as you can pile the wet dirt, but after a few rains, the slopes will take on a "natural" shape. Study photographs and get those shapes right, and you are most of the way along with realistic indoor scenery. You just learned how to—almost literally—re-create real rocks. One of the final steps in making indoor scenery, will be to add the texture and color of dirt. The "secret method"? Use real dirt.

Sift any real dirt or sand through a tea strainer. The material that passes through the strainer will do nicely for dirt. I would suggest, however, that you pass a magnet over any dirt or sand you want to use to be sure it is not magnetic; any magnetic material will eventually find its way inside the motors of the locomotives to create short circuits that can ruin the motor.

To apply the real dirt, cover the area to be made into dirt with a thick layer of latex wall paint about the same color as the dirt. Use the tea strainer, again, to scatter the dirt over the still-wet paint. Work with only a 6-by-6-inch or smaller area at a time so the paint will not dry before the dirt arrives. If you are already satisfied with the color, use artist's matte medium, straight from the jar, to cover the scenery and scatter or sprinkle the real dirt over that. You can pat the dirt gently into the paint or matte medium with your fingertips. Let the dirt dry for a day, then use a vacuum cleaner to remove the excess.

Grass and Weeds

Strange as it may seem, you can actually improve on nature in creating scale-model weeds, grasses, bushes, and trees. There are no living grasses or plants with leaves or needles small enough for even 1/22.5 scale. The plants you see in the color section of

this book look real because they are real, but their textures are grossly oversized when compared to the trains. In effect, it is possible to get proper scale-sized plants but impossible to get scale-sized textures in the real world. Indoors, you can actually buy correctly scaled grass, and the texture, if not the shape, of scale-sized leaves and pine needles.

Noch, Heki, Hannes-Fischer, Kibri, Faller, Preiser, Highball, Vintage Reproductions (all listed in Walthers's *The World of HO Scale* catalog), and Busch make loose flocking that can be applied with either an empty plastic baby powder bottle or the pumps from Vintage Reproductions by simply squeezing the bottle to force the flocking onto still-wet latex paint or artist's matte medium. The flocking takes on a static charge as it leaves the bottle and literally stands on its end in the paint or matte medium. Noch has an electric pump applicator that works even better. The grass, where needed, should be applied first, followed by the sifted-on dirt; do both while the latex paint or matte medium are still wet.

For longer and taller weeds, there is an array of special unwoven rope and fabric from Sweetwater Scenery and Woodland Scenics (both in Walthers' catalog). This material should be applied before the dirt or grass. Spread some artist's matte medium where you want the weeds or tall grass, then press clumps of the grass into the matte medium and let it dry. Follow with dirt and/or more grass.

For leafy weeds, bushes, or trees, use ground foam from Woodland Scenics, Bachmann, Life-Like, AMSI, Hannes-Fischer, or Noch. There are several sizes of the foam, and Woodland Scenics offers foam already glued to a random mesh (that is virtually preassembled tree, weed, or bush twigs) called "Foliage Material." Stretch the mesh, after removing it from the box, until it looks like lace and it is incredibly realistic. The ground foam can also be applied to piles of Woodland Scenics's bare mesh (called "Poly Fiber") to make bushes. The Poly Fiber can be tucked into cuttings from real hedges to make very realistic trees.

Scale-Model Trees

Heki, Hannes-Fischer, Kibri, Noch, Life-Like, Busch, and Model Power make a variety of trees that are at least 12 inches tall. All have molded plastic trunks and most have ground foam to simulate leaves and flocking to simulate pine needles. Most can be made more realistic by reshaping slightly and by trimming the edges into less-uniform patterns.

The most realistic trees, however, are made from weeds or bushes or the tips of hedges. Look around

your own yard and nearby woodlands, especially in the fall, for suitable tree trunk and limb structures in nature. Western sagebrush limbs, for one, make incredibly realistic trunks and limbs for a variety of trees with loose bark textures. Once you've found the basic trunk, cover it with clumps of Woodland Scenics's Poly Fiber, followed by sprinklings of fine ground foam. Common hair spray (the cheaper the better, it seems) is sprayed lightly over the Poly Fiber and the ground foam sprinkled over that. For more realism, lightly spray the foam-covered tree and sprinkle on a second, lighter color green to simulate sun-highlighted leaves.

Water for Indoor Layouts

Once again, you can re-create water indoors that looks more like scale-model water than real water. The problem with real water, even if considered in 1/24 scale, is that it is too thick. In 1/24 scale, water acts like honey. You can see it in the too-smooth waves and ripples and in the way the water creeps up the banks of rivers. Outdoors, real water looks like real water, but its scale doesn't match that of the trains.

Indoors, you can match the colors and ripples of real water in near-perfect 1/32 and 1/24 scale. No, it won't be moving, but that's only obvious at waterfalls and rapids, and even rapids can be recreated so realistically that you must look twice to be certain they really are not rushing along.

To model waterways, begin with the bottom of the river, stream, or lake. For really deep lakes or ocean docks, start with a flat surface as the "bottom." Use the two-part epoxy resins made for decoupage and sold by craft-supply stores. Buy the kind that uses equal amount of resin and hardener; it is more likely to dry

Fig. 7-13 *This is one of the larger Heki ready-made trees. There are dozens of other styles and shapes from Heki, Noch, Kibri, Hannes-Fischer and Life-Like.*

Fig. 7-14 So far, only the peaks of the mountains down to below the track level are complete on the 30-by-40-foot basement layout. The valleys will be finished last. The distant peaks are over 6 feet tall.

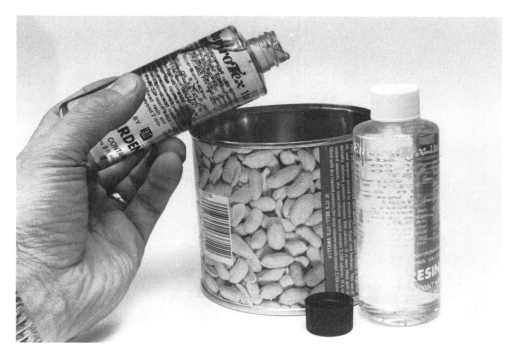

Fig. 7-15 *Simulate deeper waterways, like lakes and rivers, with decopage coatings from a craft-supply store. Use the type with equal parts resin and hardener. Pour the mixed resin into the stream or lake bottom.*

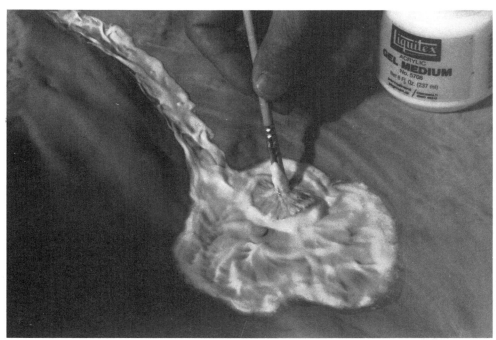

Fig. 7-16 *For shallow streams and for steep rapids, use artist's gel medium right out of the jar. The material dries clear and glossy.*

without a tacky surface than the kind for which only a few drops of hardener or catalyst are mixed in. For shallow lakes or streams, use the resin as a clear fluid. It will automatically give any real dirt or rocks the darker appearance they get when wet and they'll stay that way. For most lakes, mix equal parts black and green food color and add just a drop or two to each 4 ounces of the resin as you mix it. The color can be made darker as you add layer after layer of the resin. Just build up the depth you want by pouring in successive layers of resin. The first layers will appear darker, with the lighter earth more and more visible nearer and nearer the shore. Let each layer cure, however, before applying the next.

For swamps and 1- to 2-inch-wide streams, use artist's gel medium. Simply brush the milky fluid in the areas you want for streams or small lakes and let it dry. This stuff also works well when you want to create streams flowing down steep slopes. Just brush it over the plaster rocks and scenery. The resin will flow right down the steep slopes and collect in puddles at the bottom, but the gel stays put. The gel medium also can be applied over the top of resin streams or lakes to form rapids or waves. Apply light dabs of white acrylic paint to simulate rapids, bubbling water, and whitecapped waves.

Highways and Roads

To simulate concrete highways, use patching plaster but mix it to a consistency of oatmeal so you can spread it with a trowel and scrape the surface flat with the side of a steel ruler. Precolor the plaster with powdered cement colors so it doesn't show white if it chips. Simulate cracks and tar seams with a fine felt-tipped black pen.

For dirt roads, use real dirt sprinkled over artist's matte medium. When it dries, gently scrub the surface with a hard rubber eraser; the dirt will look like it has been run over by wagon wheels or cars.

Chapter 8

Outdoor Right-of-Way and Roadbed

MODEL RAILROADS built outdoors usually are called "garden railroads" for a very good reason: The railroad and the landscaping combine to create a new art form. The color photographs will give you a general idea of the beauty that is possible when the living landscape and the moving railroad are artfully combined. What I cannot show you, however, is the feeling that you experience when you step into one of these gardens. It really is a world of fantasy.

Fantasy or Reality?

There are two extremes in garden railroad design. The first is to create a garden that uses the railroad merely to provide animation. Often, those formal gardens are variations on the Japanese gardens, but with wooden railroad bridges and stations replacing the graceful arches and pagodas. The lovely combination of patio decks and landscaping on the layout built by John and Barbara Bierie is a fine example of the outdoor model railroad that emphasizes the garden rather than the trains. Bill and Joan Bradford's succulent plants represent a simpler form of the same theme.

The other extreme in garden railroading is to create a model railroad first and the garden second. The design and landscaping are there to enhance the believability of the railroad, and if it is as well done as Steve and Judy Arrigotti's layout, the result can be both breathtakingly realistic and a showpiece garden. Bill and Dee Baldock have used a fantasy landscape on a steep slope to create scenes that look precisely how I, at least, would expect an elf to build a railroad; yet closeup, the scenes are incredibly lifelike.

Some of us have a burning desire to create gardens like these, and honestly, these gardens are merely an extension of the basic use of bender board to divide the garden into specific areas of focus. In some cases, like the Arrigottis' layout, bender board really is used to define the track location—there are just two strips, 6 inches apart, rather than the usual single strip of bender board. You can plan the entire yard with scale drawings and surveyor's measurements of the slopes or you can just buy plenty of sectional track and use the track itself to define the areas while you position temporarily potted plants to judge the overall effect. That's how Norm Grant created his huge backyard layout and he, son Dale, and Dick Schaffer are using the same three-dimensional system to build Dick's new layout.

If the concept of making landscaping decisions seems beyond your desire, there are landscape designers in every city and town that can do the job for you, from planning to installation to care of the finished garden. There also are some specialists who build garden railroads, including Norm Grant through his firm By Grant and Paul Bussey through Garden Railways Company in Cincinnati. You can, then, choose to enjoy any single aspect of the garden railroading hobby: Design your own and let a landscape contractor build it, let a landscape firm design

Fig. 8-1 *A stone wall supports an elevated planting area around the backyard at Thomas Flynn's home. The railroad itself is virtually level.*

Fig. 8-2 *One corner of the Flynn's stone wall was removed so a tall wooden trestle could reach all the way to the lawn.*

it and you build it, or any combination of these. When the layout is complete, however, it is yours and your family's to enjoy.

A garden railroad can certainly enhance the value of any home. If and when you move, you can take the trackwork and buildings and perhaps even some special plants with you. Norm Grant moved and he was able to recover about five of the twenty tons (yes, *tons*) of rock he had imported from the Colorado Rockies and about fifty of the 300 or so plants, and all but one of the fourteen bridges. Much of Norm's layout is being brought back to life in Dick Schaffer's backyard. If you are selling a home with a garden railroad, make it clear to the real estate agent and to any potential buyers just how much of the garden you will leave behind. You may find that the garden is one of the prime selling points or features of your home and it may be worth thousands of dollars or the difference between a buyer purchasing your home or not. It is not unusual for a really fine garden to add $10,000 or more to the value of a higher-priced home. In that case, you may consider including the railroad, all the track, all the buildings, and, perhaps, even some of the locomotives and rolling stock with your home.

Establishing a Site for the Railroad

Your first decision in building a garden railroad is the extent of the railroad. Will it traverse the entire backyard like the Bierie, Baldock, Bradford, or Grant layouts? Or will you confine the layout with its own walls like the Arrigotti or Schaffer layouts? Chapter 3 will give you the information you need to decide on a minimum space for the type of layout you want to build. If you are in doubt, purchase at least a circle of the track you want to use, a pair of turnouts, and a dozen straight track sections. Use the track itself to define the shape and scope and mark the locations with small surveyor's stakes (large building supply

Fig. 8-3 *Dale Grant and his dad, Norm, moved many thousands of wheelbarrows full of dirt and boulders to build their backyard railroad.*

Fig. 8-4 *Kermit Paul moved some of the sloping dirt away from the house and used the area behind the dirt retaining wall as a waist-high bench for layout.*

Fig. 8-5 *Dale Grant is using LGB number 1600 curved track sections to plan the Thomas Flynn layout on the site.*

firms sell them). When you are satisfied, build the retaining walls, fill in the dirt, and re-create the track plan.

Track sections are also the easy way to plan a garden railroad that will extend around the backyard. It is far easier, for example, to let the track radius decide the precise shape of any borders in the garden than to try to shape the track to match the borders. You are far more likely to develop a flowing pattern and design in a garden, in fact, if you use track sections, particularly the 48- or 80-inch radius curves with a section or two of straight track between any S-bends where the curve shifts from a right hand to a left hand.

Surveying the Right-of-Way

These locomotives are powerful enough to pull a short train up a grade as steep as 8 percent, but for planning purposes, consider 2 percent to be the maximum grade. With that, you will have some margin for creativity if you decide to run the track a bit steeper uphill for a two-level area or for an over-and-under (half of a figure-8) design. Do not attempt to build a garden railroad, even on what appears to be a level backyard, without at least checking the slope of the land. If the land slopes more than about 4 percent, your layout is likely to have operating problems with trains that just can't climb some of the grades.

A simple surveying device is a 10-foot piece of a straight 1-by-4-inch board or a 2-inch aluminum angle. Support the uphill end with a short piece of 2-by-4-inch board or a brick and make a pointed 1-by-2-inch stake that can be driven in the ground for the

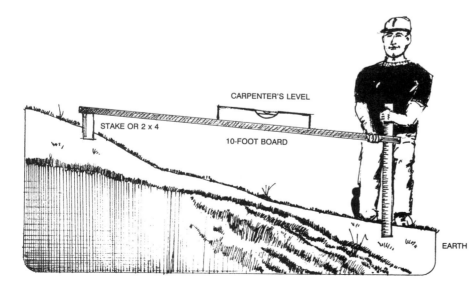

CARPENTER'S LEVEL

STAKE OR 2 x 4

10-FOOT BOARD

EARTH

Fig. 8-6 *Tape a carpenter's level to a 10-foot board with a stake at each end to support the board. Measure down from both ends of the leveled board to determine how many inches the ground slopes in 10-feet. Artwork by Dave Etchells.*

The Large-Scale Model Railroading Handbook

downhill end. A C-clamp can be used to attach the 1-by-4-inch board temporarily to the stake. Place a common carpenter's level anywhere on the 1-by-4-inch board and move the board up or down until the bubble in the level indicates the board is level. Measure the difference between the bottom of the 1-by-4-inch board and the ground at the downhill stake and subtract the thickness of the 2-by-4-inch board on the uphill end. Divide 100 into that number of inches and you'll know the percentage of slope in that portion of your yard. If, for example, the downhill end of the 1-by-4-inch board was 8 inches from the ground, you'd subtract 2 inches for the thickness of the 2-by-4-inch board and divide 6 by 100 to determine that this slope was 6 percent.

The 100-inch board has the limitations of its length. You can make a more versatile level-checking device with 50 feet or so of clear vinyl tubing. Use two stakes, one for the uphill side and the other for the downhill side. Tie the vinyl tube to the upper stake with about the last 12 inches of the tube in a vertical position. Tie the other end of the tube to the stake on the lower or downhill side of the slope you are checking. Fill the tube with water until the water level reaches within an inch or so of both ends of the tubing. You may need to move one or both ends of the tube up or down so it does not overflow. Measure the distance from the ground to the water level on the upper stake then on the lower stake. Subtract the upper dimension from that of the lower. Next, measure the distance, in inches, from one stake to the other. Divide that distance by the difference in the height of the stakes to determine the percentage of the slope. For example, if the difference in the height of the water level at the two stakes were 20 inches and the stakes were 120 inches apart, the slope would be 6 percent.

With either method, drive a surveyor's stake at both the upper and lower locations and mark on the stake the distance from the first stake, the height of each stake, and the grade. Number each stake so you have a reference. Try to start at the uppermost corner of the area the layout will occupy so that stake can be "level zero" and "stake 1"; all other stakes can then refer to stake 1 in distance and in degree of slope. If your backyard is reasonably flat, you may need a stake only in each of the four extreme corners of the layout to be able to visualize just how steep the lot slopes and in what directions.

It will be necessary to build up the downhill sides of the yard so the tracks never rise or fall more than 2 percent in the initial design. You may choose to elevate the entire layout as did Marc and Barbara Horovitz, with raised planters in the corners and long bridges in others. If only a portion of the yard has a slope, you may decide simply to use a series of bridges to carry the railroad across that area. Or, you may want to build stone or wood retaining walls and level the entire layout portion of the backyard like Steve and Judy Arrigotti did.

If you enjoy planting those stakes, you may want to survey the route of the layout. That's the system Marc

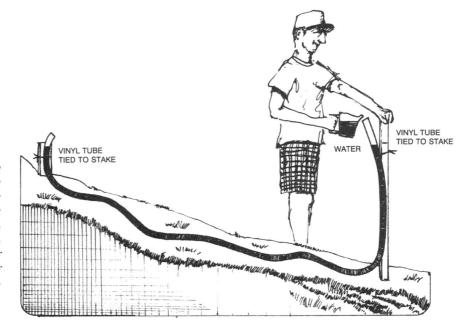

Fig. 8-7 *For larger backyard layouts, make a water level from clear vinyl tubing and fill it with water—the water will seek its own level at the extreme ends of the tubing—measure the difference in the heights of the high end and the low end of the tube to determine how many inches the ground slopes.* Artwork by Dave Etchells.

VINYL TUBE TIED TO STAKE

VINYL TUBE TIED TO STAKE

WATER

Outdoor Right-of-Way and Roadbed

Fig. 8-8 *Chris Greenwald, a friend of Marc and Barbara Horovitz, used a surveyor's trammel to locate the stakes for the track locations.*

Fig. 8-9 *This the same scene from Fig. 8-8 just two years later. This same photo appears in the color section and in Chapter 9 (Fig. 9-1) with a list of the plants in the scene.*

and Barbara Horovitz used for their backyard garden railway, with Chris Greenwald's help. The track itself was located with stakes every 2 feet. The curves were plotted with a long piece of string nailed to the top of a post in the center of the yard, to swing, for example, a measured 10-foot sweeping curve. Stakes were driven every 2 feet around roughly one-fourth of the circle in each corner of the layout. Marc tied string to each stake and, using the previously described board and level technique, moved the string up or down until it was level. He was then able to measure down from each stake to create a level main line, or where needed, to include up or down grades.

Norm Grant is using a much simpler method to build both Dick Schaffer's and Tom Flynn's layouts; he simply holds a carpenter's level over each track

section and piles dirt or bricks under the track to make it level. If an uphill grade is needed, the level can be marked at 1-foot increments with the distance it should be, at one end, above the track to achieve that grade. For a 2 percent grade, the first foot of the level should be 2 percent of 12 or approximately $\frac{1}{4}$ inch above the track. A second block, $\frac{1}{2}$ inch thick, can be taped at the 24-inch mark on the level and a third block, $\frac{3}{4}$ inch thick, can be taped to the end of a 36-inch level. With the three blocks, at least a portion of the level can rest firmly on virtually any track section. If the grade needs to be less, say 1 percent, then the blocks would be thinner ($\frac{1}{8}$, $\frac{1}{4}$, and $\frac{3}{8}$ inch at the three locations, respectively). If the grade needs to be steeper, say 4 percent, the blocks would need to be thicker ($\frac{1}{2}$, 1, and $1\frac{1}{2}$ inches, respectively).

Fig. 8-10 *Another "before" photograph of the canyon on Norm Grant's layout that appears (with the curved trestle and new wooden Howe truss bridges) in the color section.*

Railroad Roadbed

Once you have determined the precise path of the track, some provision must be made to support the track. It is possible just to lay the track on the dirt or lawn, particularly if it is attached firmly to plywood blocks at each track joint as shown in Chapter 4. There is no law stating that you must have a garden to complement a backyard railroad; you can just lay the tracks to suit your imagination and run trains. With this system, however, it will be difficult to keep weeds and grass from growing right between the ties to rest on the rails. The track is rugged but it cannot withstand the constant attack of a Weed Eater-type of lawn trimmer, and you'll soon lose patience with literally grooming the weeds from the track. If the track is not too extensive, you can certainly lift it away in long sections to mow or trim and then replace the track.

The most enjoyable way to enjoy outdoor model railroading is to make a commitment to make the railroad part of the landscape. When you do that, you can justify digging a 4- to 6-inch-deep ditch for the track and lining the ditch with weed-blocking plastic. There are about as many methods of supporting the track above that weed-free ditch as there are garden railroads. Whatever method you choose, remember that the railroad is going to be subject to the same adverse weather conditions as any other part of the earth in your yard. That can mean water and melted

snow freezing down in the ballast to push and shove the track or torrential rains washing the track to float it away.

Most of the layouts in this book use a 4- to 6-inch layer of either crusher fines, chicken feed starter grit, or squeegee. These materials are composed mostly of rice-sized gravel and dust. The dust becomes almost as firm as sandstone after it has been soaked with water. The gravel, however, allows the material to move without cracking during frost heaves or flooding. The plastic trough is simply filled with the crusher fines, starter grit, or squeegee and the track is laid on top, followed by more crusher fines, starter grit, or squeegee.

When the trough is filled—whether with crusher fines, starter grit, squeege, concrete, bricks, or boards—it is extremely important that the surface be level in all directions. The uphill grade must be a consistent slope with no sudden lurches or dips or mounds. Use a 4- or 5-foot board to smooth the length of the roadbed. The roadbed also must be perfectly level and flat across its width (parallel to the ties). Buy a foot-long level and use it constantly to be sure the subroadbed really is level. When you have smoothed the surface to perfection, flood it with water and let it settle then check it again and add more material if necessary (or move the brick or boards up or down. It's wise, in fact, to let the roadbed

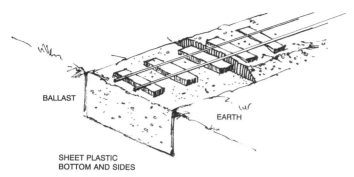

Fig. 8-11 *The simplest form of right-of-way: Dig a 2-inch-deep ditch the width of the track, line it with plastic, fill it with crusher fines, and lay the track on top.* Artwork by Dave Etchells.

Fig. 8-12 *Use a level to smooth the ballast from side to side and then position the track. Use a paper cup to spread the ballast between the rails.*

"weather" for a few months before installing the track. It's a lot easier to add or subtract crusher fines, starter grit, or squeegee, or move bricks or boards or add more concrete, than to move track up or down.

When you are satisfied that the roadbed is perfectly level with steady uphill or downhill grades, then it's time to apply the track. The track sections should be connected by something more than just the rail joiners; use bolts, set screws, special clamping rail joiners, or boards as described in Chapter 4. Set the track in place and bury it in ballast, beginning with the area between the ties. Use your hands or a toothbrush to spread the ballast, then apply a row of ballast to the outer edges of the ties. Crusher fines, starter grit, or squeegee makes fine ballast for any type of roadbed. If the track is permanently attached to the roadbed, as it is on the Arrigotti and Baldock layouts, virtually any kind of small-grain gravel or sand can be used for ballast. Please read the sections in Chapter 7 that describe the need to improve the realism of model railroad track and the methods of painting the track and using scale-sized rail. If you really want realistic outdoor track, as opposed to a caricature of real railroading, you will want to at least consider those ideas for your outdoor railroad.

Concrete Roadbed

There are two schools of thought about building roadbed for an outdoor railroad. The first suggests that it is best to allow the track to float in a thick layer of relatively loose sand. That's the system just described that uses crusher fines, starter grit, or squeegee as the ballast. The second school of thought suggests that the roadbed should be as rigid as possible to be impervious to rain, frost heaves, and ice-caused expansion. This second method involves using concrete for the roadbed or a very rigid system of posts and wood.

The layout built by Steve and Judy Arrigotti has a concrete subroadbed for rigidity, but the track itself is mounted in gravel. Their system is about as simple as concrete could be. First, they laid parallel $\frac{1}{4}$-by-6-inch strips of redwood bender board (intended for garden edging) on-edge. The two bender boards are spaced about 6 inches apart for single track and twice that for passing sidings or double track. Then they used 2-by-6-inch pieces of redwood, with the 6 inches laid vertically, as spacers between the bender boards. Steel rebars (steel reinforcing bars for concrete) are used as stakes on the outside of the bender board where needed to keep it in alignment. The area between the bender boards is then filled with a dry cement mix of five parts rock, five parts sand, and

Fig. 8-13 *Dale Grant is using his fingers to push the ballast off the tops of the ties; a stiff paintbrush will save wear and tear on your skin.*

Fig. 8-14 *The third step in ballasting is to apply the ballast along the edges of the ties. Chapter 7 describes ballast shoulder shapes.*

three parts cement, and the dry material is carefully leveled and smoothed as described earlier in this chapter. The mix is then wetted with a gentle mist of water until thoroughly saturated. It may not be quite as strong as concrete, but it is much easier to get a smooth and level surface with the dry materials than with wet concrete and easier, too, to correct any errors in level.

The Arrigottis marked the top edges of the bender boards to locate the 2-by-6-inch spacers after the track was installed and the spacers buried. The final 2 inches of the trough was filled with $\frac{1}{4}$-inch particles of crushed rock up to the level of the tops of the bender boards. The track was then laid in place using LGB rails and ties with a bending tool like the Lindsay Railbender described in Chapter 4. The track was

Fig. 8-15 *Norm Grant buried a 12-by-12-by-½-inch piece of pressure-treated and painted plywood beneath each turnout to give it a solid base.*

Fig. 8-16 *The Arrigottis used ½-by-6-inch bender boards for the edges of their roadbed, spaced them with 2-by-6-inch pieces of redwood, and then filled the cavity with dry-mixed concrete.* Artwork by Dave Etchells.

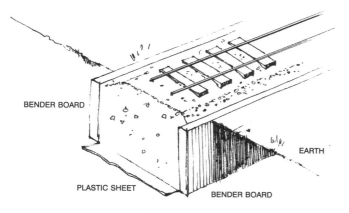

leveled along its length and from side to side, and ballast was applied to bury the ties partially. The track was then nailed to each of the 2-by-6-inch redwood spacers.

An alternate method of using concrete for roadbed would be to use the same bender board technique described for the Arrigotti layout; however, the trough would be filled to the top with wet concrete. Reinforcing bars or ¼-inch steel cables would be put in the lower portion of the trough to reinforce it. Pressure-treated pieces of 2-by-2-inch lumber would be placed horizontally in the still-wet concrete to provide places to nail the track. A loose layer of ballast would then be laid with the track on top of the cured concrete.

Indoor-Style Roadbed Outdoors

Another alternative method of building the subroadbed for an outdoor layout is to use plywood or a similar material placed below the track. Bill and Joan Bradford use sheets of ½-inch-thick insulation board for their subroadbed, supported on sand. Bill uses Rara Avis's code 250 rail and spikes and ⅜-by-9/32-by-3⅞-inch redwood ties. Rara Avis's turnout kits are also spiked to double-length ties. The ties are glued to the hard foam roadbed with construction cement in a caulking gun. The rails are spiked in place after the roadbed is installed and leveled. The final step is to cover the ties with crushed rock ballast. Fig. 8-21 shows an alternative method of support, common bricks placed on end for embankments and on their sides for lower levels. No trough would be necessary with either system.

Roadbed construction also can be of pressure-treated posts for the vertical roadbed supports. Marine-grade plywood or redwood 1-by-6-inch boards cut to the outline of the track are placed on top of the posts and attached with wood screws (number 8 or larger by 3-inch size). The complete woodwork is then buried in dirt and the track and ballast are applied on top of the wood. The track can be attached to the plywood or redwood roadbed with screws or allowed to float in a layer of ballast, depending on how severe the weather conditions are in your area.

Kermit Paul used this system on his outdoor railroad but only to span an area from a builtup earthen and wooden bench to an embankment at the rear of the backyard. For him, the vertical posts and redwood roadbed function as a wooden trestle. Kermit added ¼-by-2-inch plastic kick panel strips to the edges of the bridge to retain the ballast.

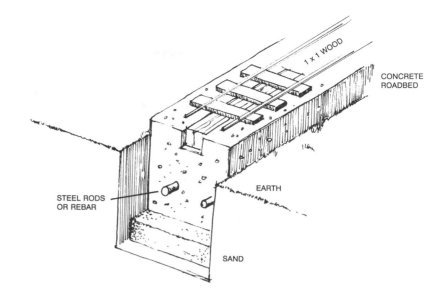

Fig. 8-17 For a solid concrete roadbed, fill a 6-inch-deep trench with an inch of sand and then lay two steel reinforcing bars or thick cable in the ditch and pour in wet concrete. Embed 1-by-1-inch redwood to serve as nail holds for the track. Artwork by Dave Etchells.

Fig. 8-18 Bill Bradford uses ½-inch thick foam insulating board and ties from Rara Avis as the basis for his trackwork and raodbed.

Fig. 8-19 The ties are cemented to the foam board with silicone construction cement.

Fig. 8-20 *The rails are spiked to the ties and roadbed on a workbench and the assembly is then laid on the leveled ground and buried in ballast.*

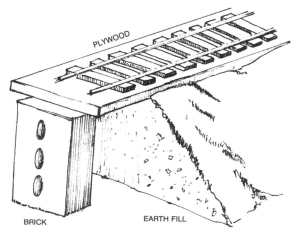

PLYWOOD

BRICK

EARTH FILL

Fig. 8-21 *This simple roadbed avoids the need to dig a ditch. Place bricks on end or on their side to support foam insulation board or treated ½-inch plywood roadbed. Ballast just the top or bury the bricks in dirt. Artwork by Dave Etchells.*

Roadbed from Plastic Pipe

Bill Baldock has developed an unusual but effective roadbed for his DSP&PRR. He uses common PVC plastic electrical conduit with the centerline of the track marked with a single run of the PVC conduit for the entire length of the layout. The pipe bends into smooth curves and the dirt holds it in place. When he is satisfied with the location and alignment of the single piece of conduit, two more pieces of PVC conduit are added, one on each side of the original. Silicone cement intended for outdoor use is applied with a caulking gun to bond the three conduits and the joining sections. In areas where bridges will be built, Bill uses one of the T-shaped support pieces sold to reinforce joints made with the conduit and a vertical section of conduit.

Bill spikes Old Pullman code 197 nickel silver rail

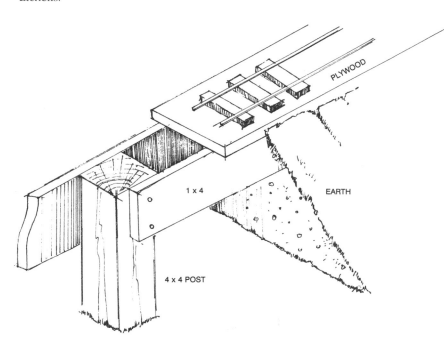

PLYWOOD

1 x 4

EARTH

4 x 4 POST

Fig. 8-22 *If you like to work with wood, the roadbed can be constructed with round or square vertical posts and wooden side spacers with an insulation board or plywood roadbed. All the wood must be pressure treated and preserved. Artwork by Dave Etchells.*

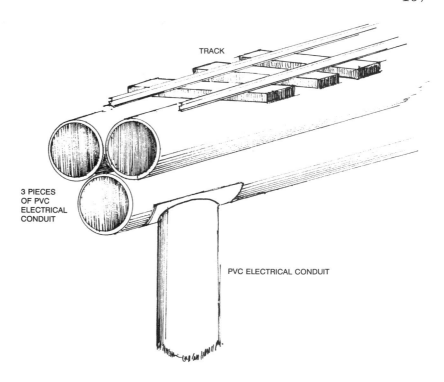

TRACK

3 PIECES
OF PVC
ELECTRICAL
CONDUIT

PVC ELECTRICAL CONDUIT

Fig. 8-23 *Bill Baldock uses three pieces of plastic PVC wiring conduit as a roadbed, cementing the conduit and the ties with silicone construction cement.* Artwork by Dave Etchells.

Fig. 8-24 *The vertical supports for Bill Baldock's roadbed are only temporary at places that will later be spanned by bridges.*

to ties he cuts from redwood on a table saw. He uses the Old Pullman turnout kits, again, spiked to longer redwood ties and uses $\frac{1}{4}$-by-$\frac{5}{16}$-by-$3\frac{7}{8}$-inch ties for single track and longer ties, cut to fit, for the turnouts. The track is built on the workbench, after bending the rail in a Railbender for the curved tracks and curved routes out of turnouts. The nearly finished track is then carried outdoors and cemented to the tops of the top two PVC plastic conduits with outdoor-grade silicone cement. Bill simply runs a continuous bead of the cement down the tops of both conduits and presses the ties in place. The conduit either will be buried in ballast or hidden by the sides of a bridge.

Chapter 9

Gardens for Gauge 1 Railroads

IN THIS chapter, I am directing your attention to the charm that an outdoor model railroad can lend to any decorative garden. You will need to make the decision about whether you simply want to add a railroad to your garden or if the railroad should be designed with a garden to complement its miniature scenes, although it is certainly possible to have the best of both worlds. At a glance, the model railroad portion of John and Barbara Bierie's backyard garden is barely visible. Viewed up close, there are dozens of realistic miniature scenes.

Garden railroading is a wonderful hobby for a couple when one is enthused about model railroads, the other about gardens, and both are willing to combine their efforts where the garden and railroad overlap. In some cases a model railroad enthusiast may even hire a landscape designer or architect to design the garden and a maintenance firm to maintain the plants so he or she can concentrate on the train portion of the hobby. Conversely, if you are more interested in gardening than actually building the railroad, there are firms that will get the trains running and come back to maintain them.

Designing the Landscape

There are thousands of books and videos available that describe exactly how to design, plant, and maintain any type of garden in any area of the country. I know of none of them, however, that describe how to incorporate a model railroad into the design. Truly, it

is an art form, and the best instruction you can find will be examples of other garden railroads. You'll see a dozen or so layouts in this book but there may be a dozen more within 50 miles of your home. I would suggest that you join one or two of the garden, gauge 1, or LGB societies listed in *Garden Railways magazine* to find out how many members are near your home. I've found that most garden railroaders are willing to share their work with neighbors, so you may discover that you can see some of the layouts in your area on a local tour or in response to a friendly telephone call. Nobody really needs your presence to approve of his or her layout, so expect some negative responses. With a bit of searching and by attending a few meetings of local and national conventions, you'll be able to see dozens of garden railroads.

If you are baffled or confused about where to start, simply run track along an existing or proposed flower bed border. If that won't fit your dream, build a simple 9-by-12-foot box edged with railroad ties or stones and fill that area with a garden railroad; that's just how the Arrigotti's incredible layout was started. Feel free to experiment. These trains will run on the grass for a day or two. Go ahead and put a layout right on the lawn and get the feeling for how these large-scale trains enhance the landscape. Notice how the track flows, especially if you can find the space to work-in a few S-curves with that 48-inch radius track. See how the scene changes when the dynamics are altered from a static but living scene to a living scene

Fig. 9-1 *See Fig. 9-2 for the list of plants on the Horovitz layout. This photograph also appears in the color section.*

with the action of a nearly real train traveling by those plants.

You can develop a garden landscape design with the aid of any of dozens of landscape books or videos supplemented, perhaps, with a consultation, at least, with a recommended landscape architect or designer. Remember, there are several elements of landscape design that you may want to consider—including shaping the terrain, rock textures, groundcover, bushes, dwarf-sized trees, larger bushes, larger trees, water, foot paths, and a model railroad.

Shaping the Terrain

Few modelers are willing to move tons of earth and rock to create hills, valleys, and mountains. Norm Grant did it and he helped Dick Schaffer create his mountains. Steve and Judy Arrigotti moved tons of topsoil, compost, and sand to the 18-by-90-foot area behind the logs they designed as their garden railroad. They did it in three nearly equal stages, completing one-third of the layout the first year, the second third the third year, and bringing the layout to the state seen in the photographs during the third and fourth years.

This is the kind of work that you will want to consider for a rented skip loader or backhoe complete with professional operator. When the heavy equipment is at work it can move some of those boulders you've collected. The final shaping can certainly be done by hand with a shovel and rake.

Real rocks are available at quarries and building supply firms. Some of the larger firms will even deliver a load into your backyard—that's what Norm Grant did, he ordered a dump-truck load of rock.

Fig. 9-2 Miniature Groundcover

These ground cover plants were used on Marc and Barbara Horovitz's garden railway. Judy Arrigotti used two kinds of miniature stonecrop ground covers (G and K) on her layout in northern California. They are numbers 22 and 23 on the chart in Figure 9-9.

Identification letter in photo	Botanical name	Common name
A	Penstemon pinifolius	Pineleaf penstemon
B	Sedum kamtschaticum	Kamtchatka sedum
C	Euphorbia epithymoides	Cushion spurge
D	Thymus pseudolanguinosus	Woolly thyme
E	Iberis sempervirens	Dwarf candytuft
F	Anacyclus depressus	Atlas daisy
G	Sedum dasphyllum	Miniature stonecrop
H	Veronica pectinata	Woolly veronica
I	Phlox subulata	Creeping phlox
J	Aquilegia species	Columbine
K	Sedum brevifolium	Miniature stonecrop

Then he ordered another and another and another and another. . . . Norm ordered mostly Colorado granite and he hand-picked the boulders and rocks he wanted; some were clean on all sides because they had been broken from larger boulders. The rocks he prized the most, however, were still covered on three-fourths of their area with the green moss that appears on "weathered" rock. He used the clean rocks for simulated cuts through the rock where his 1/22.5 scale navies would have dynamited the path through the rocks. He used the moss-covered rocks for mountaintops and cliffs.

There are some lightweight plastic boulders available for use in gardens and they can certainly be incorporated into a garden model railroad. For realism, however, you may want at least half of the rock buried so it looks like a rock outcrop rather than a gigantic boulder. You may be able to actually cut some of these rocks with an electric saber saw so you can use pieces for the peaks of mountains and other pieces for cliffs. Ask the garden-supply firm that sells the rock if it's possible to cut it.

Use the tricks that model railroaders use: shape the mountains with raw dirt (they use plaster or foam beadboard) so the rocks form only the surface texture. With this trick, you can make a few hundred pounds of rocks or boulders look like a hundred tons.

Concrete Mountains

The garden railroading version of the model railroader's plaster-soaked paper towel mountains is concrete-covered chicken wire. The technical term for the construction is ferroconcrete. The construction technique is also similar to that used with plaster-soaked paper towels on indoor railroads. First, a mountain and valley shape is formed using common chicken wire mesh. The chicken wire will need temporary supports of scrap lumber to hold the mountain peaks and mounds until the concrete cures. Use two layers of the chicken wire to ensure adequate strength. The chicken wire will give a very clear outline of the shapes of the mountains and valleys to give you an easy material to work with to achieve just the shapes you desire.

Tunnels, too, can be formed with this chicken wire and concrete technique. Use some 2-pound coffee cans, nailed to 2-by-4-inch boards, to build a form for a tunnel that is 8 inches high. Simply cover that form with the chicken wire and stop the interior at the end of the coffee can. You'll want to leave the inside of the tunnel accessible within an arm's reach. That short distance of interior will give the illusion that the tunnel is solid clear through the mountain and that the mountain is not hollow.

With the mountains and valleys and tunnels shaped in chicken wire, trowel-on premixed concrete. Lumberyards sell the stuff in bags. The larger lumberyards also sell dry powdered colors for concrete. Mix a paper-cup-full of concrete and a tablespoon of the dry color to see if the color is to your liking. I'd suggest an equal mix of brown and black, but you may want more brown and, perhaps, some reddish brown or burnt sienna color. Try three or four batches of cupfuls of concrete with more colors and different mixes of colors until you have the colors you like. Multiply the number of teaspoons by the number of cups of concrete needed or each batch you mix to match your samples to the actual construction batches of concrete. The premixed concrete is mixed with water. Apply a layer about $\frac{1}{2}$ inch thick. For maximum strength, the curing concrete must be sprinkled with water twice a day for about a week. When the concrete cures completely (in about two weeks), all the braces can be removed and the mountain should be self-supporting. You may, however, want to leave one or two vertical braces at the peaks of the mountains (they are hidden beneath the hollow mountain) so the mountain will not be cantilevered from its base as its sole support. Cover the coffee can and 2-by-5-inch tunnel interiors, too, with the concrete and push down hard with the trowel so the wet concrete squeezes through the chicken wire. When the two weeks are up, the coffee cans can be removed and, if the chicken wire is visible, more concrete can be troweled inside the tunnel. Cover the can and wood with plastic before beginning the entire procedure so you can remove it after the concrete hardens.

Bridge abutments and tunnel portals can be added after the initial scenery is complete by embedding them in small pockets of silicone construction cement and then filling in any gaps with dirt. Lake bottoms and streambeds can, of course, be built up with the chicken wire and concrete mix. I would suggest you plan any mountains or streambeds made of concrete carefully. The stuff is extremely difficult to remove once it sets. For most applications, piles of real dirt are far more practical and they may be more appealing to any potential buyers of your home should need to sell it in the future. If you limit the mountains to something you can hoist onto a pickup truck bed, you'll have a chance, at least, of hauling them away if you choose to remove or modify the railroad.

Tunnels

If the mountains are dirt, tunnels can be made by standing 2-by-6-inch redwood or pressure-treated fir on-edge for the sides topped by 2-by-4-inch boards on-edge to obtain that 8-inch interior height. The roof can be another 2-by-6-inch board. Limit tunnel lengths to about 3 feet so you can reach in from either end to rerail trains. Cover the tunnel liner with dirt and rock mountains.

Groundcover

The last choice for groundcover near a garden railroad is grass. Even the finest blades are grossly oversized for anything that might grow near a real railroad. The operative term is ground *cover;* try to find plants that—like clover, woolly thyme, or moss—cling to the ground. Generally, these plants also will have smaller leaves that are closer to the scale of the railroad. Your local landscaping or garden supply shop is the place to go to discover what will grow in your particular area. In some cases, you may need several types of groundcover that will thrive in direct sun or in shade to suit various parts of the landscape.

Judy Arrigotti took the advice of the local gardening experts in preparing her list of nearly eighty groundcover plants, shrubs, and dwarf or small trees. That list is included in this chapter with some supplemental plants from the experiments of Joan Bradford and Barbara Bierie. All three have some success with these plants, but all three do their gardening in northern California. Your local landscape experts should find this list useful because they should be able to

Fig. 9-3 *Thomas Flynn's layout. This photo also appears in the color section. The plants on Thomas Flynn's layout include (L) a Raoulia australis* New Zealand scab plant, (M) *dusty miller, (N) Alberta spruce, (O) dragon's blood sedum, (P) baby tears, and (Q) tricolor sedum.*

Fig. 9-4 *This scene on the Arrigotti layout also appears in the color section. Judy Arrigotti has identified all the plants visible in the photographs and others that were successes or failures. The numbers are from that chart (Fig. 9-9).*

recognize similar plants that thrive in your area. If they don't recognize just the names, you can show them pictures—we've identified about two dozen different plants that appear in the color section of the book with duplicate scenes in this chapter showing precisely what plants were used.

Certainly not all the ground needs to be covered with living plants. Bare dirt paths can be shaped to duplicate dirt roads. Some areas can be covered with bark until the groundcover has time to spread. Be cautious about spreading plastic sheet beneath the open areas because it will make it difficult for groundcover to spread to those areas. If you'd prefer to use low-maintenance bark rather than ground-cover, the entire layout area can be covered with plastic, then a few inches of earth and then bark are put on top. You can always pierce the plastic in a few places where you might want to plant a dwarf tree or a shrub.

Bushes and Dwarf-Sized Trees

Larger nurseries in your area should be able to supply a variety of dwarf bushes and trees that they know will grow in your climate and soil conditions. Still, you will have to experiment, and you will undoubtedly find that some survive and thrive while others will not respond to any kind of care. The most successful garden railroad builders have learned that a miniature spray system or drip irrigation system is necessary and that a nozzle or emitter is needed for each and every bush and tree if they are to survive. If you are already disciplined to turn the water on and off for your garden, you may not need an automatic

Fig. 9-5 *This scene of the Arrigotti layout also appears in the color section. The numbers identifying the plants appear on the chart (Fig. 9-9).*

Fig. 9-6 *Another scene from the Arrigotti layout that appears in the color section. The numbers identify the dwarf trees. The trees in the background are large oaks.*

timer but that, too, is considered essential for the survival of most dwarf bushes and trees. Follow your nursery's suggestions about the type and depth of soil these plants require, too. You may need to prepare large pits and then fill them with improved soil mixtures to keep the dwarf bushes and plants alive.

Again, the bushes and trees on the chart (Fig. 9-9) are the trial-and-error results of Judy Arrigotti, with some additional information from Joan Bradford and Barbara Bierie, for a specific part of the country. Your local nursery experts should be able to provide equivalent plants, with different names, that will thrive in your particular growing conditions. You will undoubtedly find that there are dozens of different bushes and trees that do not appear on the chart that will thrive in your garden. Feel free to experiment for yourself—that's part of the joy of the garden side of garden railroading. When you're looking, seek out bushes and shrubs with small leaves or very short needles. The bushes should reach peak growth at about 6 to 8 inches and trees should reach their peak growth at about 2 feet. With trees, you have the option of leaving them in containers, set in matching-sized cavities in the ground, until they exceed 3 feet. Then you can replant them elsewhere in the yard and replace them with smaller and younger trees every three or four years. The edges of the containers can be hidden with rolled-up plastic bags or covered with bark or chips.

Running Water Streams and Lakes

Small streams, reflecting ponds, and waterfalls are classic elements of gardens, and especially gardens similar to those favored for garden railroads. Bill and Joan Bradford built a semiarid scene with succulent plants, and Norm Grant created dry gulleys that only flowed during the rain or when flooded with a gar-

Fig. 9-7 *There are over a dozen dwarf trees in this scene alone. This scene also appears in the color section as part of the Arrigotti's layout. Again, the numbers are identified on Judy Arrigotti's chart (Fig. 9-9).*

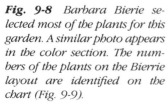

Fig. 9-8 *Barbara Bierie selected most of the plants for this garden. A similar photo appears in the color section. The numbers of the plants on the Bierie layout are identified on the chart (Fig. 9-9).*

Fig. 9-9 Typical Miniature Groundcover, Shrubs, and Trees

Judy Arrigotti's inventory of plants she and her husband, Steve, used in their garden railroad in northern California. Plant survival statistics are included. Numbers 77 through 82 are additional plants that were successful for Joan Bradford and Barbara Bierie.

I.D. # in Photo	Horticultural Name	Healthy (H) Struggling (S) Failed (F)	Common Name	Light Required	Appearance	Flowers
Groundcover						
1	Achillea tomentosa	S	Woolly yarrow	Sun/part shade	Flat spreading mat	Golden
2	Arctostaphylos uva-ursi	H	manzanita	Sun	Spreading	White/pink
3	Armeria maritima	S	Common thrift	Sun	Compact tufts	White/rose
4	Aubrieta deltoidea	S	Rock cress	Sun/light shade	Low spreading	Rose/lilac
5	Baccharis pilularis	S	Coyote brush	Sun	Dense, billowy mat	
6	Cymbalaria aequitriloba	F	Mosos basket ivy	Shade	Dainty creeper	Lilac/blue
7	Dianthus	H	Tiny rubies	Sun/light shade	Grasslike mat	Red
8	Euonymus fortunei 'Azusa'	S	Euonymus	Sun/light shade	Trails or climbs	
9	Ficus pumila	F	Dwarf creeping fig		Vine (attaches itself to wood)	
10	Galium odoratum	F	Sweet woodruf	Shade	Low spreading	White
11	Glechoma hederacea	H	Ground ivy		Trailing (leaves are a little large)	
12	Herniaria glabra	H	Green carpet	Sun	Trailing	
13	Juniperus chinensis procumbens	H	Green Mound Juniper		Shrubby, slightly mounded	
14	Laurentia fluviatillis isotoma	H	Blue Star Creeper	Part shade/full sun		Pale blue
15	Lithodora diffusa	H	Spreading lithodora	Full sun/light shade	Stems creep root along ground (faded away & came back)	Brilliant blue
16	Mazus reptans	H	Creeping mazus	Sun/light shade		White/purple
17	Mentha requienii	F	Corsican mint	Sun/part shade	Creeping mat forming	Purple
18	Parthenocissus tricuspidata veitchi	S	Boston ivy	Sun/shade	Vine, clings to walls	
19	Potentilla tabernaemontanii	H	Cinquefoil	Shade where hot	Creeper 2–6" high	Yellow
20	Sagina subulata	H	Scotch moss	Full sun/Semi shade	Mosslike masses	Tiny white
21	Saxifraga burseriana	F	Saxifrage	Full sun/light shade	Masses of tiny rosettes (We over watered)	Yellow
22	Sedum album	S	Miniature stonecrop	Full sun/shade	Creeping	White pinkish
23	Sedum dasyphyllum	S	Miniature stonecrop	Full sun/shade		White
24	Sedum spurium	S	Dragon's blood		Trailing stems	Red
25	Thymus citriodorus	H	Lemon thyme	Full sun/light shade	Erect or spreading 4–12"	Purple
26	Thymus herba-barona	H	Caraway thyme		Flat mat	Rose pink
27	Thymus praecox Arcticus	H	Mother of thyme		Flat mat	Rose pink
28	Thymus pseudolanuginosus	H	Woolly thyme		Flat mat	Purple/white
29	Thymus vulgaris	H	Common thyme		Flat mat 2–3"	Pinkish
30	Verbena rigida	H	Verbena	Sun	Spreading 10–20" tall	Pink, purple, lilac
31	Vinca minor	H	Dwarf periwinkle	Shade	Trailing	Lavender blue
32	Viola hederacca	F	Australian violet	Part shade	Spreads by stolons	White blue
Shrubs						
33	Agapanthus	H	Lily of the Nile (Peter Pan)	Full Sun	Foliage clumps 8–12" tall	Blue
34	Berberis	H	Crimson pygmy barberry	Sun/light shade	Compact foliage	
35	Buxus microphylla japonica	H	Boxwood	Full sun/shade		
36	Convolvulus sabatius	F	Ground morning glory	Full sun	Killed by freeze. Trailing to 3' wide	Lavender blue
37	Coprosma pumila verda-vista	S	Creeping coprosma			
38	Erica canaliculata	H	Scotch heath	Full sun/light shade		
39	Escallonia	F	Newport dwarf	Full sun/partial shade	10" tall spreading mound	Pink
40	Gardenia jasminoides	S	Gardenia	Full sun/filtered shade		White

No.	Botanical Name	Type	Common Name	Notes / Size	Light	Color
41	*Iberis sempervirens*	H	Candytuft	4–6" tall	Sun/partial shade	White
42	*Lavendula angustifolia munstead*	H	Lavender	Shrublets	Sun	Purple
43	*Liriope*	H	Blue lily turf	Grasslike clumps		Lavender
44	*Lobularia maritima*	F	Sweet alyssum			
45	*Lonicera nitida*	H	Box honeysuckle	Berries	Sun/light shade	White
46	*Myrtus communis compacta*	H	Dwarf myrtle	Shrub with berries	Part shade/hot sun	
47	*Nandina domestica*	H	Heavenly bamboo	Canelike stems/fine texture foliage	Sun/shade	
48	*Oxalis oregano*	H	Redwood sorrel	Bulb cloverlike leaves 2–10" tall		Pink
49	*Rhododendron impeditum*	F	Dwarf rhododendron	Dense shrub 1' tall (root rot)		Dark blue
50	*Rosa*	H	Willie Winkie	(Flowers out of scale)	Sun	
51	*Rosmarinus officinalis*	H	Rosemary	Cascadina	Sun	Lavender
52	*Zephyranthes candida*	H	Fairy Lily	Bulb	Sun	White

Trees

No.	Botanical Name	Type	Common Name	Notes / Size	Light	Color
53	*Acer palmatum*	H	Japanese maple	20' tall (Bonsai)	Filtered shade/full sun	
54	*Athizia julibrissin*	F	Silk trees (deer ate them so I took them out)	Flat topped tree (Bonsai)	Sun	Pink
55	*Chamaecyparis andelyensis*	S	Ellwood cypress	Slow growing 6–8' tall		
56	*Chamaecyparis 'Ellwoodi'*	S	Dwarf sawara cypress	20–30' tall (Bonsai)	Silvery blue	
57	*Chamaecyparis pisifera tsukumo*	H	Pygmy cypress	18" tall		
58	*Chamaecyparis pisifera 'Squarrosa' minima*	S		90' (Bonsai)		
59	*Chamaecyparis thyoides*	H	White cypress	3'		
60	*Cotoneaster horizontalis*	H	Rock cotoneaster	Low growing (Bonsai)/wide spreading berries	Sun	White pink
61	*Cryptomeria japonica tanzu*	H	Japanese red cedar	Bronze in late fall 1–2' tall		
62	*Cryptomeria japonica nana*	H	Dwarf cedar	Brownish purple in winter 1½–2' tall		
63	*Cupressus pygmaea*	S	Pygmy cypress			
64	*Lagerstroemia indica*	H	Dwarf crape myrtle		Sun	Petite pink
65	*Picea glauca conica*	H	Alberta spruce	Slow growing—7' tall in 35 yrs	Needs shelter from hot & cold	
66	*Punica granatum nana*	H	Pomegranate	3' tall	Sun	Orange/red
67	*Taxodium distichum*	F	Swamp	100' orange-brown in fall (Bonsai)		
68	*Ulmus parvitolia 'Seiju'*	S	Elm	40–60' tall (Bonsai)		
69	*Ceanothus*	S	Wild lilac			Blue
70	*Hypericum reptans*	F	Creeping Saint-John's-wart	5'–6' tall		Yellow
71	*Chamaecyparis obtusa torulosa*	S	Twisted Hinoki cypress	Ground cover	Part shade	
72	*Chamaecyparis*	S	False cypress			
73	*Pinus mugo*	S	Mugo pine			
74	*Veronica repens*	S	Veronica white			
75	*Chamaecyparis obtusa*	S	Dwarf golden cypress			
76	*Cupressus glauca*	S	Italian cypress			

Additional Shrubs

No.	Botanical Name	Type	Common Name	Notes / Size	Light	Color
77	*Raphiolepis indica*	H	Indian hawthorne/ballerina		Sun	unknown
78	*Pittosporum tobira*	H	Wheeler's dwarf		Sun	unknown
79	*Moraea*	H	Dietes		Sun	unknown
80	*Escallonia*	H	Dwarf terry		Sun	unknown
81	*Santolina chamaecyparissus*	H	Lavendar cotton		Sun	unknown

Additional Groundcover

No.	Botanical Name	Type	Common Name	Notes / Size	Light	Color
82	*Trachelospermum jasminoides*	H	Star jasmine	Tall groundcover	Sun	unknown

Fig. 9-10 *Another scene on the Bierie layout that appears in the color section. The numbers identify the plants on the chart (Fig. 9-9).*

Fig. 9-11 *The most successful gardeners with railroads, like Bill Baldock, also have small emitters or sprinklers located in each area, with buried pipes and automatic timers to keep the vegetation well supplied with water.*

den hose for operating or photography sessions, so water is certainly not an essential ingredient. These layouts focus their scenery on areas where running water would be a rare sight in the real railroad world.

Because water is such an important option in a garden, you should have no trouble locating a nursery that can provide all the plumbing and outdoor-safe pumps and filters needed and proven in use. Briefly, most waterfalls and running streams use a recycling water system in which the water flows out of a disguised pipe to cascade over the waterfalls and rapids and tumble into a lake. Somewhere on the lake is an overflow pipe that allows the water level to be maintained to the top of the pipe; excess water

spills over the edge to enter hidden pipes that lead back up to the top of the waterfall. An electric pump keeps the water moving through the system. With some systems there may be a dozen or more gallons of water flowing down the waterfalls that can overflow the lake when the system is turned off, so plan for an overflow into the yard (not the basement window well) when the system is shut off. If you live in a climate where the water can freeze, some type of full-system drain must also be provided for the winter months.

The simplest method of creating a lake and a waterfall is to buy the plastic lake beds sold by many nurseries with matching plastic rock waterfalls. You

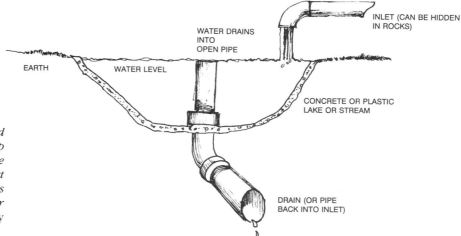

WATER DRAINS
INTO
OPEN PIPE

INLET (CAN BE HIDDEN
IN ROCKS)

EARTH   WATER LEVEL

CONCRETE OR PLASTIC
LAKE OR STREAM

DRAIN (OR PIPE
BACK INTO INLET)

Fig. 9-12 Use PVC pipe and fitting to supply water to the top of a waterfall with an open pipe at the water level of the lowest lake. When the lake's water rises to the water level, it spills over into the open drain. Artwork by Dave Etchells.

Fig. 9-13 Steve and Judy Arrigotti have two waterfalls and lakes, one on each end of their layout. This waterfall cascades down the mountain to fill a log pond beside the sawmill.

can, of course, build your own lake and streambed using the simple chicken wire and concrete method described earlier in this chapter for hollow mountains. If you want the watercourses to be watertight, the bottoms can be painted with the special compounds used to repair swimming pools. If you find that the streams or lakeshores are too smooth or even, add rocks or golf ball–sized pebbles to create a more realistic watercourse within the watertight troughs.

Roads and Highways

Dirt roads are more difficult to make than it might seem, especially if you want them to look like scale-model roads. In the real world, a dirt road is visible because it lacks vegetation and there likely will be many areas on your garden layout that lack vegetation. Real-world dirt roads are also dirt that has been hammered by passing tires into dust, even if that dust is set into clay or sandstone. Lifelike model dirt roads can be made using concrete spread between temporary sheet metal or plastic garden edging on the roadsides. Mix only sand, not gravel, with the dry cement and, after it is in place, cover the still-wet concrete with a layer of sand or dirt sifted through a door screen.

The same methods can be used to create scale-model concrete highways, but skip the overlayer of sifted sand or dirt. Paint $\frac{1}{16}$-inch-wide black lines for expansion joints or cracks.

Simulate tar or blacktop highways by using this same gravel and cement concrete mix, but add enough black concrete powdered color to produce a dark gray color. If you want an even darker color, paint the highway with dark gray (not black) flat exterior house paint. Cut a $\frac{1}{16}$-by-5-inch slit in a piece of file folder and use that as a mask to spray a yellow stripe down the center of the backtop.

The concrete can be brought right to the outer edges of the rails with any of these systems. Fill the area between the rails with a $1\frac{1}{2}$-inch-wide piece of $\frac{1}{4}$-inch-thick hardboard the width of the road. Seal the hardboard with weatherproof paint and cover the top with sifted sand or dry cement to match the road. Life-Like makes a plastic railroad crossing sign or you can build your own from $\frac{1}{16}$-by-$\frac{5}{16}$-inch basswood for the cross signs and $\frac{5}{16}$-inch-square basswood for the post using $\frac{1}{4}$-inch dry transfer letters from a drafting supply store. Echo Specialties and Rara Avis (L&P Track-works) have ready-built wooden crossing signs.

Chapter 10

Bridges and Tunnels

THE ATMOSPHERE of a real railroad is created by the structures that carry it across the valleys and through the mountains by bridges and tunnels. On a real railroad, these structures are immediate and lasting evidence that nothing will stop the railroad on its course through the countryside. It's that spirit that is worth capturing when you use bridges and buildings on your model railroad.

Railroad Right-of-Way

Real railroads use bridges as a last resort. If an embankment or fill will do, they are used with just a round culvert or two at the bottom of the embankment. Pieces of 2-inch PVC plastic pipe make fine representations of cast concrete culverts for either indoor or outdoor layouts. Lone Star Bridge and Abutment sells a nice stone bridge that is designed to mount directly beneath the track, but it would look even better at the base of, say, a 12-inch-tall embankment. Some of the HO or O scale tunnel portals that represent concrete or stone also make nice culverts for gauge 1 layouts.

To make a bridge credible, it needs to have a beginning and an end: places where the dirt or fill changes to wood or steel or stone or concrete bridge. Most of the model bridges do not include the abutments that a real bridge would use for its support. You can make them for indoor railroads or outdoor railroads by merely cutting some $\frac{3}{8}$-inch-square bass-wood (for 1/29 or 1/32 scale) or $\frac{1}{2}$-inch-square bass-wood (for 1/24 and 1/22.5 scale) into 5-, 6-, and 7-inch lengths and stacking the three into a pyramid with the ends of the bridge resting on top. This same abutment would be appropriate for the ends of a wooden or steel trestle. If you want a bridge abutment that has wings to hold back more of the embankment, make the center from a stack of three 6-inch-square pieces of wood and the wings from a stack of 2, $2\frac{1}{2}$, and 3-inch-square pieces for each right and left wing. If you want the wood to resemble concrete, paint with light gray antiskid boat deck paint.

If you are shaping the scenery, either with plaster or beadboard indoors or a ton or so of dirt outdoors, try to shape the slopes so they fall at least 6 inches below the track so there is room for a bridge, some air space, and an inch or two of real or simulated water. Most real railroads also have at least a few dozen feet of dirt fill or embankment before the bridge and after it. Again, plan the mountain slopes so the track can swing away from the mountain and out onto an embankment or fill for at least a few inches, before the bridge. If you are working outdoors, the flooding of real rainwater will erode the edges of the track to help determine where fill dirt needs to be added or, in cases of severe erosion, places where a wooden or piled-stone wall is needed to keep the water from eating into the sides of the embankment. Indoor layouts require a much more careful shaping of the hills and embankments.

Fig. 10-1 A cast simulated stone arch bridge from Lone Star Bridge on Thomas Flynn's new layout.

Fig. 10-2 An LGB number 5061 simulated steel arch bridge with Korber's number 553 abutments at each end and three Bridge Track Supports (number 554) on the right. Korber Models photo.

Bridge Installation Outdoors

Many of the sites for bridges are places where the need for a bridge is obvious because the track is crossing a very deep canyon or a designed riverbed. Outdoors, you may want to use cinder blocks or piles of brick to function truly like a bridge abutment, to hold back the dirt as well as acting for support at the ends of the bridges. Norm Grant located the abutments on the David Charles layout to match the length of one of the By Grant wooden Howe truss bridges. The railroad was located on a dirt embankment on either end of the bridge so the concrete blocks held back the dirt. Note in Fig. 10-4 (of the concrete blocks before the bridge was in place) that

Fig. 10-3 *Bachmann makes this A-frame straining beam truss bridge in plastic. Kalamazoo has a similar design with two, three, and five vertical posts.*

Fig. 10-4 *Norm Grant used cinder blocks as bridge abutments when building David Charles's layout. The stones will form the walls of a cut.*

Norm also prepared the stone walls of a cut through a mountain by building the stone walls first; the dirt was piled on later to finish the mountain.

Korber makes some cast bridge piers that can be used as tall, simulated, cut-stone bridge abutments with dirt embankment, rather than more stone, behind the abutment. The LGB number 5061 series of plastic bridge support blocks can be used in the same manner to provide bridge abutments for the ends of a bridge with a dirt embankment at either end of the bridge. The Korber and LGB piers also can be used in the middle of a valley when two or more bridges are used, end-to-end, as the center piers. The steel arch bridge in Fig. 10-2 is the LGB number 5061 and LGB makes a much shorter through steel truss bridge (in plastic, like number 5061); it is part number 5060. Narrow Gauge Machining makes a real metal deck truss bridge.

Wooden Bridges

Wood was the most common material for real railroad bridges for nearly 100 years. However, even the narrow gauge railroads used iron and, later, steel for longer truss bridges. The wooden Howe truss bridges like the Aristo-Craft, By Grant, Smoke Stack, and Trestle Works models were common on standard gauge railroads and many lasted, on branch lines, into the 1980s. Wooden trestles, too, were common on all types of real railroads, some made from round vertical posts, others from square timber vertical posts. Thousands of wooden trestles are still in

Fig. 10-5 *The same scene as Fig. 10-4, viewed from the opposite end, with one of the By Grant wooden Howe truss bridges in place on David Charles's layout.*

use on both narrow and standard gauge real railroads.

If you are building a garden railroad, some method must be used to protect the wood, especially if trestle bents or wooden bridge abutments are placed directly on the earth. Redwood is one of the best choices for outdoor wooden bridges because it needs no paint or protection unless in direct contact with the earth. Redwood also weathers to a nice gray shade that is very similar to weathered creosote-treated wood—the most common material and color on real railroad wooden bridges.

You can avoid some of the problems of wood, even redwood, in contact with the ground by resting the bottom of bridge abutments or trestle bents on bricks placed a half-inch or so above ground level

and covered with a light layer of dirt. Do not cement the bridges in place—let them "float" like real railroad bridges so they don't break or lean against their footings with extreme changes of temperature or after a severe freeze and the following thaw. Some modelers treat any wood, including redwood, with the special preservatives sold by lumber and hardware dealers.

Gagne, By Grant, and Trestle Works offer preassembled wooden trestle bents in heights that range from 3 inches to 48 inches. By Grant will even preassemble the complete trestle. Bill Baldock made his own bents, in a $\frac{1}{4}$-inch-square block plywood jig, from $\frac{1}{2}$-inch-square redwood vertical posts with $\frac{1}{8}$-by-$\frac{1}{2}$-inch braces. The track supports would usually be more $\frac{1}{2}$-inch-square timbers on their sides, but Bill needed to hide the 1-inch PVC plastic conduit he uses for roadbed, so he used $\frac{3}{8}$-by-$1\frac{1}{2}$-inch wood for the horizontal track support beams.

Wooden trestle bents also were used by real railroads as bridge abutments, especially if the track was

Fig. 10-6 *Bill Baldock leaves two of the plastic PVC conduits in place and builds the bridges around them.*

carried onto a bridge by a wooden trestle. Marc Horovitz used By Grant trestle bents for his wooden trestles, but he placed two bents just 3 inches apart at the end of the trestles to serve as supports for his By Grant wooden Howe truss bridge and his homemade simulated steel girder bridge.

Simulated wooden trestle bents also are available from Hughes and Pola. The Pola trestle is made from the same plastic used for its buildings, a material that is formulated to be impervious to ultraviolet light. Most HO scale models are made of less-expensive plastics that will actually warp like a pretzel if used outdoors. The Pola trestle bents can be used, as Marc Horovitz did with his By Grant bents, to make bridge

Fig. 10-7 *An Aristo-Craft ready-built wooden Howe truss bridge on Bill Baldock's layout.*

Fig. 10-8 *Marc Horovitz used a By Grant wooden Howe truss and By Grant wooden trestle bents to build this spectacular bridge.*

abutments. The Pola trestle, however, lacks the horizontal beams to support the track and, therefore, looks a bit light. Some $\frac{1}{4}$-by-$\frac{3}{8}$-inch redwood strips placed across the tops of the bents, one each beneath the rails of the track, would greatly improve the appearance of the Pola trestle.

The Summit trestle, on Norm Grant's now-abandoned railroad, was a scale 48 feet high and 502 feet long; that's an actual 2 feet high and an awesome 22 feet long, and it was built on a curve with about a 15-foot radius. Norm placed the redwood trestle bents right on the ground and the trestle settled over the years into a roller coaster–style bridge because the dirt beneath some of the bents settled more than beneath others. The trestle was warped before Norm could shore up the lower bents. Today, he has the experience to avoid the pitfalls. The trestle was still inline enough to carry 20-car trains, but the speeds needed to be reduced to a crawl. Precisely the same problem faced every narrow gauge railroad in the country in their declining years after World War II. This bridge was partially disassembled and some of the components sold when Norm dismantled his railroad. Several of the other trestles, however, are being built into Dick Schaffer's layout.

Metal Bridges

At present, only Narrow Gauge Machining offers ready-built metal bridges and it has a series of brass deck truss bridges. LGB has the large plastic steel truss arch bridge (number 5061) and a smaller through bridge (number 5060), both in a strong plastic that will not warp if used outdoors.

Metal bridges are always painted on real railroads so you can make them from just about any material that will survive outdoors. Hardware stores usually carry $\frac{1}{4}$-by-2-inch aluminum strips and they may have K&S brand $\frac{1}{4}$-inch brass angles. K&S also makes 0.064-by-2-inch ($\frac{1}{16}$-by-2-inch) brass strip in 12-inch lengths if you cannot find the aluminum. Hobby shops carry the K&S products. Use two 2-inch-wide aluminum or steel strips, placed on edge about 2 inches apart, as girders beneath the rails. You can attach the strips to the sides of a piece of 2-by-2-inch lumber with outdoor-quality silicone cement. Cut the $\frac{1}{4}$-inch angles into 2-inch lengths and attach them every 2 inches, as vertical braces, with the silicone cement. Cover the bottom edge of the 2-inch vertical pieces with a strip of 0.016-by-$\frac{1}{4}$-inch ($\frac{1}{64}$-by-$\frac{1}{4}$-inch) K&S brass strip attached with the silicone cement. If you need a bridge longer than the 1-foot K&S 2-inch-wide brass, just splice two pieces together, end to end, and cover the joint with one of the $\frac{1}{4}$-inch angles. The bridge will gain most of its strength from the hidden 2-by-2-inch wood.

Marc Horovitz made his deck girder bridge from $\frac{1}{32}$-inch-thick sheet brass. He bent the top and bottom over to make a shallow channel about $\frac{1}{4}$-by-2 inches

Fig. 10-9 *Marc Horovitz used sheet brass to build this deck girder bridge. The locomotive and cars are from Aristo-Craft.*

with ¼-inch angle vertical pieces. Marc used a soldering torch and resin core solder to assemble his bridge and left it unpainted. It has weathered to a dark greenish gray. The K&S 2-inch brass strip, angle, and ¼-inch strip also could be soldered rather than cemented together.

Designing Real Railroad Bridges

The National Model Railroad Association is an organization devoted primarily to indoor model railroading in the smaller scales. They have standards that most manufacturers of HO and N scale, for example, follow for track and wheels. The National Model Railroad Association (NMRA) also has standards for gauge 1 turnouts and wheels, but those standards are only needed if you are making your own turnouts from raw rail. Membership ($22.00 a year) includes the *NMRA Standards* book and twelve monthly issues of the forty-eight-page *NMRA Bulletin* magazine. The NMRA also publishes one of the best reference works on real railroad bridges, tunnels, embankments, roadbed, trackwork, and other data you can use if you want your indoor or outdoor layout to look like layouts in the real world. The *NMRA Data Book* has about 300 illustrated pages in a three-ring binder and it's only $20.00.

If you want to build your own wooden trestles, culverts, or arch bridges, the standards some of the real railroads use are in the *NMRA Data Book* with drawings. The book has drawings and dimensions for real railroad steel trestles, arch bridges, truss bridges (like LGB's), deck girder bridges (like Marc Horovitz's), and through girder bridges. The book also has dimensions of many of the narrow gauge freight cars and locomotives, the lengths of ties needed for turnouts, the proper slopes for embankments and cuts through hills, and real railroad operating data. Strangely, one of the few missing elements of real railroading are tunnels and tunnel portals.

Tunnel Portals

The portal is really just a cosmetic device for either an indoor or an outdoor model railroad. Indoors, the mountain will be hollow plaster or rough-cut layers of beadboard as shown in Chapter 7. Outdoors, the mountain may be hollow concrete or dirt with a tunnel lining of 2-by-6 and 2-by-2-inch boards for each wall and a 2-by-6-inch board for the roof. On a real railroad, the portal is really just an extension of the tunnel lining to keep the loose dirt from falling over the top and sides of the tunnel entrance and exit.

A model railroad tunnel portal can simply be glued to the edge of the plaster or concrete tunnel and mountain or to the ends of the 2-by-6-inch boards. Silicone construction cement, in a caulking gun, is the easiest adhesive to use to attach the portal. For realism, the tops and sides should be filled in with loose dirt to disguise the fact that the portal is just a facade.

Norm Grant used one of the portals now sold by Rara Avis and Steve Arrigotti made a similar portal from redwood strips cut on his own table saw. Both modelers, however, included wings on the sides of the portal; Norm's are matching Rara Avis parts and Steve used thin slabs of rock. Both types match real-world practices to keep loose debris from falling onto the track in the cut leading into the tunnel. On Norm Grant's tunnel, that loose debris is gravel. Steve Arrigotti used the slabs of stone to simulate a cut

Fig. 10-10 Norm Grant's layout had fourteen bridges and this was the largest: 48 scale feet high and 502 scale feet long.

through solid rock. Hughes and Gagne make portals similar to the Rara Avis portal. Mountains-in-Minutes, Noch, Rara Avis, and Chooch (available from Walthers) make simulated stone tunnel portals, each a slightly different design.

So far, no one makes a tunnel portal for gauge 1 trains that looks like a tunnel blasted out of solid rock. The easiest way to make such a portal would be to stack three rocks of matching colors, two for the sides and one for the roof. Fill-in the gaps with a mixture of concrete and sand (no gravel) mixed with dry color to match the rocks. The entire rock face can then be stained with a mixture of nine parts water to one part dark brown outdoor latex paint with a few drops of detergent as a wetting agent. The stain will blend the colors and place a matching stain in the crevices of both rocks and concrete.

The tunnel portal area immediately above the tracks is always black from the exhaust of steam or diesel locomotives. Mix a "wash" or nine parts water to one part black outdoor latex paint and a few drops of detergent. Use a pump-style hair spray bottle to spray the mixture over the top of the tunnel portal so the dead center is almost pure black, fading to no black at the upper corners of the portal.

Fig. 10-11 *Norm Grant used simple 2-by-6-inch boards for the sides of his tunnels with 2-by-2-inch boards on top for overhead clearance and another 2-by-6-inch board on its side for the roof. The tunnel portal is a Rara Avis product.*

Fig. 10-12 *Steve Arrigotti made two tunnels, side by side, with 2-by-6-inch redwood on both sides of both tunnels, topped by 2-by-2-inch redwood for overhead clearance and a 2-by-6-inch redwood roof. He built the tunnel portal from redwood strips cut on his table saw.*

Chapter 11

▮▮
▮▮
▮▮

Buildings and Accessories

BUILDINGS ARE an important element in any model railroad, indoors or out. They can serve to further the exact illusion you are trying to create with your railroad. Certainly, realistic replicas of real railroad and town buildings are available for those who want a realistic scene. If you are creating a railroad with a whimsical character with, perhaps, tight curves and a rainbow of rolling stock colors, then consider some of the European-style houses and even some of the Playmobil houses or castles. If you want the look of the Old West, there are dozens of buildings created to match that time period. What's more, there are realistic modern people, and vehicles, Old West people and vehicles, and fantasy figures available.

Weatherproofing Buildings

If you are creating a model railroad indoors, there is no need to wonder if the buildings you buy or build can withstand the weather. If you are careful enough to bring the buildings indoors every night, and every time rains even threatens, then you don't need to worry about the weather ruining your buildings either. Most of us don't have the patience to keep moving buildings indoors so it's worth the trouble to be sure they can withstand a thorough drenching and a few days, at least, in the sun.

Most of the plastic and foam plastic buildings sold for gauge 1 railroads are made of materials that will withstand ultraviolet rays and are impervious to moisture. The best of these, though, will fade in the sun, so you should plan to bring the buildings inside after a weekend's operations. Trestles and bridges that are supposed to look weatherbeaten can certainly remain outside. If you want some of the barns or Old West buildings to look weathered, by all means let the weather do its job. The plastics can certainly be repainted with the paints sold for model railroads like Floquil or Scalecoat, so you might want to experiment with a building or two, leaving them outside for a few weeks or months to see how they survive in your climate.

The Pola kits include cement, but I would suggest you supplement it by running a bead of outdoor-quality silicone construction cement down the inside of each seam as you assemble the model. It's difficult to get a really tight bond on the rugged plastics used in Pola and most other brands of outdoor buildings with conventional plastic cements. The silicone cement should withstand the changes in weather and humidity and keep holding the parts together.

There are also a number of brands of buildings that are made of wood, including Dees Delights, Lionel, and some Oakridge Corporation, Industrial Miniatures, and New England Hobby Supply. The wood, even if it is redwood, must be treated with the same kinds of weatherproof outdoor-quality paint or stains and oils that you would use on your house. The shingle roofs, in particular, will need painting because the wood is much thinner than conventional wood or shake shingle material. You can paint the

Fig. 11-1 *Bill Bauer created this station scene with Pola buildings and LGB figures. The railcar at the left is Delton's.* Bill Bauer photo.

shingles a light gray-green color to simulate weathered wood, because this is not the place to let nature do the weathering for you, regardless of how well it might work with redwood bridges. The wooden buildings should last about as long outdoors as a full-sized house, but they will need repainting or oiling. Protect them from the earth by placing each wooden building on its own slab of concrete. Building-supply centers sell round and rectangular walkway panels. The concrete pad should be a bit larger than the building. Disguise edges with sand, dirt, or small bark chips.

Selecting Sites for Structures

If you are building an indoor layout on a tabletop, the buildings can simply rest on the table. For greater realism, however, sprinkle some loose dirt along the edges to hide the place where the bottom of the building meets the table to give the impression the building has a foundation buried in the earth. If you are building an open-grid-style benchwork as shown in Chapter 6, cut plywood bases about ½-inch longer and wider than the base of the building and add any driveways or sidewalks to that site size. If you are elevating the track into an upgrade, the building site must be cut free even if it is a trackside building like a station or freight house. The building site segment of

plywood must be supported so it is perfectly level, not angled upward at (for example) a 4 percent grade. Real railroads try to have industrial sidings level, so you might want to do the same on your layout. Most of us, though, don't have the space to make the track level in front of every station and neither did most real railroads. It was not at all uncommon for the station on a real railroad in the mountains to have three or four steps up to the waiting room on the downhill side and no steps on the uphill side of the platform. Check the plywood building site base with a small carpenter's level to be sure it does not tilt in any direction.

Outdoors, there is not likely to be any level building site, even in the level lawn areas. You can scrape the ground bare and pour on some fine dry dirt, then level it with a board and tamp it down for each building site. You might also consider powdered clay-based soil so you can wet the site (after it is perfectly level) and the clay will harden. Use a small carpenter's level to check the outdoor sites, too, to be certain they do not tilt in any direction. If you are building a layout on a very steep slope, like Bill Baldock's DSP&PRR (in Chapter 2 and in the color section), you might want to support stations that rest on the downhill side of the tracks with a retaining wall of ½-inch-square redwood strips nailed together.

Remember to provide walkways or even stairs on steep slopes, so your railroad's passengers can reach the station and platforms.

Lighting for Your Layout

Indoors, it is most realistic to operate bulbs for interior lights or streetlights at about half their rated voltage so they glow rather than shine. Reduce the voltage by wiring a half dozen bulbs in sequence like the old Christmas tree lights; run one wire from one bulb to the light at the left and the other wire to the light at the right, repeating the chain of bulbs from the right terminal on the transformer and traveling from bulb to bulb back to the left terminal on the transformer. Experiment with different numbers of bulbs on the workbench until you find a level of light that suits your eye. If one bulb goes out, though, you will have to check them all to find the culprit. You can use Christmas tree lights but only the kind that operate from a transformer with 12 to 18 volts. *Never* use full 115-volt house current on any model railroad layout, indoors or out. Mount the bulbs on brackets of bent tin or aluminum inside the house or station or building so the bulb is somewhere near the imagined ceiling, not at floor level.

Model Power, LGB, Pola, Noch, and Life-Like sell a variety of different styles of low-voltage streetlights that can be used in town scenes or just to light the station platforms. All of these have low-voltage bulbs that can be operated from the power terminals on the transformer. I would suggest, however, that you buy an inexpensive 12-volt transformer from a hobby or electronics supply store and use it just for the lights. Garden and landscape supply stores also sell low-voltage lighting sets to provide yard illumination. You may want to use some of these to provide spot lighting for individual scenes or just to highlight the plants behind the railroad so you are not operating in pitch darkness. The lighting wires can be carried in buried PVC plastic conduit as illustrated in Chapter 5.

Dollhouse Miniatures for a Railroad

There are enough building kits now available, most in 1/22.5 to 1/24 scale, to allow you to build a complete small town with about thirty stores and offices, filling stations, churches, and forty or fifty different houses ranging from log cabins to two-story Victorians. There is also an array of details like lawnmowers and wheelbarrows and fences. To find all your choices, however, you will need to go beyond the usual hobby or toy stores or landscaping shops. Look in the telephone book's yellow pages under the headings "Dollhouses and Accessories" and "Minia-

tures for Collectors." There is a hobby as large as model railroading based on building dollhouses and single-room dioramas with every last detail—including silverware on the table and cigarettes in the ashtray. The majority of these items are 1/12 scale (1 inch is equal to 1 foot), or about twice the size of 1/24 scale gauge 1 railroads. There is, however, a growing segment of the miniatures hobby that builds in what they call "half-scale" and that is, of course, 1/24 scale. The Oakridge Corporation and Dees Delights are two major sources of building kits in 1/24 scale. You may, however, find a number of the 1/12 scale items suitable for things like garden fountains or small framed pictures for walls or newspapers or buckets that have a variety of sizes in real life.

The miniatures dealers also can supply a variety of 1/24 scale windows and milled wood for window frames and doors as well as ornate kick panels and wainscoting and eaves trim; there is a complete scale hardware store of material including door knobs, sinks, toilet paper holders, and every imaginable kind of furniture and kitchen and bath fixture in 1/12 scale, and more such items appear every day in half-scale. There are also several styles of brick, stone, and shingle material as well as wallpapers for interiors in 1/12 scale that are suitable for 1/24 scale. There are several brands of interior lighting available with operating wall switches and table lamps, if you like. It's worth your while to search out all the miniatures shops in your area and in any city you may visit to see what they have that will fit in a 1/24 scale scene. Some of the better products are produced by very small part-time manufacturers who may only sell in a limited geographic area, so you will find a different inventory in every miniatures shop you visit. There are often local custom builders who create both houses and small business buildings that you may find suitable for your layout.

Selecting Stations

If you want to pick a single building that best represents both a town and the railroad's link to the town, pick a railroad station. Most modelers in this large scale create credible towns with just a station, a store or two, and three or four houses. A real railroad station often served many functions in addition to serving the passengers. At most stations, bags of mail were dropped off and picked up by early morning mail/passenger trains. Early morning trains also used to pick up the milk from local farmers to be delivered to nearby creameries. Small and large packages that are now delivered by such shipping companies as United Parcel Service would have been carried in the

railroad's baggage cars or by Railway Express cars or compartments. All of these shipments were sometimes shipped from just the baggage compartment of a baggage/coach combine like those sold by Delton, LGB, Aristo-Craft, and Bachmann. Larger towns and stations might be served by longer trains that might have one or more mail cars like Delton's and Aristo-Craft's and baggage cars like Delton's. Full refrigerator cars might be assigned to pick up milk from the stations. Aristo-Craft has a variety of cars with authentic milk car lettering schemes and other brands of model reefers often appear with milk car lettering in limited production runs. You can, then, have a credible need for a passenger station, even if you don't operate any passenger trains.

Many full-sized passenger stations also had a freight house attached to the station. The Pola and Model Power/Pola Silverton Station and Idaho Springs Station have a platform and boxcar floor-level door that could represent a combination freight and passenger station. The baggage door on the left of the Aristo-Craft Victorian Station could be cut and modified so it would rest with the bottom sill at the height of the windows' bottom sills and a small platform built from $\frac{3}{8}$-inch-square uprights and braces with $\frac{1}{8}$-by-$\frac{3}{8}$-inch boards for the platform itself. The Pola Cripple Creek Station has an elevated platform that would make this station suitable for a combination freight and passenger station. The Pola Waldau Freight Station has the same walls as the Cripple Creek Station but a much larger roof with more overhang. The Waldau roof simulates tiles but it

Fig. 11-2 *There are stations at two levels near Snail Patch on Bill and Dee Baldock's layout.*

Fig. 11-3 *Industrial Miniatures makes a variety of ready-built 1/24 scale buildings, including this Nunda Junction Station.*

could be turned inside out and some $\frac{1}{16}$-inch-square strips cemented at $\frac{3}{4}$-inch intervals to simulate a seamed metal roof that was applied to many American buildings. New England Hobby Supply has a kit to build the wooden Passenger Platform (number 2004) that also could become a combination freight and passenger station.

Populating Your Railroad

Any model scene will appear more realistic if you add some of the clutter that appears in the real world and, perhaps, a few scale-model people. Bill Bauer used a

Pola Silverton Station on his Shawmut Line. He repainted the station a single reddish brown color similar to Floquil's Box Car Red to match the stations on the real Shawmut Line. He added a Pola baggage cart, a set of LGB Porters with Luggage (number 5229), Mountain Tourists (number 5146), Station Figures (number 5043), and Sitting Travelers (number 5147) with some barrels he located in a miniatures shop. Bill Baldock has two stations, one above the other, to serve two levels at Snail Path on his DSP&PRR. The upper station is a Pola Cripple Creek Station and the lower one is a Pola Old Time Gas Pumps canopy with

Fig. 11-4 *There are hundreds of 1/24 scale and 1/32 scale people and animal figures from all eras. These are Bachman's 1/24 scale workers.*

Fig. 11-5 *This Bachmann handcar actually runs and it comes complete with all the tools. Most of the tools are available in separate tool packs.*

the pumps relocated in one of his town scenes. The man and woman are Presier Victorian Era Standing Couple (number 5052). Noch, Pola, Model Power, and Bachmann also make 1/24 scale people.

A 1/24 scale model of a 6-foot tall man will be $\frac{72}{24}$ inches or 3 inches tall. A 1/32 scale model of a 6-foot tall man will only be $\frac{72}{32}$ or $2\frac{1}{4}$ inches tall. All of these building kits are proportioned with doors and windows to match the 3-inch-tall figures. If, however, you are using the 1/32 scale or 1/29 scale locomotives and rolling stock, you will want somewhat smaller buildings and 1/32 scale people. Preiser makes a selection of 1/32 scale people and animals and there are a number of racing car kits and military miniatures plastic kits that include 1/32 scale figures. Some larger toy stores carry the Bruder or Britains brand plastic zoo and farm animals and those series have several 1/32 scale people as well as tractors and some small buildings. There are 1/24 scale models of just about any automobile or truck imaginable as plastic kits. There are also some 1/32 scale plastic automobile kits and occasionally a 1/32 scale truck and trailer kit appears. There are also some toy cars and trucks, but the scale is not marked on the package so you'll have to measure them to determine their scale.

1/32 and 1/29 Scale Buildings

To the best of my knowledge, there are no 1/32 scale buildings on the market except for some horse stalls made by Britains and Bruder, available at a few larger toy stores. I don't even know of a source for 1/32 scale doors, although the Grandt Line 1/24 scale doors could be cut down and any of the 1/24 scale windows made by Grandt or sold by the miniatures dealers

could be used. If you want true 1/32 scale buildings, build them yourself. There is nothing made in 1/29 scale, although the smaller 1/24 scale buildings should be suitable. A 1/29 scale model of a 6-foot-tall man would be $\frac{72}{29}$ inches tall; close enough to $2\frac{1}{2}$ inches and not far from the 3-inch-tall 1/24 scale version. All of the 1/24 and 1/22.5 scale buildings are replicas of what would be very small structures in the real world so they won't look out of place on a 1/29 scale layout.

Industrial Buildings

If you want to operate your model railroad like a real one, you will want to include at least a few visible industries. Any building that looks like a warehouse can serve as a warehouse or as a manufacturing plant. The Pola Kleinbach Freight Station or Sawmill could be modified slightly to represent small industries. The Pola Sawmill can, of course, serve as a sawmill as it does on Bill Bauer's Shawmut Line. Korber Models makes several cast foam resin industrial buildings, including an Icing Platform and Ice House that could be easily modified to represent a large freight house or a small manufacturing plant. Mountains in Minutes has some two-story brick warehouses molded in polyurethane foam.

Railroad Structures

The second most popular building in gauge 1 is the railroad water tower. Smoke Stack has a fine wooden kit, and plastic models are offered by Pola and Aristo-Craft. Rara Avis produces a cast resin water tower kit and distributes an all-metal windmill that makes a nice companion model in an Old West scene.

Pola makes a single-stall and a two-stall simulated

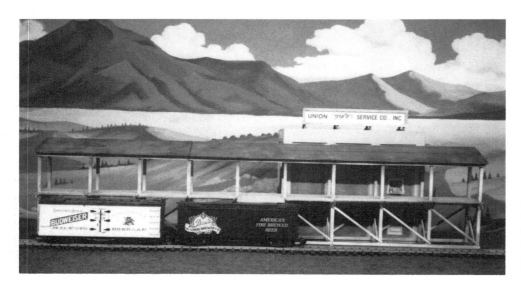

Fig. 11-6 Korber Models makes some industrial buildings, including this icehouse, which can be adapted to represent other industries. Korber Models photo.

Fig. 11-7 *Bill Bauer modified a Pola sawmill building with a platform and more wood. The Shay locomotive is an out-of-production KMT brass model.* Bill Bauer photo.

Fig. 11-8 *The Korber Models two-stall engine house is long enough for the LGB Mogul.* Korber Models photo.

Fig. 11-9 *The Korber Models three-stall roundhouse could be used, with some modifications, with the LGB turntable.*

Fig. 11-10 *Playmobil's Victorian Mansion (left) and Old West Station (foreground) with a Pola engine house in the background on the Baldocks' patio deck.*

Fig. 11-11 *The Korber Models's Aunt Millie's House is an injection-molded urethane plastic kit.* Korber Models photo.

brick engine house that are replicas of European buildings. They also have a short simulated stone single-stall engine house. Korber produces American-style two-stall engine houses and a three-stall roundhouse, both of simulated brick in molded foam plastic.

City Scenes

There are no easy-to-build plastic kit replicas of American houses. The miniatures dealers, however, often have simple-to-build wooden kits and the Oakridge Corporation carries some of those houses. Playmobil offers a snap-together Victorian dollhouse that is also available as a smaller one-story model. Korber makes a nice cast foam plastic Aunt Millie's House, which the Arrigottis used with a scratch-built barn for their farm scene. Depot G makes a wide variety of small houses and stores in high density urethane foam with separate Grandt Line windows. Pola makes a series of two-story Old West stores with minor detail changes as a Wells Fargo Express Office, First National Bank, Red Horse Saloon, and others. Depot G also has a finely detailed series of downtown buildings in high-density urethane foam plastic. Mountains in Minutes produces some urethane foam two-story downtown stores.

Kit Conversions

If you don't find a building kit that suits your needs, it is possible to modify it. I've already suggested adding

Fig. 11-12 *Columbine kits are cast polyester resin with separate Grandt Line windows, glazing, and decals. These are (l. to r.): H&A Hose Company, Public School No. 1, St. Linda's Church, and O'Malley's Mansion.* Columbine photo.

Fig. 11-13 *The Columbine series includes downtown buildings such as the (l. to r.) Jensen Bank & Trust, City Jail, Golden Cue Billiard Hall, and Olson Brothers Dry Goods. The front walls also are sold as separate kits for backdrops.* Columbine photo.

Fig. 11-14 *Aristo-Craft's Victorian Station is available ready built.*

a high level platform to the Pola Silverton Station to convert it into a combination freight and passenger station. Pola uses the same basic walls in several kits and changes the roof or adds porches or other details. You can mix and match parts from two or more of these kits to create something not available from the box.

Fig. 11-15 *Bill Baldock used two Aristo-Craft Victorian stations, one on top of the other, to make this two-story station.*

Bill Baldock has converted several kits by simple changes, including making a covered gas station platform into a passenger platform. Bill used two Aristo-Craft Victorian Station models to make his two-story station. He cut the peaked roofs from the ends with a hacksaw and made a new upstairs window from clear acetate plastic and wood strips. The staircase was taken from one of the Industrial Miniatures Pharmacy models.

Scratch-Built Structures

You certainly do not have to build all the buildings on your layout from kits. Models as large as these are relatively simple to build from raw materials or, as modelers phrase it, "to build from scratch." The walls and roof can be cut from $\frac{1}{8}$-inch-thick plywood. Cut the window openings with a saber saw after drilling a $\frac{1}{4}$-inch starter hole in one corner of the window. There are no plans for buildings as small as those commonly seen on gauge 1 railroads so draw the outline of the structure right on the plywood.

Grandt Line makes seven windows and four different doors in plastic; the doors swing and clear plastic is used for the windows. Simpson (available through Walthers) makes a selection of nine windows and five doors in plastic. There also are some preassembled wooden doors and windows sold by some miniatures dealers. Grandt Line and Simpson make chimneys, and Simpson has depot roof eaves brackets. Just trace

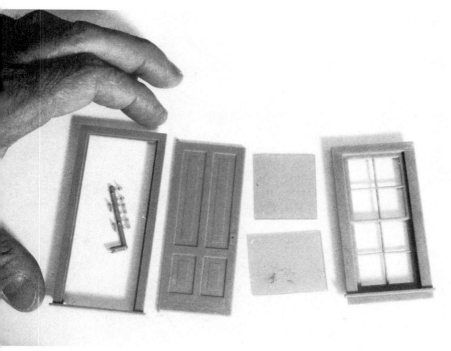

Fig. 11-16 *Grandt Line is one firm that offers plastic doors and windows for 1/24 scale models.*

Fig. 11-17 *Dave Mohr used cardboard, Northeastern wood, thick foil, and Grandt Line windows and doors to build Fritz Coal Mine No. 3 for Bill Bauer.*

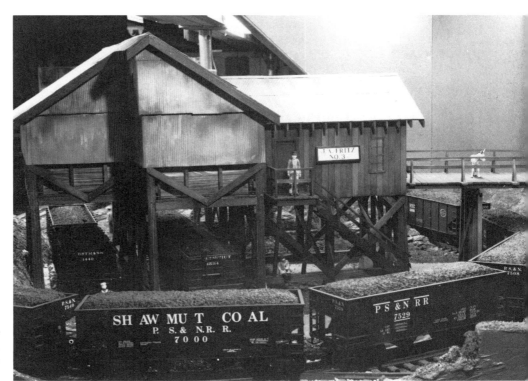

Fig. 11-18 *The back side of Fritz Coal Mine No. 3. Note the inset corner to clear the curved track on the left.*

Fig. 11-19 *George Wills built this sawmill for the Arrigotti's layout from redwood strips and panels.*

the outline of the window on the plywood and cut the opening to within $\frac{1}{32}$ inch of its outline, then file and sand the edges to match the size of the window precisely.

Miniatures dealers carry milled basswood clapboard siding from Northeastern and several types of shingles. Simpson makes metal corrugated roofing.

Dave Mohr scratch-built the Fritz Coal Mine on Bill Bauer's Shawmut Line with cardboard walls, Grandt Line windows and doors, and basswood strips from Northeastern. George Wills, Judy Arrigotti's father, built the barn and sawmill on their railroad from $\frac{1}{4}$-inch plywood with redwood beams cut on a table saw. The shingles are from a miniatures dealer. The windows were cut from the grill in the bottom of a plastic strawberry carton!

Chapter 12

Locomotive Maintenance and Upgrading

THE LOCOMOTIVE is the focal point of this hobby. The truly massive proportions of these large-scale locomotives is what sets them apart from any other form of model railroading. You have to use your imagination to believe that an HO scale or even an O scale locomotive has the power to pull a train. These large-scale locomotives look the part.

Steam or Diesel?

The old-time steam locomotives are by far the most common engines in large scale-model railroading. Bachmann has sold thousands of their 4-6-0 locomotives and few garden railroads don't have at least one of the LGB Moguls. Now that the hobby has developed beyond the Christmas tree layout stage and oval of track through a petunia garden into a hobby and a landscape design discipline, the array of models has expanded to provide as wide a selection of relatively inexpensive models as are available in O scale.

LGB is the only firm producing plastic-bodied diesels in 1/22.5 scale. The LGB number 2060 diesel is part of the least expensive set, one that is sold by some of the larger toy store chains. That diesel, like all of LGB's locomotives, is a model of a locomotive designed to operate on narrow gauge track as described in Chapter 1. LGB also produces some American-style diesels, including the twelve-wheel Alco DL-535E that operates on the White Pass and Yukon. LGB has a model of the Denver & Rio Grande Western's number 50 diesel that resides at the Colorado Rail-

road Museum. This locomotive was originally built for the Sumpter Valley in Oregon and later purchased by the Rio Grande. LGB produces another twelve-wheel diesel, lettered for the Rio Grande, that has the cab and the chassis of the White Pass Alco but a strange long hood behind the cab that is similar to the ElectroMotive Division (EMD) of General Motors SD9 diesel.

There are a growing number of models of standard gauge American diesels being produced in 1/32 scale to operate on gauge 1 track. Aristo-Craft has an Alco FA-1 and FB-1 set of eight-wheel diesels and a model of the General Electric U25-B eight-wheel diesel, and it has announced future production of an Alco RS-3 diesel. Great Trains has 1/32 scale models of the EMD F40PH used by Amtrak and some commuter railroads and EMD F7A and F7B eight-wheel diesels. Lionel produces 1/32 scale models of the EMD GP7 and GP9. Chicago Train Works produces metal EMD GP35 and F9A and F9B eight-wheel diesels. These diesels are models of the real diesels that are the most popular with HO scale modelers, and they represent the style, at least, of the most common American diesels. With the exception of the LGB White Pass diesel, all of these models are relatively short eight-wheel diesels (railroads call the wheel arrangement a B-B for two-plus-two powered axles). These compact locomotives look more realistic than longer locomotives would when traversing the relatively sharp 48-inch-radius curves, and they will oper-

Fig. 12-1 *Great Trains 1/32 scale EMD F7A and F7B plastic diesels are available with or without motors. The coupler is an optional Kadee #1-Scale.*

Fig. 12-2 *The LGB model of the Rio Grande number 50 diesel switcher.*

Fig. 12-3 *The full-sized Rio Grande number 50 switching car at the Colorado Railroad Museum.*

ate around the 24-inch-radius curves if you don't mind a toylike appearance.

Steam Locomotive Classification

LGB has been the inspiration for a lot of modelers to discover large-scale railroading, although Bachmann is the better-selling model due to a combination of much lower prices and distribution through virtually every toy store and toy catalog chain in America. Most of the garden railroads in this book, however, were started when the LGB Mogul was first introduced. This locomotive has inspired many modelers to create layouts in gauge 1.

The real railroads had two ways of classifying steam locomotives: by their wheel arrangement and by nickname. The Mogul nickname was applied to steam locomotives that had two small wheels in the front to guide it around curves and six large driving wheels. The number designation for that locomotive was 2-6-0, but modelers usually just call them Moguls. The popular Delton 1/24 scale locomotive is a model of what the real railroads call a Consolidation or 2-8-0. Lionel makes an 0-6-0T, a six-drivered locomotive with no pilot wheels and no trailing wheels and no tender—the "T" means the tender was built onto the locomotive, usually coal or oil in the rear with a water tank wrapped around the boiler—the 0-6-0T and 0-6-0 locomotives were called six-wheeled Switchers. Lionel, Kalamazoo, Bachmann, LGB, and Aristo-Craft make 0-4-0T models and Aristo-Craft and

Kalamazoo make 0-4-0 locomotives (with tenders); these were called four-wheeled Switchers. The Bachmann 4-6-0 is a ten-wheeler (although some of its catalogs list it as a Consolidation), and the Bachmann 2-4-2 is a Columbia. Kalamazoo makes a 4-4-0 American, and Aristo-Craft has medium-sized 4-6-2 Pacific and 2-8-2 Mikado locomotives. Lionel produces a 4-4-2 Atlantic. There is, among these models, at least one replica of every popular small- to medium-sized steam locomotive classification that operated in America.

The LGB Mogul

LGB selected one of the more compact steam locomotives for its first model locomotive based on an American prototype, the Mogul that was one of the last narrow gauge locomotives in operation in Colorado on the Colorado & Southern Railroad. LGB has two distinctly different versions of the Mogul, but both share the same chassis. One version has a large funnel-shaped stack with steam and sand domes that neck down in the middle and are usually brass plated. The cab has inset panels that represent all-wooden cabs. The tender has a flared-out flange around the top and a simulated wood load. This is the way the real locomotives looked when built in the late 1880s. The Colorado & Southern was originally the Denver South Park & Pacific (itself owned first by the Union Pacific). Most of the narrow gauge railroads in America purchased Moguls in the 1880–1900 period.

Fig. 12-4 *An Aster live steam Mogul double-heads with an LGB Mogul on Marc and Barbara Horovitz's layout.*

Fig. 12-5 *One of the proto-types for the LGB Mogul. Colorado & Southern number 9 has the bear trap stack common to all the C&S locomotives.* Richard Kindig photo, from the Hol Wagner collection, at Sheridan, Colorado, October 15, 1938.

Fig. 12-6 *Bill Welsh rebuilt his LGB Mogul with a new head-light and a bear trap stack, simulated canvas curtains above the cab and a light application of thinned paint with an air-brush to "weather" the locomotive.* Bill Bauer photo.

The second version of the LGB Mogul has a straight stack and domes with straight sides. The cab has simulated rivets to duplicate the later steel-sheathed cabs. The tender has square corners on the top with a smaller bunker to carry simulated coal on the top. The Denver South Park & Pacific (DSP&P) locomotives were rebuilt to this appearance in about 1915, and in 1918 a huge spark arrestor was added to the top of the stack with a pipe leading down to the track to keep any errant sparks out of the air. Those spark arrestors were called "bear traps" because they

resembled an animal trap and were big enough for bears. So far, LGB has not produced the bear trap spark arrestors, but brass kits for the arrestors are available from By Grandt. The September–October 1979 issue of the *Narrow Gauge and Short Line Gazette* has plans for the bear trap spark arrestor. Bill Welsh made his from K&S brass tube and .040-inch thick brass sheet for his LGB Mogul. LGB usually has at least one paint and lettering scheme for the earlier prototype and one for the later prototype available.

Live Steam Locomotives

There are at least a dozen brands of locomotives available to operate on gauge 1 track that are actually powered by steam pressure generated inside their boilers by a fire in a firebox. These locomotives use either alcohol or butane lighter cartridges for fuel. The most common locomotives are the little 0-4-0T engines made by Mamod and available through Diamond Enterprises and some larger toy and hobby shops. West Lawn Locomotive Works, Hyde-Out Mountain, Miniature Steam, Rara Avis, San-Val, Little Engines, and Aster also offer locomotives powered by steam. Modelers call them "live steam," as opposed to the simple simulated smoke that is available in some LGB, Bachmann, Lionel, and Aristo-Craft locomotives.

Each of these live steam locomotives has a pressure-tested boiler and automatic safety valves for steam release, but they are certainly not toys. Most are available as kits or completely assembled and tested at prices that begin at about $200 and range upward to $4,000 and more for the Aster locomotives that are replicas of real steam locomotives. Clever modelers have adapted radio-controlled systems and servo motors to operate the valves so the locomotive will have a means of remote control; all of them require frequent adjustments of the valve wheels inside the cab to negotiate a layout with any upgrades or downgrades. Live steam is, of course, designed to be used only on outdoor layouts.

There are several importers of the Japanese-made Aster locomotives, including Garden Railways and Eastern Railways. Aster has produced very limited quantities of several American-prototype models, including a Shay geared locomotive and the huge Union Pacific Big Boy 4-8-8-4 locomotive. These models are currently collector items. Aster's most recent model was their first 1/22.5 scale, another Colorado & Southern Mogul, but that one is powered by live steam with alcohol fuel. Most of the Aster locomotives have been available with 18-volt electric motors for power rather than live steam for those that prefer conventional control.

GR International (a division of Garden Railways), Eastern Railways, Precision Scale, Roberts Lines, and the Marketing Corporation of America import brass models of both steam and diesel locomotives and rolling stock from various manufacturers in Korea. These models are metal, but they are powered by electric motors for operation indoors or out on gauge 1 track. The locomotive prices range upward from $4,000 and freight cars start at $500.

Bachmann's Ten-Wheeler

Baldwin Locomotive Works was one of the largest firms building steam locomotives. In the late 1890s, it had the equivalent of some of today's diesels: a standard series of locomotives for specific duties. The common wheel arrangements at the time included 0-4-0, 0-6-0, 2-6-0, 2-8-0, 4-4-0, and 4-6-0. The 2-8-0 was considered a freight engine and most 4-4-0 en-

Fig. 12-7 *Frank Ullman upgraded his Bachmann ten-wheeler by repainting it and applying decal lettering followed by light weathering with an airbrush.* Bill Bauer photo.

Fig. 12-8 *The Bachmann 4-6-0 is available in Rio Grande Southern paint. Here's how the real locomotive looked as restored at the Colorado Railroad Museum.*

gines were used for passenger service. The 2-6-0 and some 4-6-0 locomotives with smaller drivers were considered dual-purpose locomotives. The Baldwin designs were distinct in the shape of their boilers; the smaller smoke box at the front gave way to the larger area above the firebox at the rear in a gentle taper midway up the boiler. Other builders like Cooke (who built the original Colorado & Southern Moguls) and American Locomotive Works have boilers with a more severe taper, similar to the Kalamazoo gauge 1 4-4-0 model. Bachmann picked a standard Baldwin Locomotive Works design for its 4-6-0.

The Bachmann 4-6-0 is nearly identical to the locomotives used by the East Tennessee & Western North Carolina Railroad (ET&WNCRR) Company based on plans in the July 1981 issue of *Model Railroader* magazine (out of print) along with plans for the railroad's boxcar, gondola, hopper, and caboose. The Bachmann caboose is similar to the plan, but the Bachmann boxcar, hopper, and gondola are replicas of other railroads' narrow gauge cars. That ET&WNCRR 4-6-0 was one of Baldwin's standard designs, so Bachmann produced the closest possible thing to a "generic" steam locomotive. In fact, the proportions of the model are similar to both narrow gauge and standard gauge steam locomotives from Baldwin, although the prototype was a 3-foot narrow gauge. There were nearly identical 4-6-0 locomotives sold to the Santa Fe, Baltimore & Ohio, Canadian Pacific, Colorado Midland, Denver & Rio Grande, Erie, Illinois Central, Southern Pacific, and Union Pacific that were very similar to the Bachmann model.

The most famous narrow gauge railroad to use locomotives like Bachmann's 4-6-0 was the Rio Grande Southern. That locomotive, however, has a cab with only two windows rather than the three of the Bachmann model. O & S Trains makes a Sheet styrene cab side with two windows to modify the Bachmann cab to match the Rio Grande Southern locomotives. In fact, the Rio Grande Southern locomotives were not made by Baldwin but by the Schenectady Locomotive Works for the Florence & Cripple Creek Railroad and were acquired in 1916 for scrap value by the Rio Grande Southern and numbered 20, 22, and 25. There were only minor differences between the three. Numbers 22 and 25 were scrapped in 1940 but number 20 survives as a display at the Colorado Railroad Museum in Golden, Colorado. Bachmann now offers a Rio Grande version of the 4-6-0 with a two-window cab.

Bachmann's first 4-6-0 models, introduced in 1988, were powered by radio control with on-board batteries and all-plastic track. In 1990, that model was superseded by one with conventional control of its DC electric motor. Bachmann also introduced its plated sheet steel track. The radio-controlled locomotives and all-plastic track are no longer made by Bachmann. Bachmann has offered the later 4-6-0 in a variety of paint and lettering schemes, including a maroon Santa Fe model, a dark blue Baltimore & Ohio model, and a black Rio Grande Southern version with number 25 on the side of the cab. Most of the radio-controlled ten-wheelers were green and silver. Frank Ullman repainted one of the Santa Fe models in a dark flat black with a silver smoke box. That's about all the colors the locomotives carried on the Rio Grande Southern. Frank also used an airbrush from an artist's supply store to apply a thin wash of lighter gray in streaks to simulate weathering with some darker gray to simulate smoke stains on the smoke box. Now that is truly how those locomotives looked in service. Steve Arrigotti uses the same technique to age and weather his freight cars. Frank did not change the cab windows but he did cut the cylinder saddle and cab mount to remove about $\frac{1}{4}$ inch of plastic to lower the boiler and cab.

Locomotive Maintenance

Large-scale locomotives can roll up some long hours of operation in a relatively short time because the layouts are often large and it's so enjoyable to just watch them run. To be safe, perform a complete series of maintenance steps on each locomotive every 8 hours it operates. The procedure takes only a few minutes and it can prevent damage to the gears and motor.

Dirt is the major problem with large-scale locomotives, especially those operated outdoors. Keep a stiff-bristled, $\frac{1}{4}$-inch-wide brush and some pipe cleaners at the operating panel and clean the locomotives after every long operating session. The pipe cleaner can be used dry unless there is caked mud or great gobs of grease. Use the brush and damp pipe cleaners to remove mud; do not hold any of these locomotives under running water or use a garden hose to wash them. If grease will not rub off, buy one of the contact cleaners sold by electronics hobby stores or one of the model railroad track-cleaning fluids. Do not use alcohol; it is highly flammable and it can coat the brass rails with a mysterious substance that impairs the flow of electricity from the locomotive to the rails.

Dirt and oxides also must be removed from the locomotives' drivers or wheels and from the wheels of the rolling stock. Use a hard rubber eraser, like the Bright Boy sold by model railroad shops, to scrub the drivers or diesel wheels clean. Clean the pickup shoes on the LGB locomotives with same material. Do not use any type of sandpaper or emery board, because they can leave scratches that will oxidize even faster than a new driver or wheel and help grip and hold dirt. Plastic wheels, however, can be scraped gently with a hobby knife to remove any really sticky scum.

The track, too, must be cleaned if the locomotives are to operate properly. Again, avoid the use of any sandpaper. LGB sells a Cleaning Block (number 5004) that can be used. John Row developed a clever cleaning device that attaches permanently to one of the tender trucks on a locomotive or to a freight car. It has two wheels that spin with the friction of passing rails. The wheels effectively scrub the track while the locomotive operates. San-Val has a similar device called a Lil Wheelie Wonder. Those devices do not, however, solve the problem of cleaning track after a winter of nonoperation; that's when the Bright Boy or LGB Cleaning Block will be needed.

Fig. 12-9 *Use a pipe cleaner and toothbrush to clean behind the drivers.*

Fig. 12-10 *A hard rubber eraser, like a Bright Boy, is best for cleaning drivers.*

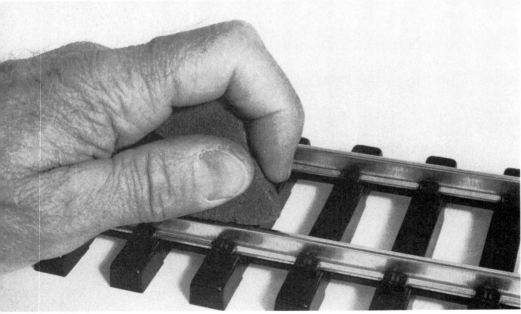

Fig. 12-11 *Clean the track with a hard rubber eraser or one of the special track cleaning pads sold by hobby dealers.*

The gears on the driver axles and on the motor also must be lubricated every eight hours (of use) or so. On most locomotives, there is a cover plate that can be removed from the bottom of the locomotive. On some, however, the superstructure must be removed to gain access to the gears. Four screws hold the bottom cover plate on the LGB Mogul. Note carefully (in Fig. 12-12) how the spring and pilot truck are mounted as you remove the plate and note

the position of the $\frac{1}{8}$-inch-wide metal contact strips that run from front to rear drivers. The LGB track wiper system just slides into the bottom of the chassis (shown) so you can lift it out to clean inside.

Use a pipe cleaner, a lint-free rag and a brush to remove any traces of dirt and any dirty grease from the axles, bearings, and all gears. Apply fresh plastic-compatible grease like the LaBelle (number 106) grease sold by hobby shops. Apply just a pinhead-sized bead of the grease around the gear and in each axle bearing. Use plastic-compatible oil like LaBell's (number 102) to lubricate the moving side rods at each pivot point. Do not use any oil on the tender trucks or on any freight or passenger car axles. Remove the wheels by spreading the side frames and clean out the bearings in the side frames with a pipe cleaner dipped in contact cleaner.

Troubleshooting Locomotives and Track

There will be times when the locomotives simply refuse to run. On an outdoor railroad, the cause is

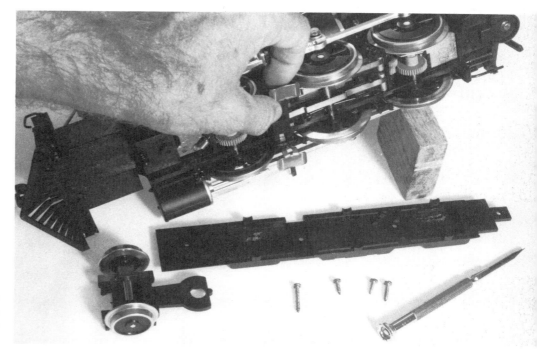

Fig. 12-12 Remove the four screws that retain the bottom cover plate on the LGB Mogul to gain access to the gears.

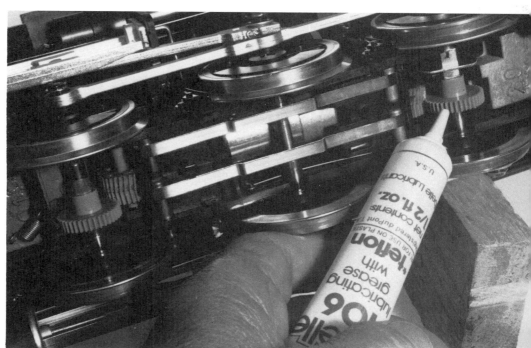

Fig. 12-13 Use plastic-compatible grease, like LaBelle number 106, for lubricating the gears and driver or diesel axles

Fig. 12-14   Locomotive and Electrical Troubleshooting

Trouble	Probable Cause of Trouble	Solution
Locomotive does not run (and head-light does not glow).	1. Power pack not plugged in, or the outlet is faulty.	1. Plug in the power pack or check the other appliance in the outlet.
	2. Track wires may be attached to the "AC" terminals of the power pack.	2. Connect the track wires to the two "DC" terminals.
	3. Wires may be improperly connected to the track terminals.	3. Check the "rules" and diagrams in Chapter 5.
	4. Insulated rail joiners may not be in correct positions.	4. Check the "rules" and diagrams in Chapter 5.
	5. Locomotive may be off the track.	5. Rerail the locomotive.
	6. Wheels or track rails may be dirty.	6. Clean the tracks.
	7. Nails, wires, tinsel, or other metals may be causing a short circuit by laying on the track.	7. Remove the material.
	8. Locomotive may be sitting on the plastic frog of a switch or crossing; on an insulated rail joiner; on a track with an operating-signal man or operating crossing gates.	8. Move the locomotive.
Locomotive does not run (but head-light does glow)	1. Check all of the above probable causes. Number 2 is the most likely.	1. Be sure to turn the power pack off immediately while you search for and correct the problem.
Locomotive does not run, and none of the above 8 checks solves the problem.	1. Use an operating light or model street light as a "test light." Touch the two wires to the "DC" terminals of the power pack with the "throttle" on. If the light glows, the pack is fine.	1. If the light does not glow with the power pack plugged into a working outlet and with the throttle full on, have the pack checked by your dealer's service department.
	2. Touch the street-lamp wires to the terminals on each of the terminal tracks with the throttle full on and the "Blocking Switch" (if any) for each block turned on. If the light glows, the problem is likely in the locomotive. If the light does not glow, there is a break in one or both of the wires from the power pack to the terminal.	2. Replace the wires.
	3. Place the locomotive on the terminal track that you just checked and found to be working. If the locomotive runs, then the problem is a loose or missing rail joiner or incorrect wiring.	3. Check every track joint and see that any complex wiring is correct according to the "rules" and diagrams in Chapter 5.
	4. If the locomotive does not run on a terminal track you know is getting power, and you have preformed every other troubleshooting check, the problem is likely to be the locomotive. Try another locomotive as a double-check; if it does run, the fault lies in the first locomotive.	4. Have locomotive checked by your dealer's service department.
Locomotive runs but in a series of jerks and stops.	1. Dirty track or locomotive wheels, or, on some steam locomotives, dirty truck-pivot area.	1. Clean everything as outlined.
	2. Loose wire connections or loose rail joiners.	2. Check EVERY one in the areas behind and in front of places where the locomotive stalls, and check the terminal track and the power packed wires.
	3. Lack of lubrication on the locomotive (but this is highly unlikely).	3. Lubricate as outlined in this chapter.
	4. Worn motor brushes.	4. Replace.

most likely a blade of grass or leaves or bugs that have been caught on the locomotive wheels, drivers, or LGB's pickup shoes. Some cleaning fluids and wind-borne fertilizer fluids or weed-control liquids can form nonconductive films on the rails. Even alcohol can create a nonconductive film on some brass rail. If the trains run slower and slower, suspect dirty track and drivers or wheels first. The "Probable Cause of Trouble" column in the chart (Fig. 12-14) includes a list of the possibilities in order of most frequent first, so run down the list after you've checked for clean track. The chart applies to potential problems on either indoor or outdoor model railroads.

Chapter 13

‖‖‖

Locomotive Performance Reports

WHENEVER ONE of us model railroaders sees a new locomotive, one of the first questions that comes to mind is "How does it run?" We can see how it looks and we can judge if its price is within our budget, but we really don't know the dynamics of the model until we get it home and onto our track. I've gathered as many different locomotives as I could find to include in this book so you can see how they look. Your local hobby dealer or toy store will tell you how much they cost (because prices fluctuate, any prices I would give here would not be accurate by the time you read them). I can, with the help of Robert Higgins, give you an idea of how some of the most popular locomotives run.

The Test Procedure

Robert Higgins developed a locomotive test program for the National Model Railroad Association (NMRA)

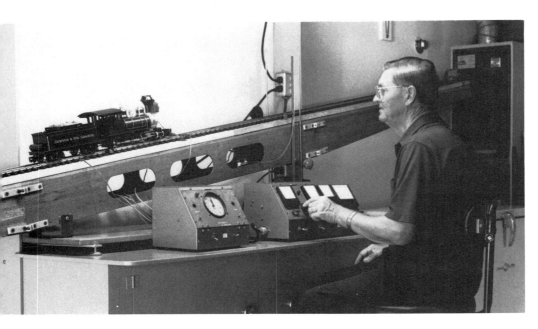

Fig. 13-1 *Robert Higgins built this 12-foot-long locomotive test rig in the 1960s.* Photo by Robert Higgins.

back in the 1960s. The NMRA holds annual conventions and some members wanted to build their own drive systems for their locomotives or fine-tune and improve factory mechanisms that could be entered in performance contests at these conventions. Bob established the basic standards for performance and built a portable 12-foot-long test track of milled stainless steel with a hardwood support. The rig looks like a giant teeter-totter and, in a way, that's how it works: One end can be elevated to make an uphill grade of any slope from 0 to 50 percent.

Bob modified the rig for testing gauge 1 locomotives by installing sections of LGB's number 1061 1,200-millimeter ($47\frac{1}{4}$ inch)-long straight track. The testing procedure also uses a pair of photoelectric cells at the ends of a 2-foot-long timing section at the end of the track. An electric timer records the time it takes for the locomotive to pass between those cells, and Bob converts that time into hours, then divides the hours by $\frac{1}{22.5}$, $\frac{1}{24}$, $\frac{1}{29}$, or $\frac{1}{32}$ (to match the scale of the model) to determine scale miles per hour that is accurate to within about $\frac{1}{10}$ mile an hour.

The test circuit is powered by the LGB's number 5000 14-volt transformer with a voltmeter, ohmeter, and ammeter in the circuit. Usually, Bob uses a special 12-volt power supply, but many of the gauge 1 locomotives need a full 14 volts to achieve maximum pulling power. Bob began publishing the results of his locomotive tests in the *NMRA Bulletin* and continued to publish those reports into the late 1970s. He still does an article every few years for the *NMRA Bulletin*, but his test reports have appeared every month in *Railmodel Journal* (which I edit) since the first issue in June 1989. Most of his monthly reports cover N, HO, O, or S scale locomotives, but he averages about five gauge 1 locomotive reports a year. Bob no longer attends NMRA conventions, but there is a second test rig that appears at some national events.

Minimum Speed Performance

For most model railroaders, one of the most critical aspects of locomotive performance is how slow the locomotive will operate. This makes it easier to per-

Fig. 13-2   Gauge 1 Locomotive Performance

Robert Higgins's reports, in Railmodel Journal, *measure the basic performance of a locomotive so you can compare one model to another to determine which one best meets the needs of your railroad.*

Model Manufacturer	Prototype Locomotive	Minimum Speed (over LGB no. 1200 turnout in smph)	Maximum Speed (smph)	Maximum Pulling Power (ounces)	Magazine Cover Date
Diesels					
Aristo-Craft	ALCO FA-1	3.79	68.2	15.25	July 1990
LGB	ALCO DL-535E	2.67	48.0	27.01	April 1990
Lionel	EMD GP7	0.38	55.6	14.74	May 1991
Steam Locomotives					
Aristo-Craft	0-4-0	0.94	72.7	12.13	February 1992
Aristo-Craft	0-4-0T	0.94	72.7	16.83	February 1992
Aristo-Craft	4-6-2	1.15	51.9	28.08	October 1991
Bachmann	4-6-0 (radio-controlled)	0.55	25.2	28.81	June 1989
Bachmann	4-6-0 (track-powered)	5.50	38.4	11.23	October 1990
Delton	2-8-0	0.12	40.9	17.0	December 1989
LGB	2-6-0	2.65	54.8	22.45	December 1991
Lionel	0-4-0T	0.12	54.5	9.6	October 1989
Kalamazoo	0-4-0T	0.48	50.1	13.57	January 1991
Kalamazoo	4-4-0	0.82	67.1	13.18	January 1991

Note: smph indicates scale miles per hour.

Fig. 13-3 *Aristo-Craft's FA-1 in one of many optional paint schemes.* Photo by Robert Higgins.

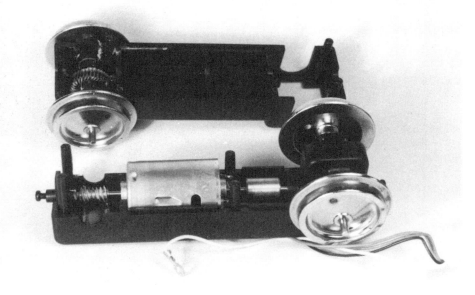

Fig. 13-4 *The trucks for the Aristo-Craft diesels include the motor and gears.* Photo by Robert Higgins.

Fig. 13-5 *The motors for the LGB White Pass Alco DL-535E are in the trucks.* Photo by Robert Higgins.

form switching maneuvers like those illustrated in Chapter 15. Modelers realized that real locomotives are far more likely to be seen traveling 2 miles an hour than 82. Bob has always tested the slow-speed performance of locomotives, but I wanted to add another factor: Does the slowly creeping locomotive stall when it rattles over a turnout? Hence, an LGB number 1200 right-hand turnout has been added to the testing. Bob uses an appropriate Atlas N or HO scale turnout and a Roco turnout for O scale test reports.

The slow-speed tests provide two answers: how slow the locomotive will move without lurching and whether the electrical pickup system is designed so

Fig. 13-6 *Lionel's 1/32 scale EMD GP7 includes digital sound.*

Fig. 13-7 *The motors in Lionel's GP7 and GP9 are also in the trucks.*

Fig. 13-8 *Aristo-Craft's 0-4-OT is a model of a real Pennsylvania Railroad locomotive.* Photo by Robert Higgins.

Fig. 13-9 *The motors for the 0-4-OT and the 0-4-0 lie behind the drivers.* Photo by Robert Higgins.

Fig. 13-10 *When the tender is added to the Aristo-Craft 0-4-0 locomotive, the coal bunker is removed.* Photo by Robert Higgins.

Fig. 13-11 *The Aristo-Craft 4-6-2 on the test fixture.* Photo by Robert Higgins.

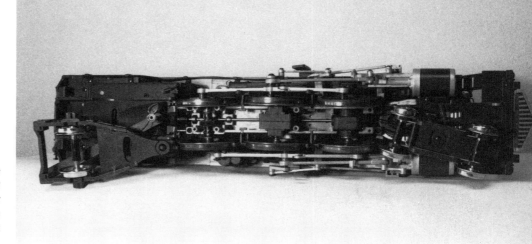

Fig. 13-12 *Each of the three axles in the Aristo-Craft 4-6-2 has its own enclosed gearbox (here the cover is removed from number 3).* Photo by Robert Higgins.

the locomotive will not stall when it bounces through a turnout. That usually means that both the drivers and the tender wheels on a steam locomotive must pick up power and, on a diesel, at least eight wheels must pick up power. The little four-wheeled 0-4-0T steam locomotives without tenders should not fare well in this test, but the designers have found ways of allowing the driver axles to move enough so each of the four drivers is in contact with the track.

Every locomotive Bob tests is disassembled and inspected to be certain it has proper lubrication (and not too much of it) and that there are no burrs or rough spots on any of the moving parts. These results may not, then, be what you could achieve with an out-

of-the-box locomotive. Most modelers who use gauge 1 equipment, however, take the time to maintain their locomotives. Often, a well-broken-in locomotive will run even better than the ones Bob tests.

These are most certainly not tests you can duplicate at home. In fact, the locomotives may run even slower and smoother on your own track or they may have higher or lower top speeds or they may pull more or less cars than the ones Bob tests. The figures here are really meant for comparison with one another. On the chart (Fig. 13-2) you can see, for example, that a Bachmann 4-6-0 has a somewhat higher slow speed than the other locomotives. Do not, however, take those slow speeds as something like an

Olympics score; any locomotive that will creep along at 3 scale miles per hour (5 mph) or less is going about as slow as you can watch it travel. If slow speed is important to you, then you might want to take some special care in cleaning the Aristo-Craft FA-1 or the Bachmann 4-6-0 and removing any burrs or rough spots so the bare models roll smoothly. Apply just a trace of grease and break them in by running for three or four 4-hour sessions before applying fresh lubrication. You can make these models operate more smoothly at slow speeds with careful tuning.

Maximum Speed Tests

These large-scale models have far more realistic maximum speeds, as a group, than a similar assortment of HO or N scale locomotives. The top speed of full-sized diesel locomotives can be altered by changing the gearing and the range of top speeds is well within the speeds exhibited by all three of the diesels on the chart. Most of the steam locomotives have a top speed comparable to the prototype they represent. The 4-4-0 prototype for the Kalamazoo model was supposed to exceed 60 miles per hour (mph), especially in passenger service. The Aristo-Craft 0-4-0 and 0-4-0T run about twice as fast as the real ones, and it's doubtful that many Colorado & Southern Moguls, like LGB's model, ever exceeded 40 mph.

The locomotives with overly high maximum speeds can certainly be operated at half-throttle to keep their speeds within the range of the real thing. The disadvantage, to the modeler, is that it will be more difficult to adjust their speed smoothly when

Fig. 13-13 *The Bachmann 4-6-0 is one of the least expensive gauge 1 locomotives.* Photo by Robert Higgins.

Fig. 13-14 *The Delton 2-8-0 is a 1/24 scale replica of the Rio Grande C-16 class.* Photo by Robert Higgins.

Fig. 13-15 *A vertical motor drives the third axle on the Delton 2-8-0 and the side rods carry the power to the other drivers.* Photo by Robert Higgins.

Fig. 13-16 *The Lionel 0-4-0T is offered in a variety of paint schemes.*

Fig. 13-17 *A heavy weight fills the boiler on the Lionel 0-4-0T. The motor and gears are enclosed in a plastic case behind the drivers.*

only half the throttle can be used. The throttle response is also a measure of how easy the locomotive is to control.

Maximum Pulling Power

What you really want to know is how many cars it will pull. But which brand of cars? Around how tight a curve or through what series of S-curves? Up how steep a grade? With how clean a set of rails? Again, these pulling power numbers should be considered just that—*numbers*. Compare one locomotive's number to another to see which will pull more. Most of

you have at least one of these locomotives, and you already know how much it will pull around your layout (and how slow and how fast it will go and how it responds to the throttle). If your LGB Mogul will pull eight cars around your layout, a Bachmann ten-wheeler should pull about half that many, or four cars. This should be no surprise, because the Bachmann model is far lighter and has a less powerful motor. Do not be misled by the high pulling power of the radio-controlled Bachmann 4-6-0; it had especially sticky traction tires, and because of its unusual drive and control system, it provided an unrealistic

Fig. 13-18 *The Kalamazoo 0-4-OT is a free-lance design based on some small logging locomotives and switchers of the 1880 era.* Photo by Robert Higgins.

Fig. 13-19 *The Kalamazoo 4-4-0 has the trim lines of many 1880s era locomotives.* Photo by Robert Higgins.

result. In the real world, the radio-controlled Bachmann 4-6-0 only pulls a bit less than the later track-powered versions.

Bob uses the inclined test fixture to obtain these pulling power figures. He tilts the test fixture at about an 8 precent grade to see if the locomotive will climb that steep a grade. He raises the ramp a degree at a time until the locomotive will no longer start on that steep a slope. He then backs the angle down a degree, or more if needed, until he determines exactly how steep a grade the locomotive alone will climb. Because he knows the rolling resistance and the slope, he can compute how many ounces a locomotive will pull. The effect is about the same as you could record with the locomotive pushing against a postal scale laid sideways on the track. These numbers, though, are extremely accurate and the tests can be repeated with predictable results. Locomotives Bob tested back in 1969 or 1989 can be compared with locomotives tested in 1991 or later. Notice that the ounces are pulling power, not the weight of the cars that will be pulled.

These test results are intended to give you some idea of how a locomotive you might want to buy performs as compared with a locomotive you already own. They are not meant to be a comparison or rating chart. If you are, for example, unhappy with the throttle response of one of your locomotives, you might compare the top speed to others. If your locomotive has a relatively low top speed, then you might consider a new throttle or power pack for better response instead of a new locomotive.

Chapter 14

▚▚

Painting and Lettering Rolling Stock

MOST OF us just call them cars but the railroaders call them "rolling stock" to avoid excluding cabooses or passenger cars. The vast majority of locomotives and rolling stock for gauge 1 layouts is sold virtually ready-built. Some brands include loose ladders and doors that the modeler must install, but the basic car body is painted and ready to go.

Recently, Bachmann began to offer their rolling stock in unpainted kits instead of assembled and painted. The modeler can save a bit, depending on where he or she buys the kits or the ready-builts, and be able to paint and letter the car in some paint scheme that that is not available ready painted. Simpson (available through Walthers) and Rara Avis offer precut wood kits to build a variety of reefers, boxcars, gondolas, flatcars, and log cars. The kits include metal fittings and trucks. Other firms advertise limited production runs of similar kits in *Garden Railways* magazine.

Scale-Model Freight Cars

The concept of scale is explained in Chapter 1, but here is an opportunity for you to see the difference in some specific freight cars. The train of Colorado & Southern equipment includes both 1/24 and 1/22.5 scale models, but any variation in size you might perceive could easily have been apparent in a real train of similar equipment. There are no standard heights, lengths, or widths for narrow gauge cars and only the width of about 10 feet is standard for stan-

dard gauge cars. The width of narrow gauge boxcars ranged from 6 feet 2 inches to 7 feet 9 inches.

The National Model Railroad Association's *Data Book*, described in Chapter 10 for its use in bridge and right-of-way information, also has a sheet that compares all the dimensions of twelve once-common narrow gauge boxcars, including four different Rio Grande cars; and cars from the Colorado Central; Denver, South Park & Pacific; Rio Grande Southern; Florence & Cripple Creek; East Broad Top; East Tennessee & Western North Carolina; and two Colorado & Southern cars. The car lengths varied between 22 feet, 1 inch (for the early Rio Grande cars) and 37 feet (for the ET&WNCRR cars). Car heights from rail to running board ranged from 8 feet, 11 inches to about 11 feet, 6 inches for the same two cars; 10 feet is close to the average height.

The dimensions for the car I feel is closest to the prototype for the LGB model—the Denver & Rio Grande Western number series 4000 through 4099—and to the Delton model—the Denver & Rio Grande Western number series 3000 through 3749—are shown on the chart. Because I am using one of the Delton cars (from Depot G Hobbies) to represent the Colorado & Southern number series 8293 through 8417, I've included the dimensions of that car for comparison in the chart (Fig. 14-3). Notice that the LGB and Bachmann cars which are sold as 1/22.5 scale models can fit nicely as 1/24 scale cars even though their dimensions increase effectively when

Fig. 14-1 *Different brands and scales do mix with gauge 1 models.*

Fig. 14-2 *CDS sells dry transfers to back date rolling stock to match the bright paint schemes on some LGB Moguls.*

Fig. 14-3   1/22.5, 1/24, and 1/1 Narrow Gauge Boxcars
A comparison of the sizes of Bachmann, LGB, and Delton models, if each was measured with a 1/24 scale and a 1/22.5 scale ruler. Willow Works offers a stainless steel ruler marked with feet and inches for 1/32, 1/24, 1/22.5 and 1/1 (full-sized).

Model Manufacturer	Body Length	Height to Running Board	Body Width
Dimensions of Real-Life Boxcar at 1/24 Scale			
Bachmann	30 feet, 7 inches	10 feet, 7 inches	7 feet, 9 inches
Delton	29 feet, 8 inches	11 feet, 2 inches	7 feet, 7 inches
LGB	29 feet, 0 inches	11 feet, 2 inches	8 feet, 0 inches
Dimensions of Real-Life Boxcar at 1/22.5 Scale			
Bachmann	28 feet, 7 inches	9 feet, 9 inches	7 feet, 4 inches
Delton	27 feet, 2 inches	10 feet, 6 inches	7 feet, 1 inch
LGB	27 feet, 1 inch	10 feet, 6 inches	7 feet, 6 inches
Dimensions of Real-Life Boxcars at 1/1 Scale			
Denver & Rio Grande Western Railroad (numbers 4000–4099)	27 feet, 6 inches	10 feet, 8 inches	7 feet, 4 inches
Denver & Rio Grande Western Railroad (numbers 3000–3749)	30 feet, 0 inches	10 feet, 5 inches	7 feet, 9 inches
Colorado & Southern Railroad (numbers 8293–8417)	30 feet, 0 inches	10 feet, 1 inch	7 feet, 1 inch

Fig. 14-4 *The Delton reefer is available in C&S markings from Depot G Hobbies.*

compared with other 1/24 scale models. Conversely, the Delton 1/24 scale cars can fit nicely within the sizes of 1/22.5 scale equipment.

If you want to build accurate models of Colorado & Southern cars to match your LGB Mogul, you can obtain plans for most of them in old issues of the *Narrow Gauge and Short Line Gazette* with the LGB number 6 Mogul itself (complete with bear trap stack) in the March–April 1978 issue. No two Colorado & Southern four-wheel cabooses were the same and plans for most of them appeared in the March–April 1985 issue. Plans for the reefer appeared in the July–August 1982 issue; the boxcars, in the September–October 1980 issue; the gondolas, in the January–February 1984 issue; the stock cars, in the November–December 1987 issue, and the baggage/coach combine, in the March–April 1988 issue. The stock car and boxcar also were used on the Rio Grand Southern, and those plans appear with the Colorado & Southern cars. You may have to search for back issues or contact advertisers selling copies in current issues. Photographs of nearly all the Colorado & Southern freight cars appear in Volume 8 of Robert Grant's *Narrow Gauge Pictorial Series* (published by R. Robb Limited, P.O. Box 649, Union City, CA 94587). Volume 6 includes photographs of the Colorado & Southern narrow gauge locomotives.

Standard Gauge Cars

The models produced by Lionel, Aristo-Craft, USA Trains, and MDC are reproductions of standard gauge rolling stock. LGB has added a model of a standard gauge boxcar to its line as part number 4091, painted in Rio Grande orange and silver. There are photo-graphs (Figs. 1-7 and 1-8) of the car in Chapter 1. Aristo-Craft specifies that their models are 1/29 scale and MDC specifies that theirs are 1/32, but neither LGB nor USA Trains specifies a scale. All operate on gauge 1 track. All these cars, including the reefers from Lionel, MDC, Aristo-Craft, and USA Trains are based on real cars that are 40 feet long over the ends.

Because the size of the models varies considerably, you might want to know how they compare. In Figure 14-6, I've listed the actual measurements of each model, rather than scale feet and inches as in Figure 14-3. The LGB boxcar appears in both charts (Figs. 14-3 and 14-6) to give you a comparison. The dimensions for the full-sized car were taken from a Pullman-Standard 40-foot boxcar with a 10-foot, 5⅜-inch interior height, in the 1957 *Car Builders' Cyclopedia* (published by Simmons-Boardman, now out of print). This was the standard car from about 1953 until the 50-foot and longer cars replaced it in the 1970s.

Three things stand out from Fig. 14-6: First, the Aristo-Craft car really is a pretty accurate 1/29 scale model; second, LGB's car is very close to the same scale as the Aristo-Craft car; and third, there really are no accurate 1/32 scale models although Lionel's would be if it were about ½ inch narrower. MDC's car, however, could be a reasonable stand-in for some of the 40-foot boxcars and reefers built in the early 1930s, which were about a foot shorter than the Pullman-Standard car. The real railroads' standard-gauge cars did vary that much in their height, so the MDC car could represent a "low" car and the Lionel car a "high" car.

Frankly, most modelers are not going to care if the

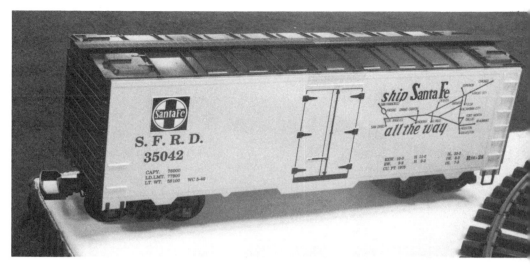

Fig. 14-5 *MDC has both reefers and boxcars in 1/32 scale.*

Fig. 14-6 *Standard Gauge Boxcar and Reefer Sizes (in Inches)*

Manufacturer	Body Length	Body Width	Overall Height
Full-Size Car	40 feet, $8\frac{1}{8}$	9 feet, $9\frac{5}{8}$	14 feet, $10\frac{9}{32}$
Exact 1/29 scale	$16\frac{3}{4}$	$4\frac{1}{32}$	$6\frac{3}{32}$
Exact 1/32 scale	$15\frac{3}{8}$	$3\frac{3}{4}$	$6\frac{3}{32}$
LGB (number 4091; no scale noted)	$16\frac{5}{8}$	$4\frac{1}{4}$	$6\frac{1}{4}$
Aristo-Craft (1/29 scale)	$16\frac{7}{8}$	$4\frac{1}{8}$	$6\frac{7}{16}$
Lionel (1/29 scale)	$14\frac{5}{8}$	4	$6\frac{5}{32}$
MDC (1/32 scale)	$14\frac{1}{8}$	$3\frac{7}{8}$	$5\frac{1}{4}$
LGB's simulated wood 1/22.5 scale boxcar (number 4067)	$14\frac{1}{2}$	4	$5\frac{5}{8}$

boxcar is a replica of any particular car. Most, in fact, will operate a mixture of replicas of narrow gauge cars with standard gauge cars becauuse they all roll on the same track. Remember, the narrow gauge models are built to a larger scale (1/22.5 or 1/24) than the 1/29 or 1/32 scale cars. Just for comparison, I've included LGB's model of a narrow gauge boxcar in 1/22.5 scale (in Fig. 14-3). That LGB model is very close, indeed, to being a standard gauge 1/32 scale model, except for the door, which is about a scale foot too wide to represent an accurate standard gauge car. For most of us, Fig. 14-3 simply proves that you can operate any of these cars with any others and there will not be much of a visual difference. Also, if you want an accurate 1/32 or 1/29 scale standard gauge train, the models are there, as are the models in Fig. 14-3 to recreate an accurate 1/24 or 1/22.5 scale narrow gauge train.

Painting Railroad Models

There is no accurate model of the Colorado & Southern gondola to match the LGB locomotive and Depot G boxcar and caboose. D.A.N. makes a high-side gondola, but the lettering is too simple for an accurate reproduction. Bachmann has a car similar to the real Colorado & Southern gondola in most dimensions but the two center side posts should be a bit closer. I decided the Bachmann car was close enough to the prototype.

First, disassemble the car so you don't paint the trucks and grab irons (see Figs. 14-8 through 14-16 for the complete sequence). These are usually made from a slippery and flexible plastic that won't hold paint well so it's wise to avoid later paint peeling by just not painting them in the first place. A single screw holds each truck and coupler unit and four screws retain the body. On this car, I decided to gamble on

Fig. 14-7 *D.A.N. offers 1/22.5 scale narrow gauge cars, including this gondola.*

Fig. 14-8 *The Bachmann 1/22.5 scale gondola before repainting and lettering.*

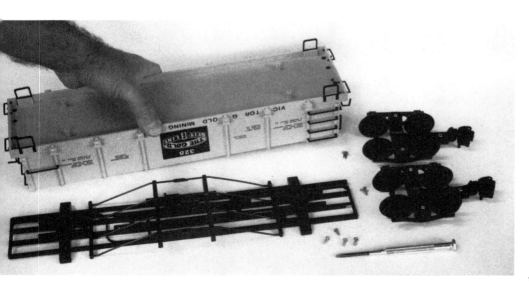

Fig. 14-9 *Remove six screws to free the trucks and frame from Bachmann's model.*

The Large-Scale Model Railroading Handbook

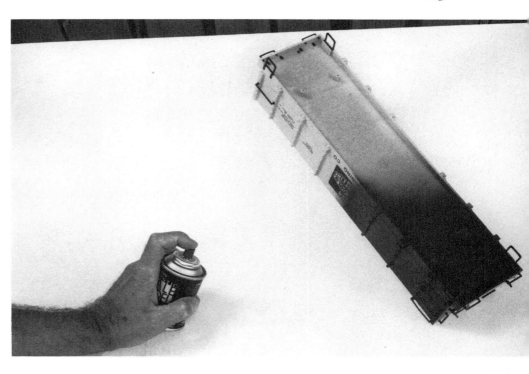

Fig. 14-10 *Wash the model in detergent and let it dry. Then paint with an aerosol, moving the model back and forth under the spray pattern.*

painting the grab irons with the theory that the real ones would have had peeled paint, so it didn't matter if mine did peel.

The plastic used for these cars is tough enough so that most spray paints will not attack it. I could not find a brown I liked in hardware store aerosols so I used a flat finish (no gloss) Pactra military enamel called Dark Earth. Gloss paints are fine for this application and decals will actually adhere better to a shiny surface than a dull one. Spray the finished car with clear flat to hide the decal shine later.

Applying Decal Lettering

I used Walthers's decals but Micro Scale, Robert Dustin, Old and Weary Car Shops, and William McIntyre make decals for these models. CDS also makes fine dry-transfer or rub-on lettering in 1/24 scale. When using decals, begin by cutting each decal from the sheet. Use tweezers to dip the decal into a cup of warm water for about 10 seconds. Set the decal on a paper towel for about a minute or two while the water soaks through the paper backing to dissolve the glue behind the decal. You can try moving the decal on the paper and, when it's free, pick up both decal and paper with tweezers.

Moisten the area that will be beneath the decal with decal-softening fluid like Walthers's Solvaset or Micro Scale's Micro Sol. Position the decal and its paper backing precisely where you want the decal. Hold the decal lightly in place with a fingertip wetted with water while you slide the paper backing from beneath the decal.

Flood the surface of the decal with the decal-softening fluid. You can use a small paintbrush both to apply the fluid and to move the decal into perfect alignment. Repeat the process with all the decals on one side or end of the car and let it dry overnight. Apply the decals to the opposite side or end of the car and let it dry overnight. When the fluid is dry, gently scrub the surface of the car with a paper towel or cotton swab and water to remove the residue from the glue behind the decal. Let that dry overnight.

Finish the model by spraying the entire surface with a light layer of Testors's Dullcote (hobby shops and some hardware stores sell it). This fluid dries clear and leaves a flat, no-gloss finish that makes the decal shine match that of the rest of the car so the decal appears as though it were printed or painted right on the car.

Applying Rub-On Lettering

"Dry transfers," the modeler's term for rub-on lettering, also should be cut into individual groups or letters. Cut each letter from the sheet that will fit between the ribs of the gondola so the sheet does not need to be bent around the ribs. Cut close to the

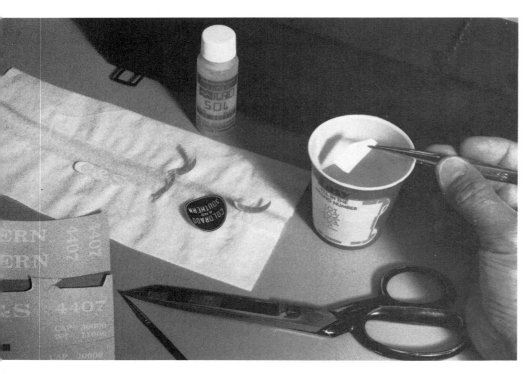

Fig. 14-11 *Cut the decals near the colors, then dip them briefly in water.*

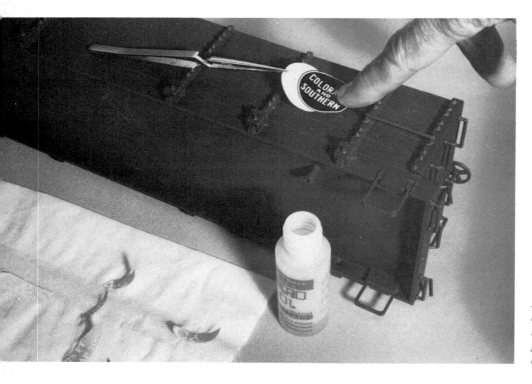

Fig. 14-12 *Coat the side with decal-softening fluid, then position the decal with a wetted finger and slide the paper from beneath it with tweezers.*

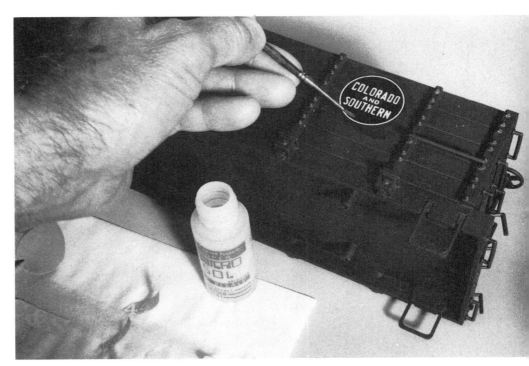

Fig. 14-13 *Cover the decal with several coats of decal softening fluid.*

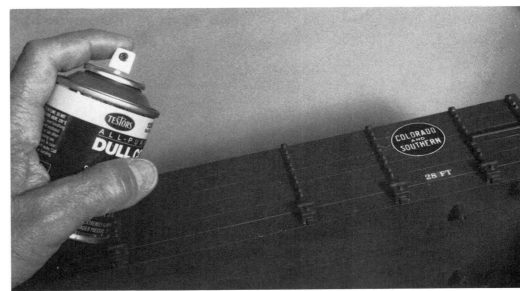

Fig. 14-14 *Spray the finished car with a light coat of Testors' Dullcote.*

Fig. 14-15 *The finished model is about an 85-percent-accurate replica of a Colorado & Southern car, and it fits in nicely with the Delton cars.*

Fig. 14-16 CDS offers dry transfers. Cut the letters apart close to their outline and tape each set of lettering in the precise position before rubbing over the face of the plastic covering with a soft pencil.

letters, too, so the clear surface doesn't touch adjacent grab irons or other raised details. Position the dry transfers exactly where you want them and tape the top edge in place with drafting tape (it's not as sticky as masking tape and so won't lift the paint). Get it precisely right because you cannot move it. Rub firmly over the plastic covering with a slightly dulled number 2 pencil or with one of the special burnishing tools sold by drafting supply stores. Rub right and left, then up and down. Gently peel back the clear plastic and peer beneath it to see if any of the lettering is still stuck to the clear plastic. Thanks to that drafting tape "hinge" you can put the plastic back down and finish rubbing over any areas that did not stick the first time.

When all the lettering is in place, place the paper backing sheet over each lettered area and rub over the paper to burnish the letters firmly into the surface. If you have trouble with a decal or a dry transfer over a large rivet, wet a fingertip and use that to push the decal tightly over the rivet. If the decals or dry transfers cross deep panel lines, use a new hobby knife blade, guided by a steel ruler, to slice through the decal or dry transfer and cover the dry transfer with the paper and burnish it into the edges of the panel lines with the pencil tip. Finally, spray the entire surface with Testors's Dullcote to protect the dry transfers. CDS is the only firm that makes a range

of dry transfers, but they do offer them for nearly all the narrow gauge railroads.

A Colorado & Southern Caboose Kit Conversion

It's ironic that there is no caboose to match the LGB Mogul. Delton did announce production of a four-wheel caboose, but the model has not yet entered production. The Colorado & Southern (C&S) did have a center cupola caboose, numbered 1002, that is similar to the LGB number 4065 with, of course, C&S lettering. The cupola on the number 1002 was about three-fourths the length and height of the LGB cupola. Most of the Colorado & Southern cabooses had offset cupolas like number 1009, which survives at the Colorado Railroad Museum. Numbers 1000 and 1003 were nearly identical to number 1009 but had a facia strip along the top of the side walls. Numbers 1005, 1006, and 1008 were about 10 percent smaller.

The LGB number 4065 is within a scale 6 inches of being an accurate model of the 1009 except for the size and location of the cupola. I decided I could live with the size and simply cut the roof to allow the cupola section to be moved to the rear of the wall. The job is really simple because the roof snaps off the LGB caboose. Use a razor saw for cuts and make the first one in line with the outer wall of the cupola, opposite the smokestack. Make the second

Fig. 14-17 *All but one of the Colorado & Southern cabooses looked like number 1009. Modify an LGB center cupola caboose to complement the LGB Mogul.* Photo from the Hal Wagner collection.

Fig. 14-18 *Cut the roof across the edge of the cupola and then across the opposite end to leave three pieces. Reassemble them as shown. The pencil points to the second seam, already cemented.*

Fig. 14-19 *Enlarge the windows on one end of the sides and install a Grandt Line window with a modified mullion.*

Fig. 14-20 *Fill the remaining two windows, one on each side, with pieces of Evergreen Scale Models' styrene.*

Fig. 14-21 *Paint the model caboose red or Boxcar Red and apply CDS dry transfers.*

cut in line with the two interior tabs of the roof that hold it in place. With the roof in three pieces, simply turn the cupola section end-for-end and the cupola will move from the center to the end of the car as shown. Use 5-minute epoxy to cement the three roof sections and the three matching running board sections together.

Use a small square file to enlarge one of the side windows to match the Grandt Line O scale number 3725 window. Modify the window by cutting the mullions out with a sharp hobby knife and cementing one back in as shown Fig. 14-19. Fill the face of the remaining LGB window with a piece of Evergreen-brand number 4150 styrene plastic Novelty Siding that just happens to match the boards on the LGB body. Attach the filler with epoxy and use a knife-edged jeweler's file to blend the grooves on the filler piece into the grooves on the side.

The strange bars between the wheels can be cut away to make the chassis seem more American and the two European buffers cut from the ends with a razor saw. Short Line Foundry's number 350 brake cylinder is similar to the C&S cylinder. Attach it to the underframe below the car number on the right side of the car. Kadee's smaller gauge 1 couplers would look even better than these number 835 Kadee G-Gauge couplers. Finish the model in bright caboose red paint to match the car at the Colorado Railroad Museum or use a more accurate Box Car Red and CDS number 24-223 dry transfers. CDS offers both the modern Colorado & Southern round herald and the block-style large *C&S*. I lettered one side of a Delton boxcar and reefer and one side of the Bachmann gondola with the old style CDS lettering and one side of each of the cars with lettering to match the caboose. Photographs taken as late as the early 1940s show some of the earlier block-style lettering although the cars were officially repainted with round heralds in 1928.

Chapter 15

Operating a Real Railroad

THE FRUSTRATING thing about writing a book on large-scale railroads is that I cannot show you the best the hobby has to offer. I have certainly found what I believe to be the best indoor and outdoor model railroads in the country and the photographs do, I hope, convey some of the breathtaking beauty and, in some cases, realism. The best this hobby has to offer, however, is the action. As nice as these scenes look in two dimensions, they are only flat images compared with actually being there. First, the scene itself literally comes alive with every breeze or every subtle movement of your eyes. It's the motion of the trains through those scenes, though, that make them so indescribable. The best image I can convey is for you to imagine your surprise at actually seeing an elf dancing through a garden; that's what these trains look like in motion. The sight is beyond realistic, it's a dream come true.

Garden Railroads in Action

If you are a model railroader, you will undoubtedly have plans to operate your garden railroad in a manner similar to that developed by other model railroaders for their indoor layouts. Anything you can do indoors, you can duplicate outdoors. If you really do want 100-car trains, however, you had best have at least an acre of land and lots of money. The sheer size and bulk of these trains dictates relatively short trains and, compared to garage or basement-sized model railroads built with HO or N scale equipment, a relatively compact track plan. The trackwork, locomotives, and rolling stock are available, ready to run, in gauge 1 to duplicate anything you might imagine for an indoor HO or N scale layout.

You may, however, discover that your intentions of operating an outdoor layout like it was a real railroad change after you actually build your first garden railroad. The simple sight of a single track and train meandering through the world you have created, perhaps to meet or pass one or two other trains along the way, is positively captivating. These railroads are *Real*! You no longer have to imagine that there is a "real world" outside your basement or garage. An outdoor railroad is part of that real world. Somehow, many of the tricks that have been developed for indoor railroads to make them seem more real are not necessary with a garden railroad. It is no longer necessary to pretend that the track going into the tunnel really leads to San Francisco or Atlanta or some other real-world place because your trains are already running in the real world.

Many model railroaders have explained to me that they would rather watch their garden railroads amble through the landscape than be in the basement or garage imagining that their HO or N scale trains are in the real world. The lesson is that simple trackwork with the barest number of passing sidings and only a few industrial tracks is more than enough to keep you mesmerized with an outdoor layout. Most of us can forget the twenty-track freight yards and roundhouses and tracks that loop back over themselves six times within a 3-by-3-foot area. I understand that there is a large following for that complex kind of layout in Europe, and there are plenty of track plans and photographs of such layouts in the *LGB Track Planning & Technical Guidebook* but, so far, I have yet to see one of these European-style layouts in the United States. If you want one, buy the LGB book from an LGB dealer and build one; the track and trains are waiting.

Automatic Coupling and Uncoupling

These large-scale trains are allowing modelers to fulfill dreams they may have worked on with a basement railroad for years. The gauge 1 trains are almost realistic by definition because they are so large. The installation of track and roadbed—and the adaptation of Mother Nature's work to the smaller scale, while still leaving her in charge—is explained in the previous chapters. Some garden railroad operators are content just to watch the trains run. Turnouts are needed only to allow one train to park while another takes its place or as places for two trains to pass. After a time you may want to direct the trains to move in a manner that duplicates the movement of a real train instead of just a forward path through the world. However real these scenes may be, the trains do pass the same place a lot more often than real ones do. Adding some back and forth movements to train operations will break up the trips. Follow all the suggestions in this chapter and those places the trains pass will seem even more a part of the railroad.

Virtually every car and locomotive in this book is supplied with at least one type of automatic coupler. The LGB, USA Trains, Great Trains, and Kalamazoo cars and locomotives and MDC's cars are equipped with a book-and-loop-style coupler that is very similar to a brass coupler that was the most common HO scale coupler in the 1940 to 1960 period (made by Mantua). All of the modelers whose layouts appear in this book have replaced those couplers with one of the knuckle-type couplers that match the shape of a real railroad coupler. Aristo-Craft, Lionel, Bachmann, Delton, and D.A.N. cars and locomotives are all supplied with knuckle-style couplers. Some of these also include a loop-style coupler that can be installed if you want to couple their equipment to LGB's standard coupler. LGB and MDC sell the loop-style couplers if you need them.

The standard coupler for model railroaders who actually perform switching operations is made by Kadee. The Kadee coupler has the shape and opening knuckle of a real coupler, but it also has a bent metal wire extending almost to track level below the coupler. This wire vaguely resembles the hanging brake hoses on all real railroad equipment that is fitted with air brakes (everything operated after about 1905). The advantage of the Kadee coupler is that it can be operated by remote control by merely stopping the train with the couplers over a magnet placed between the rails. The magnet is virtually invisible if painted a color similar to the ballast or disguised as a road crossing or a handcar-entry point. The LGB replacement knuckle couplers also can be operated by a

Fig. 15-1 Some of the knuckle-style couplers (l. to r.): Kadee's G-Scale, Bachmann, Aristo-Craft, Lionel, and Delton, with a pair of LGB's number 2019/2 in the foreground.

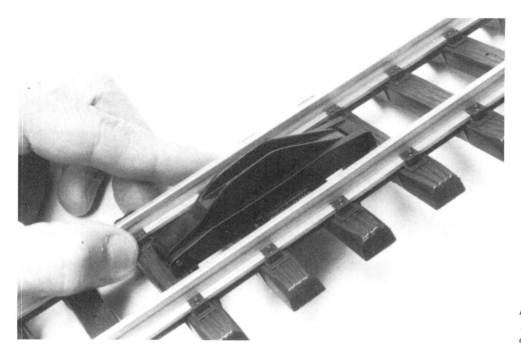

ramp placed between the rails—the same ramp that is used to operate their loop-and-hook couplers. The functional difference between Kadee's and LGB's couplers is that Kadee's can be set to uncouple at the ramp and the car can be pushed anywhere on the layout without the coupler recoupling. You need a ramp everywhere you want to uncouple with the LGB system.

Even though all the knuckle-style couplers look alike, I found that the current Aristo-Craft coupler would not couple automatically with Bachmann, Lionel, or Delton knuckle couplers; however, Aristo-Craft will couple with Kadee and LGB knuckle couplers. The Aristo-Craft coupler will fit inside the Bachmann, Lionel, or Delton coupler, but both couplers must be closed and the couplers lifted up and interlocked by sliding one into the other. With that exception, any coupler on these cars or locomotives will couple automatically by simply pushing two cars or a locomotive together with both couple knuckles open. The trick here is that the coupler knuckles must be open, and that is something you must do by hand by reaching into the coupler and pulling the plastic pin upward.

So far, only the LGB coupler has uncoupling ramp (number 1052) for their knuckle coupler, and it only operates with the LGB knuckle coupler. If you use the standard operating knuckle couplers, the easiest method of coupling and uncoupling is to do precisely what the real railroads do: Stop the train, go to each of the couplers that are to be either coupled or uncoupled, pull the pin (that's a real railroad expression, by the way), and then move the locomotive to couple or uncouple. Some modelers take pride in the need to duplicate that real railroad maneuver.

Magnetic-Action Uncoupling

If you would rather not reach down every time you want a car or locomotive to couple or uncouple, then install either the LGB or the Kadee system. LGB offers a coupler only to fit its equipment, so you may need to do some drilling and trimming to adapt the coupler to other brands. Kadee, because couplers are its business, has made a quick-installation kit for all the popular brands and styles of locomotives and cars. What's more, Kadee makes two sizes of couplers, a G-Scale coupler that is close to the size of the couplers on all the models and a #1-Scale coupler that is about three-fourths the size of the other couplers. The larger coupler will couple with all the others, but the #1-Scale coupler is a bit too small for reliable automatic coupling, although you can force-fit it into most other brands. Even the Kadee #1-Scale coupler is at least twice as large as it should be for a 1/22.5 or 1/24 scale coupler; all the other brands are grossly oversized—one of the few truly toylike aspects of nearly all brands of garden railroad cars and locomotives. If you want a coupler that is nearer to scale and operates, use the Kadee #1-Scale. If you really want just a scale coupler, George Randeall makes a one-piece cast metal coupler without an operating knuckle. Bill Bauer uses them on all his equipment, and his layout is shown in Chapter 2.

Kadee offers the advantages of a coupler that will couple anywhere and, once the train stops to set the couplers over a ramp, that will uncouple anywhere. If you decide on the G-Scale Kadee couplers, they can be changed over gradually, because they will at least couple manually with any of the other knuckle couplers. If you want more realistic appearance, too, then use the #1-Scale Kadee couplers.

On most locomotives and rolling stock, a Kadee coupler can be installed by simply removing the original coupler-attaching screw and putting a Kadee cou-

Fig. 15-3 To install Kadee couplers, remove the stock coupler and purchase a Kadee to match the brand you need from Kadee's chart. This is a number 832 going on an LGB Mogul tender. The Kadee G-Scale couplers are easier to install than the smaller #1-Scale Kadee couplers because Kadee has special mountings for the larger couplers. You may need to use plastic shims and drill a hole to mount the smaller couplers.

Fig. 15-4 Attach the Kadee coupler with the screw provided.

Fig. 15-5 *The Kadee G-Scale coupler is about 10 percent smaller than the couplers furnished with most gauge 1 models, such as this Bachmann gondola.*

Fig. 15-6 *The Kadee #1-Scale coupler (right) and G-Scale coupler mounted on the special coupler-height gauges Kadee sells to ensure correct mounting.*

pler in place of the original. On some installations, the support for the original coupler must be cut short with a pair of diagonal cutters, a razor saw, or a hacksaw. In some rare cases, you may need to drill a single hole in the plastic and use the self-threading screw supplied with the coupler. Kadee has a complete application list of their various couplers to help in your choice. Kadee also has a coupler height or mounting gauge so you can judge correctly if the couplers are the proper height. If the couplers are too low, it may be necessary to bend or file the mount or to use a different coupler from Kadee. If the couplers are too high, the mounting may be bent down or shims added between the coupler and mounting to lower the coupler.

All of the Kadee couplers, from the Z and N scale Micro Trains couplers to the HO and O and G and number 1 size couplers, have a unique "delay" fea-

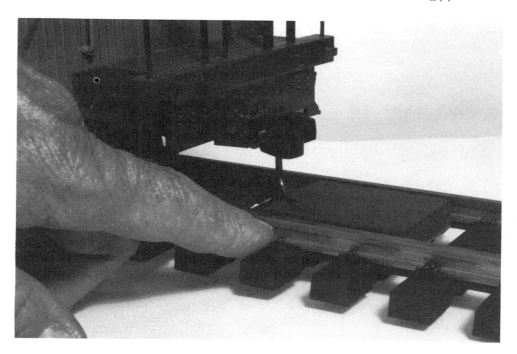

Fig. 15-7 *The Kadee magnetic ramp can be purchased already installed in LGB or Delton track or as a glue-on kit.*

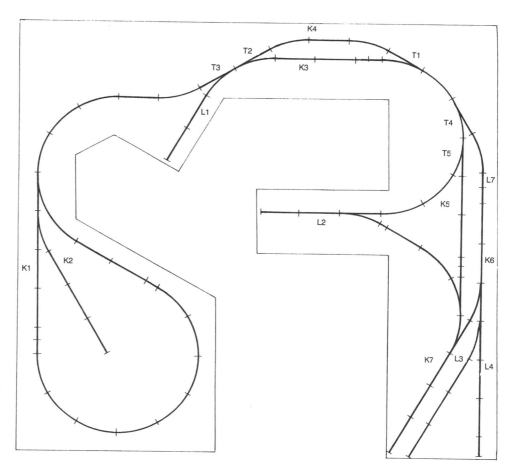

Fig. 15-8 *The letters K1, etc., identify where to install Kadee uncoupling ramps. LGB ramps also would be needed at those locations as well as at the locations marked L1, etc.*

ture. A small lip on the coupler knuckle allows the coupler knuckle to open when the coupler is over one of the Kadee magnetic uncoupling pads or, as modelers call them, "ramps." Once the coupler knuckle is open, the train can back up and the car will be left where it sits. If, however, you want the car to be left somewhere on a siding a few feet or a few hundred feet beyond the ramp, the locomotive can simply shove the car until the car is at its desired location. When the locomotive stops and backs up, the car will remain behind. That little lip prevents the couplers from recoupling until the couplers are actually apart when the locomotive backs away.

Kadee's delayed action uncoupling feature means that only a few ramps are needed to allow cars to be left on sidings anywhere on the layout. The track plan from Fig. 3-26 (Chapter 3) is repeated here to show you where the Kadee ramps need to be located to make this layout completely "hands-off" for both uncoupling and coupling with Kadee couplers. The ramp at K1 is needed so a train can be left by the locomotive while it makes other switching moves after the train arrives by traveling the lower-left reversing loop in a clockwise direction. The ramp at K2 allows cars to be left on that siding or for the locomotive to use both the main line and the siding to rearrange the train. So far, either Kadee or the LGB systems would do just as well.

The actual train movements needed to leave cars at the siding near K3 are shown, step-by-step, later in this chapter. Thanks to the Kadee delayed feature, however, only the ramps at K3, K4, and K5 are needed. With the LGB system, a ramp also would be needed at L1. The Kadee delay feature also allows cars to be left at L3, L4, or K7 by simply stopping the train to open the couplers over a Kadee ramp at K5 or K6. The ramp at K5 is needed for outbound trains traveling counterclockwise around the layout. The Kadee ramp at K7 serves a double-duty, allowing cars to be left at K7 or the locomotive to head into the siding at K7 with the car behind it, stop at the K7 ramp, then back on into siding L2 to leave the car at L2. On this layout, only seven Kadee uncoupling ramps are needed, but if you use LGB couplers ramps will be needed at those seven locations plus four more. The LGB ramps are also one-way, so a pair will be needed at all seven Kadee locations (but one-way LGB ramps will be okay at L1, L2, L3, and L4).

Real Railroad Switching Moves: Spotting a Car

The track configuration in the photographs (Figs. 15-9 through 15-30) duplicates the general shape of the

Fig. 15-9 *You can duplicate any of these switching moves with the couplers that are furnished with any model.*

track plan in this chapter (Fig. 15-8) and in Chapter 2. In the photographs, however, the tight LGB number 1100 curves (from the plan) and number 1200 and 1210 turnouts have been replaced with the larger (approximately 48-inch) radius LGB number 1600 curved track sections and number 1605 and 1615 turnouts. To make these sections fit properly, two number 1008 straight track sections, each 52-millimeters ($5\frac{1}{8}$-inches) long, are needed with one standard number 1000 straight on the siding and four on the main line. Micro Engineering makes a similar array of track sections, as shown in Chapter 3.

If the train's operating crew has orders to leave ("spot" or "drop" are the real railroad terms) a car on the passing siding at K4, the switching moves are simple:

Move 1. The train stops and uncouples from the caboose at K3 to leave the caboose on the main line.

Move 2. The train pulls forward and stops when the reefer has cleared the points of turnout T2. Those points are then thrown to route the trains to the passing siding.

Fig. 15-10 *The beginning of the switching series for spotting a car using a trailing-point switch.*

Fig. 15-11 *Spotting a car, move 1.*

Fig. 15-12 *Spotting a car, move 2.*

Fig. 15-13 *Spotting a car, move 3.*

Fig. 15-14 *Spotting a car, move 4.*

Fig. 15-15 *Spotting a car, move 5.*

Move 3. The train backs into the siding and stops with the reefer at K4. The reefer is uncoupled from the locomotive.

Move 4. The locomotive alone pulls forward until it clears the points of turnout T2. The turnout is then reset for the main line.

Move 5. The locomotive reverses and backs to K3. It stops and the caboose is coupled to the locomotive.

Move 6. The locomotive pulls forward with the caboose to continue its journey around the layout.

The turnout's moving parts—the points—point in the direction the locomotive is moving in this sequence, and real railroaders call it a "trailing-point turnout." The action of dropping a car in a siding fed by a trailing-point turnout is the simplest movement in real or model railroading switching. You can repeat this sequence endlessly to rearrange a train of 5 or 105 cars simply by spotting one or more cars on either track.

Real Railroad Switching Moves: A Facing-Point Turnout

This move is needed when the train crew has orders to pull that gondola at siding L1 (see Fig. 15-8). The turnout leading into L1 is one where the points head toward the locomotive's pilot, in the direction opposite to the direction the train is moving. It is far more complicated to accomplish this maneuver, or switching sequence, than the trailing-point turnout. However, this is a challenge that faces the operating crews of real railroads every working day. To a model railroader, it is simply challenging fun. On this model railroad plan, it would be much faster for the train to simply continue around the layout and around the reversing loop past K1 to return to turnout T3 from the opposite direction. This would make T3 a trailing-point turnout and the six switching moves listed previously would be used to pull the gondola at L1. It's your railroad and you may do just that if you wish.

Remember, these same movements are needed if you are using standard knuckle couplers rather than Kadee or LGB couplers and ramps. The difference is that you must reach each coupler, without the Kadee or LGB ramps, to couple or uncouple. To some modelers, that is far more realistic than just standing back and watching. Others find the interference of a 1/1 scale human hand detracts from the mood of recreating real railroad switching movements.

I've complicated this sequence just a bit by also stipulating that the reefer left by the last move at K4

must be returned to K4 when the switching moves to pull the gondola at L1 are completed.

Real railroaders use the term "pull" to mean pick up or remove a car. The sequence of movements would simply be reversed if the gondola were in the train as it arrived (as, we imagine, it did earlier) with operating instructions or "orders" to drop the gondola at L1. Here, the train consists only of the locomotive and a caboose. (Remember, Fig. 15-8 shows the locations of the various positions.)

Move 1. The locomotive would stop to uncouple the caboose at K3 to leave the caboose on the main line. The turnout points at T3 would also be thrown from the main line to the siding.

Move 2. The locomotive would pull forward into the siding and stop to couple onto the gondola. The turnout points at T2 also would be set for the passing siding.

Move 3. The locomotive would back into the passing siding and stop long enough to couple onto the reefer and for the crew to throw the points of turnout T1 for the siding.

Move 4. The locomotive would push both the gondola and the reefer back until the gondola could be left at K4, where the locomotive would stop again and uncouple.

Move 5. The locomotive would continue backward until its pilot cleared the points of turnout T1. It also would uncouple from the reefer. If the couplers are Kadee's, the reefer can be left there; if the couplers are LGB, another ramp—L7—will be needed to uncouple the reefer. The crew also would throw the points of turnout T1 back to the main line.

Move 6. The locomotive would pull forward and stop behind the caboose at K3 to couple onto the caboose. The crew would throw the turnout points at T2 back to the main line.

Move 7. The locomotive would continue forward until its rear tender wheels cleared the points of turnout T2. The crew then would throw the points of turnout T2 for the passing siding.

Move 8. The locomotive would reverse to couple onto the gondola at K4 and stop so the gondola could be coupled.

Move 9. The locomotive would back just far enough so the caboose could be left at K4 and stop so it could be uncoupled. The crew would then throw the points of turnout T1 to the siding.

Move 10. The locomotive would continue backward to stop and couple onto the reefer left at L7. The

Fig. 15-16 *Switching a facing-point turn-out, move 1.*

Fig. 15-17 *Switching a facing-point turn-out, move 2.*

Fig. 15-18 *Switching a fac-ing-point turnout, move 4.*

Fig. 15-19 *Switching a fac-ing-point turnout, move 6.*

Fig. 15-20 *Switching a facing-point turnout, move 7.*

Fig. 15-21 *Switching a fac-ing-point turnout, move 8.*

Fig. 15-22 *Switching a fac-ing-point turnout, move 9.*

Fig. 15-23 *Switching a facing-point turnout, move 12.*

Fig. 15-24 *Switching a facing-point turnout, move 13.*

Fig. 15-25 *Switching a facing-point turnout, move 14.*

Fig. 15-26 *Switching a facing-point turnout, move 15.*

Fig. 15-27 *Switching a facing-point turnout, move 16.*

Fig. 15-28 *Switching a facing-point turnout, move 17.*

Fig. 15-29 *Switching a facing-point turnout, move 18.*

Fig. 15-30 *Switching a facing-point turnout, moves 19 and 20.*

crew would walk forward and throw the points of turnout T1 back to the main line.

Move 11. The locomotive would pull forward (another car-length more than when the photographer caught it) and stop to leave the reefer at K3.

Move 12. The locomotive would stop and uncouple from the reefer while the train crew walked forward to throw turnout T2 for the main line.

Move 13. The locomotive would pull forward far enough so its tender's wheels would clear the points of turnout T2 and the points would be thrown back to the siding.

Move 14. The locomotive would reverse to push the gondola just far enough to couple with the caboose at K4.

Move 15. The locomotive would pull forward a bit further than before so the caboose would clear the points of turnout T2. The crew would then throw the points of T2 for the main line.

Move 16. The locomotive would reverse and push the caboose just far enough to couple with the reefer at K3. The crew would throw the points of turnout T3 for the main line.

Move 17. The locomotive would pull foward far enough so the reefer would clear the points of turnout T2. The crew would throw the points of T2 for the siding.

Move 18. The locomotive would reverse far enough to leave the reefer back at K4 once again and stop to uncouple from the caboose.

Move 19. The locomotive would pull forward until the caboose cleared the points of turnout T2 and the crew would throw the points back to the main line.

Move 20. The locomotive and its now two-car train would proceed on to their next switching assignment.

Trolleys and Electric Locomotives

LGB makes a variety of models that are replicas of European locomotives that draw their operating energy from overhead wires. The practice was common in the United States until the 1940s, but now only some parts of the Northeast Corridor between Boston and Washington, D.C., have true electric locomotives. The locomotives that are standard in America are called diesels, but in fact, the diesel engines really turn generators; there's an electric motor on each axle. Electric locomotives merely bypassed the need for an onboard engine and generator. Because these

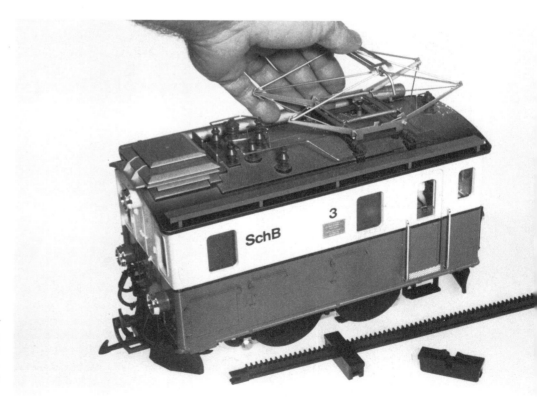

Fig. 15-31 *The LGB number 2146 rack locomotive with a section of the rack and clips to hold it to the track. This locomotive will climb a 25 percent grade.*

are European prototypes, they are beyond what I wanted to include here.

LGB offers a model of an electric prototype locomotive (number 2146) that is also operated on a rack railroad. A large gear beneath the locomotive engages a strip of gear teeth or a rack placed between the rails. The system also was used in the United States at Mount Washington in New Hampshire, and a diesel still pulls passengers up the rack railroad (we call it a cog railroad) to the top of Pikes Peak near Colorado Springs, Colorado. With the LGB number 1021 rack between the rails, the locomotive will climb a 25 percent grade.

A few brass models of the Pennsylvania Railroad GG-1 electric locomotives have been imported in 1/32 scale for operation on gauge 1 track, but they sell for in excess of $4,000. The only inexpensive models of real American railroad equipment that are currently available are the four-wheel streetcars that Bachmann offers. Two models are available—one has open sides and visible seats and the other is a conventional model with windows on the closed sides. They operate on track power, but the real ones drew electricity from overhead wires. Both LGB and Depot G offer overhead wire systems. I've included these trolleys and this chapter because their operation nearly always was limited to special trackage. You might want to put a loop around a downtown city scene, but they would not be part of any recreation of other real-world operations. The electric locomotives, of course, served just as diesels do today, but no American prototypes are currently available.

Two-Train Operations

There are two different philosophies behind the operation of two or more trains in a garden railroad setting. For the first, the model railroaders have a desire, based on their experiences or dreams, that trains will operate on some kind of schedule or, at least, a sequence that simulates the ordered coming and going of real trains. The other extreme of two-train operation is revealed in the unpredictability of two trains that appear and disappear from the scene, sometimes passing each other and often just winding their own way through the scenery. You can see these differing philosophies by tracing the routes of the trains on the track diagrams in Chapter 2.

One of the most realistic outdoor railroads—that of Steve and Judy Arrigotti—is deliberately designed so three trains can be kept in motion at once without ever sharing the same tracks. There's an isolated oval at the far end of the layout with another oval option, half-hidden in a tunnel, beneath it. A third train has the option, itself, of tracking a folded-inside-itself oval or a large figure 8. Bill and Dee Baldock's layout can be divided neatly into two layouts: a figure 8 on the patio deck and a large convoluted oval outside. The 30-by-40-foot indoor layout on the basement floor (seen in Fig. 2-30) is the most complex plan in this book but, with care, you can trace a reverse loop to reverse loop into the mountains at the far left and an oval all on the floor at the far right, with a third path weaving its way around the outer right of the room that overlaps just 3 or 4 feet of the first loop-to-loop option. These are multitrain operation layouts in which the trains can be set in motion and pretty much left to run with no chance they'll ever collide.

Passenger and Express Trains

All of the layouts are large enough so two trains can chase each other for dozens of laps before one will catch the other. More interesting, though, are operations where trains travel in opposite directions. There's room enough on Norm Grant's layout for that kind of operation, and three passing sidings provide a place fo the trains to wait. A real railroad would certainly only route the trains over the layout once a day and the trains would have priorities over one another so that, for example, a train of empty cars would have to wait on the siding until the passenger train had passed. On real railroads passenger trains almost always have priority over all freight trains. The top-priority freight trains would include trains of perishable fruit and high-speed freight express trains where overnight delivery was guaranteed.

If you have three trains on your layout, one can be designated a passenger train (even if it only carries passengers in the caboose); one can be a "hot shot" or express freight; and one can be a low-priority freight train of empty cars or coal or a similar commodity. Stipulate on your "timetable" that the coal train waits for the passenger and the express and that the express waits for the passenger train. Park the two lower-priority trains on sidings and make them wait until the passenger has passed, then allow the express to depart and pass the waiting train of empties or coal, and, finally, let the freight train depart. The train of empties may only have time to duck into the next siding before the express or passenger train passes.

The whole concept of multiple train operation can keep you and several friends busy operating an indoor or outdoor model railroad. Chapter 5 includes a variety of methods of controlling the trains independently, but you can run two on most power packs and use sidings and electrically isolated blocks to hold one train while the other catches up with it or passes it. The sidings can be double-ended with a turnout on each end or simple stub-end sidings that the train must either back into or back out of. Real railroads used both types on branch lines.

Yard Operations

The most noticeable ommission in this book (to a long-time model railroader) is the lack of any six- to twenty-car freight yards. There are plans for those in the LGB *Track Planning and Technical Guide*, but those layouts are in Europe. Large yards are rare in American gauge 1 railroading. There certainly are plenty of large freight yards in HO scale; I'd guess there are more than one thousand. Somehow, the appeal and the cost of such an operating feature and the cars to fill it are just not part of gauge 1 railroading. With the larger trains, the layout owners and operators find more than enough to keep themselves and a half-dozen friends busy for a Sunday afternoon and evening.

The track plan in this chapter (Fig. 15-8) has the major elements of a yard in the lower right-hand corner. There's a wye for turning locomotives or cars and a passing siding so locomotives can "run around" their trains to perform facing-point turnout switching operations, and there are two tracks, L3 and L4, that can be considered as yard tracks for the makeup or breakdown of arriving and departing trains. With the large-scale models, however, a very long train might have four or five cars. Two- and three-car trains are common, so a large yard is not really needed, especially for an indoor layout. If I were to build the plan shown here outdoors, I'd use the larger-radius curves and double the length of everything. As it is drawn, the passing siding at K3 will only hold a train consisting of a Mogul and one car, although another car or two could be temporarily parked at L1. The runaround siding at K5 and K6 will hold a Mogul and three cars.

All-Season Operations

If you build your gauge 1 model railroad indoors, you won't need to think about winter snows or spring rains. When you build a railroad outdoors, however, it doesn't matter whether it is 1/1 scale or 1/22.5 scale, the weather will bring operating problems to solve. Those weather problems, however, are enough of a challenge to make places like Denver and Cincinnati two of the most popular cities in the nation for garden railroad construction. The roadbed construction suggested in Chapter 6 includes proven techniques to make an outdoor railroad as weatherproof

as possible. Other chapters suggest weatherproofing techniques for wiring and structures.

You won't really know what's going to happen to the railroad during heavy rains, however, until those heavy rains occur. You will probably find that water collects in lakes in places that, perhaps, should provide bridges or culverts made from 2-inch PVC pipe to allow drainage. If some particular stretch of track is continually washed-out by the rains, you may want to build some water diversion levees beside the tracks or, better, install a long, low wooden trestle so the water can flow freely.

Most garden railroads, even in the snow belt, operate all year long. You might have to wait for the ice to melt on some shaded portion of the layout, but out-and-back operations are certainly possible. Firms like By Grant occasionally advertise custom-made metal snowplows for locomotives like the LGB Mogul, and those plows really work. You can buy a square-shaped 6-inch-wide garden spade and use your own shoulder power to clear the snow from just the tracks. The same fairyland delight that happens with trains running through the garden happens when those same colorful trains wend their way through the snowbanks.

Freight for Your Freight Trains

If you ever tire of just watching the trains work their magic in your garden or of watching their travels around your indoor layout, you may want to follow the path taken by thousands of modelers who have built layouts in N, HO, and O scales. A large proportion of the builders of indoor model railroads perceive their model railroads as merely smaller-scale version of real railroads. Yes, the locomotives and the rolling stock are scale models of real railroad equipment, as are the buildings and the scenery. These modelers carry it one step further: The trains actually operate just as they do on a real railroad.

At first thought you might believe that your trains operate just like the real ones: The train is guided by the rails and the locomotive pulls the first car, which pulls the second, and so on. The trains take sidings by a turnout being operated so the points redirect the train's route. Most of these gauge 1 locomotives, in fact, run at speeds very nearly correct in scale miles per hour and they can pull about as many cars as the full-size equivalents. But there is more to running a real railroad than just running trains—*lots* more.

Real railroads exist solely to carry either freight or passengers from one place to another. Tourist railroads, like the East Broad Top in Pennsylvania and the Durango & Silverton in Colorado, exist to run back and forth past some very pretty scenery. You certainly may choose to operate your model railroad in just that fashion, whether you run freight trains or passenger trains. Modelers interested in some serious fun, however, have established some systems to make it seem that their railroads really do haul something from somewhere to somewhere.

The true experts at making imagination work are the folks who play the simulation games such as Dungeons & Dragons and a thousand others that simulate air warfare, ground wars, and even peaceful events like building a railroad. These people use scraps of paper or cardboard to represent a dozen army tanks. Model railroaders have it much easier. We don't have to simulate either the equipment or the terrain. Instead, we model them both in living color and three dimensions, and with outdoor railroads, in living *everything*. What's more, our game-playing pieces move under their own power. Where we fall short is in the goal of our game; we enjoy watching the movements so much that we forget, if we ever knew, why those trains existed in the first place.

The missing element in our simulation games that recreates real railroading is the stuff the trains carry. Some of us have real logs on our log cars and real coal in the hopper cars, but few actually pick up or delivery those loads. In fact, the actual loading or unloading of logs or coal can become far more of a chore, and often a more toylike device is used than anything seen in the real world. No, real loads are not the answer in simulating real-world railroad shipments. Hundreds of model railroaders, especially those that enjoyed the hobby in the 1940s when Lionel and their O gauge operating log and coal loaders and barrel loaders and magnetic cranes were popular, tried real loads. Lionel still offers one or two reproductions of those devices each year, and most are large enough for gauge 1 indoor layouts if you want to try them yourself.

Model railroaders developed a very simple system that simulates both the loads and the drudgery of paperwork, both elements of real-world railroading most tof us would rather not re-create. This is a hobby for fun, not a means of creating busy work. The systems evolved over the years, and even today, there are as many minor variations as there are operators. Pioneer railroaders in the 1930s, like Frank Ellison and Lynn Westcott and John Page and their more sophisticated followers in the 1960s like Roy Dohn, Doug Small, Terry Walsh, and especially Doug Smith, developed what is now called the "Car Card Operating System" of simulating the loads that are carried by real railroad cars and how those loads affected the movements of the cars.

The Car Card Operating System

The Car Card Operating System works because it carries the simulation game we play when we operate our trains to its real-life conclusion: Real-world loads are destined for real-world places. The Car Card System has been known by a number of names, including the Waybill System (because that's its origin, in real-world paperwork). In essence, it is the shipments and the shippers that direct how a real railroad operates, not the railroad dispatcher or the engineer. There are thousands of reefer loads of fruit heading east from California each year and an equal number of empty reefers headed west. There are still hundreds of log cars carrying logs to sawmills and empties going back up the hill. No railroad customer orders a train of reefers or log cars, but somebody does say, "We want to move fruit or logs," and the railroads respond by supplying the proper type of car and moving that car where the shipper wants it to be moved.

The real railroads prepare a piece of paper for every carload shipment, which is called a waybill. The shipper, receiver, and shipment are all listed on the waybill. For modeling purposes, it's the perfect playing piece in our simulation game. Modelers use 3-by-5-inch or smaller index cards and, thanks to the trial-and-error efforts of the pioneer operators, modelers simply print or type four or five cards or waybills for each car and that is the beginning and end of the paperwork. Because we do not need to be paid for our services, we can keep the waybill and use it again and again. The real railroads use the waybill to prepare the invoices to bill their customers. We will recycle all our waybills.

In the real world, each car has a pocket or a board where the waybill can be placed so it travels with the car to the customer. Duplicate copies are mailed. Even with these large-scale models, there is no convenient place to keep an index card without destroying part of the realism. For our purposes a small clear plastic packet the size of the index card is used to simulate the waybill board on a real railroad car. A self-adhesive label, in one corner of the card, gives the type and number of the car and that envelope stays with the car forever as it travels over our system. You may want to provide a few small boxes to hold the car envelopes and loose waybills near some of the places where you might spot or drop cars. That's all there is to it: a handful of index cards, an envelope

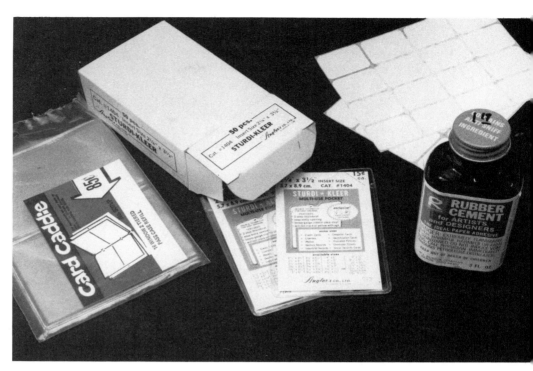

Fig. 15-32 *The materials for the Waybill System are available at any stationery store.*

for each car, and a few boxes. You don't even need a pencil or a paper clip.

I found that 2½-by-3½-inch index cards were large enough for all the information I wanted, but you can use larger ones if you like. Buy a pack of fifty index cards at an office supply or hardware store or, if you prefer, simply photocopy Fig. 15-33 in this book and make fifteen or twenty copies. I've even used different colored paper for different types of cars so the waybills are color-coded by car type (red for boxcars, yellow for reefers, white for flat cars, black for hoppers, blue for tank cars, pink for stock cars, and beige for gondolas made sense to me). Just insert the colored paper in the photocopy machine. Also buy enough matching 2¼-by-3½-inch clear plastic envelopes to match the number of freight cars you have or hope to purchase in the next year or so. Finally, buy an equal amount (or more) of ½-by-¾-inch self-adhesive labels. You can color code them, too, if you wish, with felt-tipped pens. Empty business card boxes may be available at some printing companies and they make nice boxes to hold the cards and plastic envelopes.

Setting Up the Operating System

This is the first and last time you'll be doing paperwork, but it may be an enjoyable exercise. Let your imagination run wild. First, list each type of car

you own or intend to buy in the near future and leave a half-page below each listing. Write down every imaginable commodity that might be shipped in that car. They did ship hay in stock cars and lumber (that's why they have doors in the ends). Gondolas usually carry things that can be shoveled or removed with a clamshell-type of digger or a magnet, including scrap metal, lumber, logs, pulpwood, rail, ties, sand, barrels, machinery, and sugar beets but rarely coal. Hoppers usually carry coal, sand, or ballast. You can figure out the rest.

When you have some commodities listed, take a look at your layout and decide how many places you want to have a pretend (whoops, simulated) industry. You do not need to have a turnout and a siding for each industry; cattle often were loaded right on the main line of the narrow gauge, for example. Also, one siding, even if it only has one piece of straight track or is a passing siding, can serve more than one industry. Before trucks took over most of the shipments to small towns, every town had what was called a "team track," which was a simple siding, often with a loading ramp sloped up to car-door-sill height. Anything imaginable could be shipped from a team track, from barrels of oil to tractors to pickles.

Make a second list of the industries and what type of commodities would be shipped by such an industry. Try to think of industries that receive and other industries that ship. It's nice to be able to pick up a loaded car that you spotted as an empty the day before, but the simulation is more credible when there are at least a few cars spotted to be unloaded. Cattle, for instance, often spent their spring days in the meadows and are shipped by rail to the high meadows in the late spring and then back to harvested sugar beet fields in the fall. Rough-cut wood is often shipped to finishing mills where finished lumber is shipped out.

One of the most active "industries" on any real railroad is the interchange yard in every major city. This is the place where the railroad exchanges cars with its competitors. You can use the interchange yard as the place where your railroad reaches out beyond the walls of the basement or beyond the garden fence to the world outside. In railroad terms, you might designate it as "AT&SF Westbound Interchange" or "Conrail Eastbound Interchange." In reality, you might place a small sign beside the track nearest the door into the house. That sign would note the place where you put cars onto the track from indoor storage shelves and remove cars to be stored. When you ship a car *to* the AT&SF Interchange, what you're really saying is that the operating crew should leave that car by the sign and you'll pick it off the track and put it away. Similarly, when you designate the order *from* Conrail Eastbound Interchange, you are asking to take a car off the shelf, of the type directed by the waybill, and place it on that track for the next train to take to its destination on your railroad. The interchange track can, of course, be an actual siding where the cars are stored or, on a large layout, it might be one track in a six-track yard. Absolutely anything can be shipped to or from an interchange track. If you want to simulate the single most common operating sequence of a real railroad, make cards that route cars both *from* AT&SF Eastbound Interchange and *to* Conrail Eastbound Interchange; those cars simply make a lap of the layout. You take them off the shelf, the train picks them up and runs around the layout, and drops them back off so you can put them back on the shelf.

Now go back to your list of industries and be sure that each industry has listed all the commodities it might either ship or receive. Write the word *in* in red beside each commodity the industry might receive and the word *out* in blue beside each commodity the industry might ship.

Make two more columns under each industry, one marked *To* and the second column marked *From*. List the imaginary city and the industry that would ship that commodity to your industry under the *To* column—these are the places where the carloads are going to be shipped *into* your industry. The *From* column will be easier; list the industry that would receive the commodity shipped by your industry and imagine some city, if you wish. The operations will be more interesting if at least three-fourths of both the *From* inbound shipment and *To* outbound shipment industries are on your layout. Remember, the team track can take just about anything, including oil or gas delivered to waiting (if imagined) tank trucks and trailers.

Now you are ready to prepare the waybills. If you are using photocopies on paper from this book, cut the copies apart as indicated by the lines and fold them in half. Use rubber cement to glue the folds back to back. The folded and glued paper will be about as stiff as an index card. After you have used the cards for a month or two so you know the information is correct, you can prolong their life almost indefinitely by spraying them with clear enamel.

Use the list of industries and shipments as the source of information to fill out the waybills. First, write *To* on the side of each waybill that ends with the sentence "Place card in 'Yard' file." Next, write the name of the town on your layout where that industry is located and, below that, the name of the industry. List the type of car that would be used (a boxcar, for example) for the commodity that the industry receives from that list of "in" commodities. Then write "Empty—For Loading."

Turn the card over to the side that ends with the words "and file the waybill and packet in the 'Town' set-out box." Write *To* at the top of the card and then pick one destination from your list of "to" places for that industry's products. If the commodity is coming from Miami, write, "From Miami, via _____" [meaning through] and fill in the name of the town on your layout with the interchange, followed by the word *interchange*. If the commodity is coming from some town and industry that is actually on your layout, just list that town and the industry below the word *To*. Below this, write the type of car, just as you did on the opposite side of the waybill, but here add the word "Loaded" and write down the commodity the car will actually be carrying.

Make at least four of these cards, each with a different destination, for every industry on your layout. If, however, you are shipping loaded and empty cars back and forth between two industries, both on your layout, you will need only one card. Examples might be logs going to a sawmill from a log-loading platform and coal traveling between a mine and coke oven. With these cars you'll just have

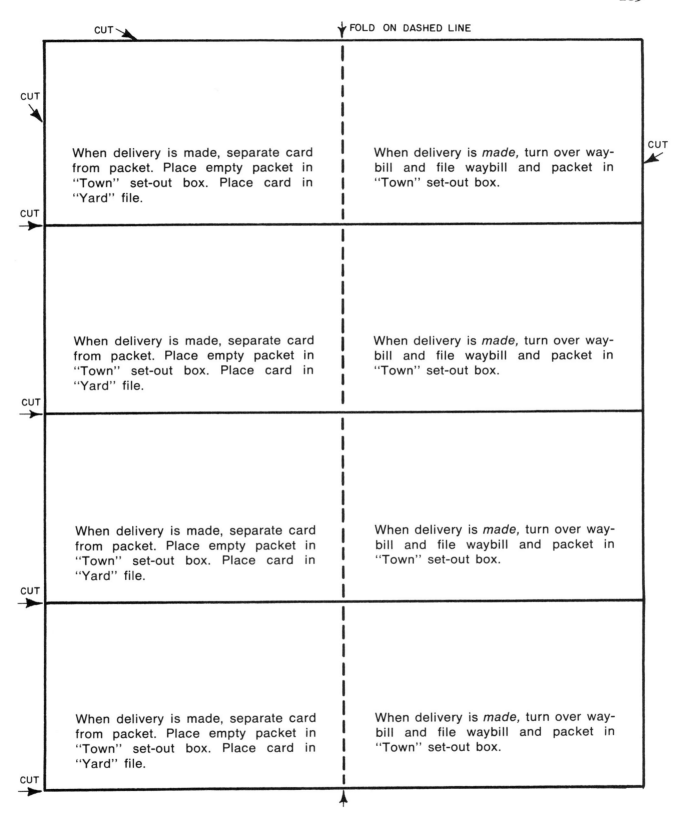

CUT →

FOLD ON DASHED LINE

CUT

CUT →

CUT

CUT →

When delivery is made, separate card from packet. Place empty packet in "Town" set-out box. Place card in "Yard" file.

When delivery is *made,* turn over waybill and file waybill and packet in "Town" set-out box.

CUT →

When delivery is made, separate card from packet. Place empty packet in "Town" set-out box. Place card in "Yard" file.

When delivery is *made,* turn over waybill and file waybill and packet in "Town" set-out box.

CUT →

When delivery is made, separate card from packet. Place empty packet in "Town" set-out box. Place card in "Yard" file.

When delivery is *made,* turn over waybill and file waybill and packet in "Town" set-out box.

CUT →

When delivery is made, separate card from packet. Place empty packet in "Town" set-out box. Place card in "Yard" file.

When delivery is *made,* turn over waybill and file waybill and packet in "Town" set-out box.

Fig. 15-33 *Four waybills that can be photocopied and cut apart.*

Operating a Real Railroad

to pretend that the logs are unloaded or the coal dumped unless you want to make quickly removeable one-piece piles of logs you can lift from the cars or use the one-piece coal loads available from Korber and Depot G.

Make a car packet for each car with clear plastic 2¼-by-3½-inch envelopes with a sticker in the upper-left corner. Write the initials of the railroad marked on the car side, followed by the car number. If, for whatever reason, the car has no railroad reporting marks, use decals or dry transfers, as described in Chapter 14, to apply them to the car. Then list the type of car.

You will need an empty box to hold the cards and

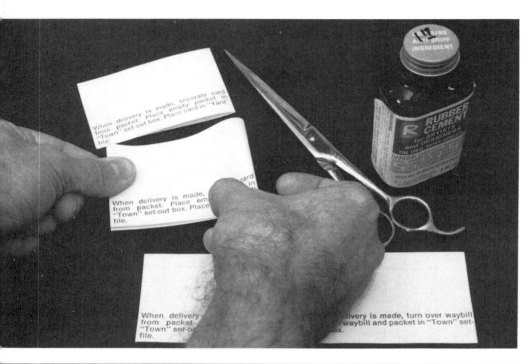

Fig. 15-34 *Cut apart the photocopies of the waybills, then fold them as shown to glue the backs together with rubber cement.*

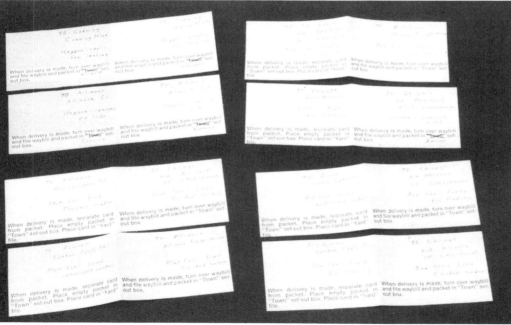

Fig. 15-35 *Samples of eight waybill variations (unfolded only so you can read both sides).*

Fig. 15-36 *A waybill file box is needed for each town, plus a "master" yard file for the waybills themselves and for empty-car envelopes.*

Fig. 15-37 *The cycle for each standard type of waybill and plastic envelope for each car follows this pattern.*

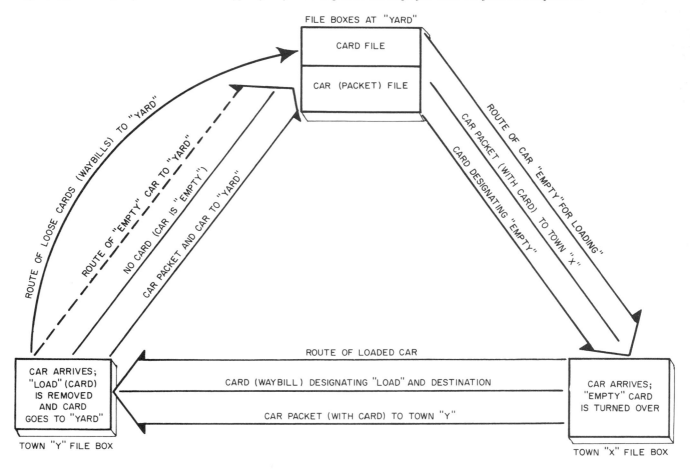

envelopes at the main operating point for your railroad—you can call it a "yard" even if it's just a sign beside the track. You also will want a box for every other town on the layout. I'd suggest a minimum of three towns, including the yard, so you have three possible destinations for the shipments. Those "towns" can be simply a turnout and a siding or, again, just a hand-lettered sign with the town name. I'm calling them Town "X," Town "Y," for purposes of illustration.

Operating the System

Park at least one car at each of the towns and put its car packet in the box marked with the town name. Put the rest of the cars in the Yard for now, even if that means you make up a six-car train and park it by the Yard sign. Put the car packets for those cars in the box marked Yard. Pick some waybills at random from the pile you prepared and insert just one that matches each of the cars in all the towns and in the Yard into the car packets. For now, don't worry, which side of the waybill is up. The "up" for a car packet is the side on which you placed the sticker with the car number and description.

From now on, just follow the directions on the cards. The system should run by itself as long as you follow the instructions printed on the waybills. Keep the extra waybills in the Yard file box and, when loose waybills are available, put them at the back of the pile. Pick a fresh waybill card each time you are ready to operate a train. Fig. 15-37 shows the "cycle" for each standard type of waybill and the plastic envelope for each car. Notice how the car (with its matching clear plastic envelope car packet) can begin the operating sequence wherever the car may be. The cycle can begin in the Yard where the waybill is first inserted into the car packet. When the car arrives at its destination, the waybill is turned over and placed back in the envelope unless the car is unloaded at that industry. The waybills for unloaded cars go back to the Yard and the car travels with an empty envelope.

When the car is dropped off, it can rest there for as long as you wish. The next train through can pick it

Fig. 15-38 **Whistle and Horn Signal Codes**

Real railroad engineers seldom use the steam locomotive whistle or a diesel horn just to "honk." They have a specific combination of short and long notes, similar to the Morse Code used by telegraph operators, that is understood by all the operating crew. Here, the short whistle or horn sounds are noted with a dot, and the longer whistle or horn sounds are noted with a dash.

·	Apply brakes, stop.
- -	Release brakes, procede.
- - -	Train parted or uncoupled.
· · ·	Back up or reverse.
——	(A prolonged sound) Used when approaching railroad stations or railroad crossings with other railroads.
- - - -	Approaching grade crossings with highway.
· · · · · ·	Alarm for persons or livestock on track.
- ·	Used when running against the normal flow of traffic to warn approaching trains and stations.

up or, if you want a variation on the system, make a card that says "Hold two days for unloading" on one side and "Hold one day for unloading" on the other side. The first train through turns the card over to the "one day" side and the next train through removes the card so the third train through can pick up the empty (or loaded) car.

You certainly do not need to use the Waybill or Car Card Operating System every time you run the trains. When you want to use it, you will need to match the cars to their car packets and, perhaps, insert or remove a waybill to get the car back into the system. You may discover that the creation of the waybill system will allow you to see your model railroad in a completely different way: as a transportation system. When you take the time to realize what those cars could be carrying, the trains seem to take on a purpose, with or without the Waybill System, that makes the operations seem more like running a real railroad.

Glossary

▌▌▐▐▌▌▐▐▌▌▐▐▌▌▐▐▌▌▐▐▌▌▐▐▌▌▐▐▌▌▐▐▌▌▐▐▌▌▐▐▌▌▐▐▌▌▐▐▌▌▐▐▌▌▐▐▌▌▐▐▌▌▐▐▌▌▐▐▌▌▐▐▌▌▐▐
▌▌▐▐▌▌▐▐▌▌▐▐▌▌▐▐▌▌▐▐▌▌▐▐▌▌▐▐▌▌▐▐▌▌▐▐▌▌▐▐▌▌▐▐▌▌▐▐▌▌▐▐▌▌▐▐▌▌▐▐▌▌▐▐▌▌▐▐▌▌▐▐▌▌▐▐

AAR The Association of American Railroads, the real railroad organization that establishes standards for equipment and safety.

Articulated A steam locomotive, like the LGB number 2085 European-style or the Union Pacific's Big Boy, with two sets of drivers under a common boiler. The front set is allowed to move from side to side so the locomotive can travel around tighter curves than a locomotive with a rigid chassis.

Bad order The term real railroads use to describe a malfunctioning car.

Ballast The crushed stone, rock, or cinders used to hold the railroad ties in place.

Block A section of track on either a model railroad or a real one that is isolated from the rest of the track for electrical control of model locomotives or, on the real railroads, for signaling.

Bolster The two places on the underbody of a freight or passenger car or steam locomotive tender where the trucks attach and pivot.

Branch line A portion of railroad track and route that leaves the main line to reach some remote town or industry.

Bumper The device used at the end of a stub-end siding to prevent cars or locomotives from accidentally rolling off the end of the track.

Caboose The rolling office and living quarters for the railroad crew. Most cabooses have a small box on the top or on each side with windows so the crew can see along the train to identify any smoking and overheated wheel bearing journals. Sometimes called a bobber, cabin car, crummy, or way car.

Carrier control *see* Command control

Catenary Overhead wires where electric locomotives pick up current through pantographs on the roof of the locomotives. The wires on a trolley line are simply called "overhead."

Coaling station A building where coal is stored to be delivered into a steam locomotive's tender. The coal may simply be shoveled by hand or hoisted by bucket. In some designs the coal is stored in an overhead bin, carried by conveyor from a dump bin beside the building, so the coal can be delivered by gravity down a chute and into the locomotive's tender.

Command control A system of electronic control for model locomotives. The rails carry a signal for the locomotive to speed up or slow down. Each locomotive has its own receiver and frequency so it will respond only to electronic commands from the throttle with a matching frequency. Up to eighty locomotives may be controlled at once on the same track as long as there are eighty throttles. Keller and Power Systems, Inc. make command control systems suitable for gauge 1 trains.

Crossing When two tracks cross each other on the same level, like the 90-degree crossing in some figure-8 model railroad layouts.

Crossover The pair of turnouts that allow a train to travel from one track on a double-track main line to the other track.

Cut Places where the railroad builders had to dig or blast dirt and rock from a hill so the railroad right-of-way could go through. Also, a few railroad cars coupled together as a cut of cars.

Cyanoacrylate cement Often known under the trademark Super Glue, it is a quick-setting clear liquid cement that will bond almost anything (including your fingers).

DPDT An electrical switch that is used by model railroaders to reverse the flow of current and change the locomotive's direction of travel or, with altered wiring at the switch, to select alternate electrical blocks or to operate remote-controlled electric turnouts. Literally, a *double-pole, double-throw* switch.

Draft gear The mounting boxes located under the extreme ends of the cars or locomotives for couplers. The coupler is sprung or cushioned to absorb part of the impact of coupling and of sudden stops or starts.

Fiddle yard A hidden track or small yard used by modelers to store or rearrange trains by lifting or moving the cars and locomotives into different order by hand.

Fill When a real railroad builds an embankment of dirt or rock to carry the roadbed and track over a valley.

Flange The protion of any railroad wheel or driver that guides the wheel down the rails. The flange extends around the circumference of the wheel or driver as its largest diameter.

Frog The point where the rails in a turnout actually cross and the same point in a crossing where the rails cross.

G gauge An earlier term for the models and operation of narrow gauge–style models on gauge 1 track.

G scale The term sometimes used to describe the 1/22.5 scale models of narrow gauge prototypes that operate on gauge 1 track.

Gap A break in the rails to isolate electrically some portion of the track from another to prevent short circuits or to allow for multiple train operation on the same stretch of track.

Gauge The distance between the inside edges of the tops or heads of the rails. Standard gauge in America is 4 feet, 8½ inches.

Grab iron The steel handholds or bars on the sides, roof, and ends of rolling stock.

Grade The gradual rise or fall of the track, from level, enabling the track to follow the contours of the land or rise to pass over another track.

Ground foam Synthetic rubber ground to approximately the size of coffee grounds for use as simulated leaves.

Head end cars The cars in a passenger train that normally are coupled nearest to the locomotive, including express reefers, milk cars, express baggage cars, baggage cars, mail cars, railway post office (RPO) cars, and combines.

Helper A locomotive that is added to a train to supply the extra power that may be needed to surmount a steep grade.

Hostler The real railroad man or woman who moves the locomotives around the maintenance yard or engine terminal to service the locomotive or prepare it for the engineer.

Hotbox A bearing or journal that has become overheated from lack of lubrication so that the oil or, in earlier years, the cotton waste actually smokes and burns.

Interchange A segment of track or several tracks where one railroad connects with another so complete trains or individual cars can be moved from one railroad to the next.

Interlocking A system of mechanical or electrical contacts to ensure that only one train at a time can move through an interchange or through a crossing.

Interurban Real railroads that were powered by electricity taken from overhead wires with either self-propelled electric passenger cars or small electric locomotives to pull short trains. The pre–World War I equivalent of today's light rail with the option of freight service.

Journal The bearing around the end of a locomotive or car axle that actually supports the load of the car.

Jumper wire A short length of wire to carry electrical current across a rail joint or across the back of a DPDT electrical switch.

Kingpin The pivot point of a freight or passenger car or tender truck where it connects to the bolster.

LCL *Less than carload lot;* freight shipments too small to fill a complete freight car.

Main line The most heavily trafficked routes of the railroad.

Maintenance-of-way The rolling stock or structures that are directly associated with maintaining the railroad or with repairing and righting wrecked or damaged trains.

Mallet A particular type of articulated steam locomotive that used some of the still-unused steam energy exhausted from the rear set of cylinders and drivers to power the front set of cylinders and drivers.

Module A portion of a model railroad that is designed to be both portable and to interface with similar modules at both ends. Modules are usually built by individual members of a club so the members can bring their modules together to assemble a large layout.

Narrow gauge Railroad track built with the rails spaced less than the standard 4-foot, 8½-inch gauge. The most common narrow gauge in America was 3 feet, but some railroads in the Northeast used 2-foot gauge.

Open grid A type of table for model railroads without a solid top, where 1-by-4-inch or similar-sized lumber is placed on edge to create a series of open-top-and-bottom boxes in a waffle or grill pattern.

Passing siding Where a second track leaves the main track through a turnout to run parallel to the main track and reconnect through a second switch. Trains can pass each other, without either needing to reverse, if one train can pull into the passing siding to wait for the second train to pass.

Piggyback Modern railroading's special flatcar service to transport highway trailers or intermodal containers. Sometimes called TOFC, meaning *trailers on flatcars.*

Points The moving parts of a turnout that actually change the train route from the main line to the siding.

Point-to-point A type of track plan or train operating pattern that simulates real railroad operations from one town to another but within the confines of a room or yard.

Power pack The box of electrical components that change 115-volt AC household current to the 14-volt DC current used by most gauge 1 locomotives. It may or may not include a throttle to control the locomotive's speed, a reversing switch, and an on-off switch.

Prototype The term used to describe the real railroad version of what the model duplicates.

Pullman The passenger train cars, usually sleeping cars, diners, or parlor cars, that were owned and operated by the Pullman Company.

Rail joiner The bent piece of metal that holds two pieces of rail together.

Reed switch An electrical switch with a thin metal pedal that opens or closes the electrical circuit. The pedal or reed often is moved by the attraction of a passing magnet.

Reefer Insulated cars that are cooled either by ice in bunkers or by mechanical refrigeration units.

Reversing loop A track configuration that allows trains to enter in one direction and, by traversing the loop, leave traveling in the opposite direction. A method of reversing the direction of trains with no need for the train to stop.

Right-of-way The property and track adjacent to the track.

R-T-R An abbreviation for *ready-to-run* models. It usually includes models with simple snap-in or snap-to-gether assembly.

Runaround A switching move in which the locomotive uncouples from the front of the train and, using a passing siding, runs around to couple onto the rear of the train.

Snowshed Protective buildings that cover the tracks, usually in mountain areas, so that a snowslide or avalanche will not cover the tracks.

Spot A switching move whereby the locomotive delivers a car to a designated siding or a desired position on a track, usually so the car can be unloaded.

Stub siding A track that leaves the main line from a turnout and ends in a bumper.

Superelevation Banking on tracks in a curve so trains can travel at a designated speed with a minimum of load on the outer wheels and rails and a minimum of sway.

Switch Often used to describe the part of a railroad's track, more correctly called a turnout. Also, an electrical device like an on-off switch or a DPDT switch to provide electrical control.

Switch machine The electrical solenoid or motor used to move the points of a turnout by remote control.

Talgo Model railroad trucks with the couplers mounted to the truck rather than on the body of the car.

Tangent Straight stretches of track.

Tank engine A steam locomotive without a tender where the coal or fuel oil is carried in a large box behind the cab and the water in a tank over the top of the boiler.

Tender The car behind most steam locomotives that carries water and coal, fuel oil, or wood for fuel.

Throat The point where the yard tracks begin to diverge or fan out into the multiple tracks used for storage and switching.

Timetable A schedule, usually printed, to tell railroad employees and customers when trains are scheduled to be at certain points or stations on the railroad.

Traction The term used to describe all prototype locomotives and self-powered cars, like trolleys and interurbans, that are powered by electricity taken from overhead wires above the tracks.

Transistor throttle An electronic speed controller for model locomotives that is used in place of the older wire-wound rheostats.

Transition curve A length of track that begins at a straight and gradually bends into ever-tighter radii until the curve itself is reached. Also called an easement.

Turnout Where two diverging tracks join. Also called a switch.

Trolley Self-propelled electric-powered cars that ran almost exclusively on city streets (as opposed to interurbans, that ran through the country between cities and towns).

Truck The sprung-metal frame with four or six wheels under each end of a car.

Turntable A rotating steel or wooden bridge, pivoted in the center, to turn locomotives or cars and reverse their direction, route them into storage tracks, or into roundhouse tracks that fan out from the edges of the turntable.

Vestibule The enclosed area, usually at both ends of a passenger car, where patrons may enter the car from the station platform and where they walk to move from one car to another.

Way freight A freight train that switches cars in and out of the train at most towns along its route from terminal to terminal. Also called a pedlar freight.

Wye A turnout where the diverging routes are curved away from each other. Also the triangular-shaped track pattern or plan where trains or locomotives can be reversed.

Supply Sources

When writing to any of these firms, enclose a self-addressed stamped envelope if you expect a reply. Some sell catalogs that range in price from $1.00 to $5.00.

American Craft Products, Inc.
1530 N. Old Rand Road
Waucona, IL 60084

☐ 1/24 scale dollhouse miniatures

American Model Builders
1408 Hanley Industrial Court
Saint Louis, MO 63144

☐ Wood and metal car kits and car parts

American Standard Car Co. (Great Trains)
P.O. Box 394
Crystal Lake, IL 60014

☐ 1/32 scale locomotives and cars

AMSI (Architectural Model Supplies, Inc.)
P.O. Box 750638
Petaluma, CA 94975

Aristo-Craft
346 Bergen Avenue
Jersey City, NJ 07034

☐ 1/29 scale cars, locomotives, and buildings

Aster Hobby USA, Inc.
P.O. Box 90643
Pasadena, CA 91109-0643

☐ Metal live steam locomotives and kits

B. & W. R. Railway Line
Bruce K. Bates
1008 Teal Drive
Santa Clara, CA 95051

☐ 1/24 scale locomotive kits

Bachmann Industries
1400 E. Erie Avenue
Philadelphia, PA 19124

☐ 1/22.5 scale locomotives, cars, and accessories

Brandbright Limited
The Old School, Cromer Road
Bodham, Holt, Norfolk NR25 6QG
ENGLAND

☐ Live steam locomotives and kits

Britains (see San-Val)

Bruder (see San-Val)

By Grant
1709 Geneva St.
Aurora, CO 80010

☐ Bridge kits and locomotives, custom outdoor railroad construction

Caboose Industries
1861 Ridge Road
Freeport, IL 61032-3637

☐ Turnout operating levers

California and Oregon Coast Railway
P.O. Box 57
Rogue River, OR 97537

☐ Wood ties

Campbell/Fortney Corporation
2217 W. State Street
Alliance, OH 44601

☐ Sound systems

CDS Lettering Limited
P.O. Box 2003, Station "D"
Ottawa, Ontario K1P 5W3
CANADA

☐ Dry transfer lettering

CMI (Chicago Model International)
P.O. Box 170
Deerfield, Il 60015

☐ Starr-Tec power supplies, throttles, and sound systems

Chicago Train Works (CTW)
698 Springhill Circle
Naperville, IL 60563

☐ 1/32 scale diesel locomotives

Columbine Hobby Company
OS 371 Florida Lane
Winfield, IL 60190

☐ 1/24 scale building kits and accessories

CTT Incorporated
109 Medallion Center
Dallas, TX 75214

☐ Track planning template for LGB

D.A.N.
13000 Stuck Road
Delton, MI 49046

☐ 1/24 scale rolling stock

Decker's Trains
Route 1, Box 102
Hot Springs, SD 57747

☐ 1/22.5 scale car kits and parts

Dees Delights, Inc.
3150 State Line Road
North Bend, OH 45052

☐ Structure kits and accessories, dollhouse miniatures

Delton Locomotive Works
120 Maple
Delton, MI 49046

☐ 1/24 scale locomotives and cars

Depot G Hobbies
OS 371 Florida Lane
Winfield, IL 60190

☐ 1/24 scale cars and accessories, Peco gauge 1 track

Diamond Enterprises and Book Publishers
Box 537
Alexandria Bay, NY 13607

☐ Mamod live steam locomotives

Robert Dustin
334 Aubuerndale Avenue
Newton, MA 02166

☐ Decals

Dynatrol (see PSI)

Eastern Railways
RD 1, Box 254
Beech Creek, PA 16822

☐ 1/32 scale locomotives

Echo Specialties
P.O. Box 27433
Hollywood, CA 90027

☐ Railroad signs

EDA Electronics
15 Boies Court
Pleasant Hill, CA 94523

☐ Radio-control power and throttle conversion kits.

Evergreen Scale Models, Inc.
12808 NE 125th Way
Kirkland, WA 98034

☐ Sheet and strip styrene plastic

F & H Enterprises
7501 McFadden Avenue
Huntington Beach, CA 92647

☐ Peco track and Busch trees

Floquil-Polly S Color Corp.
Route 30 North
Amsterdam, NY 12010

☐ Paints and brushes

Bill Gagne's Railroad Accessories
8 N. Munroe Terrace
Dorchester, MA 02122

☐ Wooden bridges, ties, and tunnel portals

Garden Railway Company
2008 Madison Road
Cincinnati, OH 45208

☐ 1/32 scale locomotives and cars, custom outdoor railroad construction

Garich Light Transport
6101 Glenwood Drive
Huntington Beach, CA 92647

☐ Track, rail, and turnouts

Gary Raymond
P.O. Box 1722
Thousand Oaks, CA 91360

☐ Metal wheel sets

Grandt Line Products, Inc.
1040 B Shary Court
Concord, CA 94518

☐ Plastic windows and doors

Grant (see By Grant)

Great Trains (see American Standard Car Co.)

Hartford Products, Inc.
6523 Old Farm Lane
Rockville, MD 20852

☐ Metal freight trucks and kits

Heki (see Portman)

Hughes (see San-Val)

Hyde-Out Mountain
89060 New Rumley Road
Jewett, OH 43986

☐ Live steam locomotives

Industrial Miniatures
Route 1, Box 169-B
Milbank, SD 57252

☐ 1/24 scale structures

I.S.L.E. Laboratories
P.O. Box 636
Sylvania, OH 43560

☐ Mountains-in-Minutes scenery supplies

ITTC (Industrial Train Technology, Inc.)
P.O. Box 5042
West Hills, CA 91308

☐ Walk-around throttles

Kadee Quality Products
P.O. Box 1726
Medford, OR 97501

☐ Couplers

Kalamazoo Trains, Chicora Corp.
655 44th Street
Allegan, MI 49010

☐ 1/22.5 scale locomotives, cars, and track

Keller Engineering
200 San Mateo Avenue
Los Gatos, CA 95030

☐ Onboard command-control system

Kenosha Railway Supply (see By Grant)

Korber Models, Division of Scale Modelers
    Industries, Inc.
18B Delaware Street
Paulsboro, NJ 08066

☐ Cast resin structure kits

L & P Trackworks (see Rara Avis)

LGB of America
6444 Nancy Ridge Drive
San Diego, CA 92121

☐ 1/22.5 scale locomotives, cars, track, and accessories

Life-Like Products, Inc.
1600 Union Avenue
Baltimore, MD 21211

☐ Signs, trees, and accessories

Lindsay Machine Works
1004 S. Washington Street
Denver, CO 80209

☐ Railbender rail-curving tool

Lionel Trains, Inc.
P.O. Box 748
Mount Clemens, MI 48045

☐ 1/22.5 and 1/32 scale locomotives, cars, track, and
accessories

Little Engines
194C Bodo Drive
Durango, CO 81301

☐ Live steam locomotives

Llagas Creek Railways
2200 Llagas Road
Morgan Hill, CA 95037

☐ Track, turnouts, and rail

Lone Star Bridge and Abutment
901 Oak View Court
Arlington, TX 76012

☐ Bridges and tunnel portals

Dave Manley
5122 Ellester Drive
San Jose, CA 95124

☐ Rail joiners

Marketing Corporation of America
P.O. Box 225
Birmingham, MI 48012

☐ 1/32 scale brass locomotives and cars

MATRA
18 Karin Court
East Northport, NY 11731

☐ Conversion kits for Delton locomotives

William McIntyre
528 Vine Street
Orrville, OH 44667

☐ Decals

Micro Engineering Company
1120 Eagle Road
Fenton, MO 63026

☐ Track, turnouts, rail and joiners

Microscale Industries, Inc.
P.O. Box 11950
Costa Mesa, CA 92627

☐ Decals and decal softeners

Midwest Products Company, Inc.
P.O. Box 564
Hobart, IN 46342

☐ Precut wood strips and sheets

Timothy I. Miller Co.
P.O. Box 86757
San Diego, CA 92138

☐ Economy R/C radio control throttles

Miniature Plant Kingdom
4125 Harrison Grade Road
Sebastapol, CA 95472

☐ Mail-order living plants

Miniature Steam Railways
P.O. Box 110192
Arlington, TX 76007

☐ Mamod live steam locomotives and accessories

Model Die Casting, Inc.
P.O. Box 926
Hawthorne, CA 90250

☐ 1/32 scale rolling stock

Model Power
180 Smith Street
Farmingdale, NY 11735

☐ Pola building kits, track, and accessories

Model Rectifier Corporation (MRC)
200 Carter Drive
Edison, NJ 08817

☐ Power packs

Mountains-in-Minutes (see I.S.L.E. Laboratories)

Narrow Gauge Machining
% Mike Bigger
1815 Orchard Avenue
Boulder, CO 80304

☐ Metal bridges and track rail

New England Hobby Supply
71 Hillard Street
Manchester, CT 06040

☐ 1/24 scale structure kits

Northeastern Scale Models, Inc.
P.O. Box 727
Methuen, MA 01844

☐ Bass wood strips, sheets, and windows and doors

Northeast Narrow Gauge
P.O. Box 191
Wiscasset, ME 04578

☐ 1/24 scale wagon kits and accessories

North West Short Line
P.O. Box 423
Seattle, WA 98116

☐ Motors, metal wheel sets, and rail

O & S Trains
835 Delaware
Denver, CO 80204

☐ Locomotive conversion kits and R/C throttles

Oakridge Corporation
P.O. Box 247
Lemont, IL 60436

☐ Dollhouse miniatures; 1/24 scale structures, wagons, and automobiles

Old and Weary Car Shop
104 Oak Street
Orangeburg, NY 10962

☐ Decals

Old Pullman Model Railroads, Inc.
8195 25th Street
Vero Beach, FL 32966

☐ Code 197 rail, assembled turnouts, spikes, and rail joiners

Onboard (see Keller Engineering)

Ozark Miniatures
P.O. Box 22
Linn Creek, MO 65052

☐ Switch stands and metal detail parts

The Parker Company
P.O. Box 1546
Camarillo, CA 93011

☐ Custom-made turnouts with wooden ties

PBL
P.O. Box 769
Ukiah, CA 95482

☐ Resistance soldering equipment

P.H. Hobbies, Inc.
185 Jay Street
Coldwater, MI 49036

☐ Power packs

Pola GmbH
Am Bahndamm 59
D-8734 Rothhausen
WEST GERMANY

☐ Plastic structure kits, people, and accessories

Portman Hobby Distributors
851 Washington Street
Peekskill, NY 10566

☐ Heki trees and scenery products

Precision Scale
3961 Highway 93 North
Stevensville, MT 59870

☐ Metal detail parts and rail

PSI (Power Systems, Inc.)
56 Bellis Circle
Cambridge, MA 02140

☐ Dynatrol command-control system

Peco (see Dept G and F&H Enterprises)

Railway Design Associates
241 Silver Street
Monson, MA 01057

☐ 1/24 scale structure kits

George Randeall
429 Linden Avenue
Wilmette, IL 60091

☐ Cast metal nonoperating couplers

Rara Avis Trains
5650-H Imhoff Drive
Concord, CA 94520

☐ On track R/C throttles, car and structure kits, and accessories

Remote Control Systems
37 Woodmason Road
Boronia, Victoria 3155
AUSTRALIA

☐ Radio-controlled throttles

Richard Hillman
P.O. Box 1253
Lodi, CA 95421

☐ Rail clamp rail joiners

Roanoake Electronics
7035 Amhurst
Saint Louis, MO 63130

☐ Sound systems

Roberts Lines
P.O. Box 96
East Rochester, NY 14445

☐ 1/32 scale brass locomotives and cars

Rondel Wood Products
2679 Washington Road G
North Waldoboro, ME 04572

☐ 1/24 scale wagon kits

Roundhouse Engineering
Unit 6, Churchill Business Park
Churchill Road Wheatley
Doncaster DN1 2TF
ENGLAND

☐ 1/24 scale live steam locomotives

Ryan Equipment Company
749 Creel Drive
Wood Dale, IL 60191

☐ 1/24 scale metal freight car trucks

San-Val Trains
7444 Valjean Avenue
Van Nuys, CA 91406

☐ Conductor rail joiners, track cleaners, Mamod live steam, Bruder horses and buildings, Hughes bridges, and Britains figures and accessories

Short Line Car and Foundry
14918 Lake Forest
Dallas, TX 75240

☐ 1/24 scale freight cars, trucks, and detail parts

Smoke Stack Hobby Kit Company
358 Lincoln Center, Unit A
Lancaster, OH 43130

☐ Wooden bridges and abutments

Starr Enterprises, Inc. (see CMI)

Tempest Electronics
P.O. Box 265
Ferntree Gully
Victoria, 3156
AUSTRALIA

☐ Radio-controlled throttles

Trackside Details
1331 Avalon Street
San Luis Obispo, CA 93401

☐ Metal locomotive and car detail parts

Trestle Works
% Hess Manufacturing
5321 E. 29th Street
Long Beach, CA 90815

☐ Wooden bridges, tunnel portals, and abutments

Tru-Scale Buildings
607 North A Street
Lake Worth, FL 33460

☐ 1/24 scale structures

USA Trains
P.O. Box 100
Malden, MA 02148

☐ 1/29 scale plastic freight cars

Wm. K. Walthers, Inc.
5601 W. Florist Avenue
Milwaukee, WI 53218

☐ Decals, loads, and catalogs

West Lawn Locomotive Works
P.O. Box 570
Madison, WI 53701

☐ Live steam locomotives, including Aster

Westlund Manufacturing
1415 Airline Drive
Jackson, MI 49203

☐ Cast resin structure kits

Willow Works
P.O. Box 150581
Nashville, TN 37215

☐ Steel scale ruler for 1/22.5, 1/24, 1/32, and 1/1

Woodland Scenics
P.O. Box 98
Linn Creek, MO 65052

☐ Scenery supplies

Publications

Big Train Operator
LGB Model Railroad Club of America
Mary Lentz, Secretary
P.O. Box 15835
Pittsburgh, PA 15244-5835

☐ Newsletter included in membership. Send a self-addressed stamped envelope for current membership charges.

Garden Railways
P.O. Box 61461
Denver, CO 80209

☐ Edited by Marc and Barb Horovitz. Bimonthly magazine devoted to large scale model railroading outdoors primarily with gauge 1 but occasionally with other gauges. $18.00 per year.

Garden Railway Guide
Garden Railway World

℅ West Lawn Locomotive Works
P.O. Box 570
Madison, WI 53701

☐ Two magazines, both published in England. Contact West Lawn for current subscription rates. Sample copies of *Garden Railway Guide* are $7.00 each; *Garden Railway World*, $6.00 each.

LGB Telegram
P.O. Box 187
Harrisburg, PA 17108

☐ Published four times a year by LGB. Subscriptions are $24.00 per year.

Model Railroader
P.O. Box 1612
Waukesha, WI 53187

☐ The largest-selling model railroad magazine. Usually has one or two gauge 1 layout tours and locomotive reports a year. Subscription rate is $28.95 per year.

Narrow Gauge and Short Line Gazette
P.O. Box 26
Los Altos, CA 94023

☐ Bimonthly magazine devoted to both model and prototype narrow guage with plans and photographs. Usually has two indoor large scale layouts a year. Edited by Robert Brown. Subscription rate is $21.00 per year.

National Model Railroad Association (NMRA)
4121 Cromwell Road
Chattanooga, TN 37421

☐ Indoor model railroading (HO and N scale) organization. They publish *NMRA Standards, NMRA Bulletin,* and the *NMRA Data Book.* Membership is $22.00 per year.

Railmodel Journal
2403 Champ Street
Denver, CO 80205

☐ Monthly magazine primarily for standard gauge modeling. Edited by Robert Schleicher. Usually features two gauge 1 layouts a year and one or two how-to-do-it features and test reports on four or five gauge 1 locomotives each year. Subscription rate is $28.00 per year.

Garden Railways magazine publishes a monthly list of clubs in the United States for gauge 1 model railroaders. Usually, these clubs have regular visits or tours of members' layouts. The listing includes the address and telephone numbers of those to contact for more information. A sample copy of *Garden Railways*, which will include the most current list, is $3.50 from P.O. Box 61461, Denver, CO 80206.

Index